BLANK SPOTS
ON THE MAP

Trevor Paglen

BLANK SPOTS
ON THE MAP

THE DARK GEOGRAPHY OF THE
PENTAGON'S SECRET WORLD

DUTTON

29358I7

DUTTON
Published by Penguin Group (USA) Inc.
375 Hudson Street, New York, New York 10014, U.S.A.
Penguin Group (Canada), 90 Eglinton Avenue East, Suite 700, Toronto, Ontario M4P 2Y3, Canada (a division of Pearson Penguin Canada Inc.); Penguin Books Ltd, 80 Strand, London WC2R
0RL, England; Penguin Ireland, 25 St Stephen's Green, Dublin 2, Ireland (a division of Penguin
Books Ltd); Penguin Group (Australia), 250 Camberwell Road, Camberwell, Victoria 3124, Australia (a division of Pearson Australia Group Pty Ltd); Penguin Books India Pvt Ltd, 11 Community Centre, Panchsheel Park, New Delhi – 110 017, India; Penguin Group (NZ), 67 Apollo Drive,
Rosedale, North Shore 0632, New Zealand (a division of Pearson New Zealand Ltd); Penguin
Books (South Africa) (Pty) Ltd, 24 Sturdee Avenue, Rosebank, Johannesburg 2196, South Africa

Penguin Books Ltd, Registered Offices: 80 Strand, London WC2R 0RL, England

Published by Dutton, a member of Penguin Group (USA) Inc.

First printing, February 2009
10 9 8 7 6 5 4 3 2 1

Map on pages viii–ix created by Darin Jensen. Photo on page 7: courtesy of the USGS; page 80:
courtesy of the Department of Energy; page 152: courtesy of the USAF; page 168: courtesy of
National Parks Service; page 186: courtesy of the Library of Congress. All other photos courtesy
of the author.

Ⓟ REGISTERED TRADEMARK—MARCA REGISTRADA

LIBRARY OF CONGRESS CATALOGING-IN-PUBLICATION DATA

Paglen, Trevor.
Blank spots on the map: the dark geography of the Pentagon's secret world / Trevor Paglen.
p. cm.
ISBN 978-0-525-95101-8 (hbk.)
1. Military bases—United States. 2. Intelligence service—United States. 3. Defense information,
Classified—United States. 4. Military bases, American. I. Title.
UA26.A2P2716 2009
355.3'4320973—dc22   2008042862

Printed in the United States of America
Set in Minion

CONTENTS

BLANK SPOTS
ON THE MAP

Stare Kiejkuty

Bagram
Kabul The Salt Pit

Some Entry Points to the Secret World

Prologue

"We need to find an old man," says Maiwand. We're standing on a street corner in downtown Kabul. The traffic around us is a tempest of battered 1970s Toyotas occasionally punctuated by a U.N. Land Cruiser or an American Suburban. We're trying to find a taxi driver who knows the back road to Bagram, a road that has been so dangerous for so long that driving on it would have been unthinkable until recently. We need to find someone who remembers the route from before the Soviet invasion in 1979. An old man.

Eventually we find a driver who knows the road and wants $15 to make the trip, a week's salary for someone lucky enough to have a steady job outside the opium business. We get into the man's beat-up Toyota wagon and bounce toward Kabul's outskirts. At the traffic circle near the military's heavily fortified Ka-bul Compound around the corner from the bunker-like American embassy, we see a two-story-high paint-chipped and weathered sign instructing locals to turn in any terrorists they may know.

Kabul itself is occupied by a gaggle of American military units, private military contractors, European troops from the Interna-tional Security Forces, United Nations development outfits, and other assorted nongovernmental organizations, but their trap-pings fade away as our cab drives northeast past the airport to-ward the back road to Bagram. Once we're outside town, houses give way to sprawling junkyards erected *Mad Max*–style on the Afghan plains. Guard towers protect the compounds' precious scrap metal and junk. Solitary furnaces from distant brick facto-ries lace the air with black smoke. A few oversized pickup trucks with homemade turquoise-blue paint jobs adorned with intricate gold and red markings ramble past, their backs overladen with burlap sacks bearing food from Afghanistan's agrarian bread-basket to the north.

After ten dusty miles, the walls of a compound rise in the dis-tance, and we come to an old-world traffic jam: an elderly shepherd wearing baggy Afghan garb herding a flock of goats across the bat-tered road. The man turns around to look at us. He's wearing a baseball hat. Unusual attire for a traditional Afghan, to say the least. Emblazoned on his cap are the same initials I'd seen printed on identity cards hanging from the necks of Bagram-bound contrac-tors in Dubai. KBR: Kellogg Brown and Root, the construction firm that had until recently been a subsidiary of Halliburton, Dick Cheney's old company.

And there it is in the distance. The top of the crumbling old brick factory once known as the Hecht-hochtief, which found new purpose as one of the first black sites of the war on terror's geog-raphy. A secret prison called the Salt Pit, built shortly after Sep-tember 11 as the Northern Alliance, the CIA, and American

Special Forces fanned though Afghanistan. Like so many other secret places, it had been built as a "temporary" facility but stayed open long after the initial invasion was complete, eventually holding scores of the CIA's "ghost" prisoners who'd been "rendered" from all over the world. When the CIA abducted a man named Khaled El-Masri from Macedonia and brought him here, his black-clad interrogators told him that he "was in Afghanistan, where there are no laws . . . 'We can do with you whatever we want.'"

What was once a single, crumbling building was now an entire complex spanning dozens of acres and surrounded by high brick walls and a barbed wire fence. Outside the walled gates was another wind-blasted and paint-chipped sign in Dari and English: NO PHOTOGRAPHY. I start snapping pictures.

Black SUVs pull out from the far side of the compound, a telltale sign of some kind of "special" American unit: CIA, Special Forces, or contractor. Realizing that there's a checkpoint ahead, I pull out the memory card on my camera, stash it under the car seat, then pull out another and shoot off a few more pictures. If the guards demand to see what pictures I've taken, they will see that I have indeed taken forbidden photographs. I plan to play dumb. I'll pretend not to have seen the billboard-sized sign, admit to taking the photos, and apologetically erase them or forfeit the camera and memory card. The good stuff will be safely under the car seat. The images on the card are far more valuable to me than the easily replaceable camera equipment.

But none of that will be necessary. As we pull up toward the ramshackle checkpoint, the rail-thin Afghan guard lazily asks where we're going. Maiwand tells them we're going back to Kabul.

"What is this place?" we ask.

"Training facility," says the disinterested guard.

"Are there Americans here?"

"Yes, lots of Americans."

We turn around to go back the way we came; two Humvees painted desert-tan pass by.

Every year, the United States spends more than $50 billion to fund a secret world of classified military and intelligence activities, a world of secret airplanes and unacknowledged spacecraft, "black" military units and covert prisons, a secret geography that military and intelligence insiders call the "black world."

It is a global world. It extends from secret prisons in dusty Afghan hinterlands to ice-encrusted radomes near the North Pole, and from remote eavesdropping stations in the Australian outback to makeshift camps and dirt landing strips in South American jungles. But this black world is more than a collection of places. It is an economy of secret dollars, a world of security clearances and secrecy oaths, code names and classifications tucked away in archives larger than the nation's greatest libraries.

But you don't have to scour the earth's corners to find the blank spots on maps characterizing this secret world. The vast majority of this secret world is not found in the remote corners of the earth, but is instead startlingly close to home. And its scale is tremendous.

Approximately *four million* people in the United States hold security clearances to work on classified projects in the black world. By way of contrast, the federal government employs approximately 1.8 million civilians in the "white" world. The black world, then, represents millions of jobs. It also represents accumulated knowledge and history.

A 2004 study by Peter Galison at Harvard University concluded that, in terms of information, the "classified universe as it is sometimes called is certainly not smaller, and very probably much larger than this unclassified one." Using data from 2001, Galison noted that there were 33 million classification actions.

Assuming that each action represented, on average, ten pages, he deduced that 330 million pages were classified that year. About 80 million were declassified, leaving a net gain of about 250 million classified pages in secret archives. Galison found that if you measure accumulated human knowledge by numbers of pages, the amount of classified knowledge produced in a single year is about five times as great as the amount of knowledge going into the world's greatest repositories of public knowledge. And the classified universe continues to expand.

This book is a guide to the geography of the classified universe, a circumnavigation of the black world, and an examination of the secret state that has grown and matured as a shadow part of the American government.

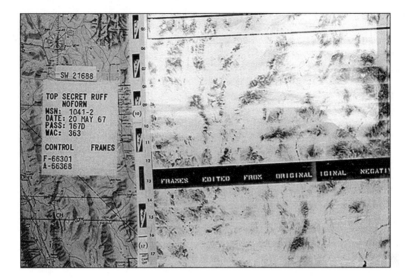

1

Facts on the Ground
Berkeley

The geography department at U.C. Berkeley lies on the relatively quiet north side of campus near the corner of Hearst and Euclid avenues in a building named after a former CIA director. The department's home is on the fifth floor of McCone Hall, a name commemorating John McCone, whom Kennedy appointed CIA head after the Bay of Pigs disaster. Having a geography building named after a CIA director somehow makes sense. The building, after all, plays host to a handful of social scientists who spend much of their time traveling around the world, collecting, analyzing, and publishing information about faraway, and sometimes not so faraway, places. A social scientist's work can be remarkably close to that of an intelligence analyst for the CIA or NSA. The lines separating academia from state power can get exceptionally blurry. Across campus from the geography department, at the Boalt law school on the corner of Bancroft and Piedmont avenues on the eighth floor of Simon Hall, is the office of John Yoo. While working in the Bush administration's Office of Legal Counsel, Yoo authored legal opinions authorizing everything from CIA renditions to "enhanced interrogation techniques" to warrantless surveillance of Americans by the National Security Agency. Upon leaving the Bush administration in 2003, Yoo returned to his professorship at Berkeley. In an age where information is power, it doesn't take much investigative work to find all sorts of connections among the academy, the military, and the intelligence industries. One doesn't even have to walk across campus. Every spring, like clockwork, recruitment letters from the National Geospatial-Intelligence Agency show up at McCone Hall, encouraging young scholars to join the intelligence community's own version of the geography department.

When most people hear the word "geography," they're reminded of traumatic elementary school quizzes on the names of rivers, mountain ranges, and state capitals. People think of maps. But although the discipline finds its origins in Renaissance exploration and the imperial mapmakers of royal courts, contemporary geographic research has come a long way. Geographers nowadays do everything from building elaborate digital climate models of potential global warming scenarios to picking through bits of fossilized pollen to reconstruct prehistoric agricultural practices, and from tracing the light-speed flows of international capital to documenting localized effects of nature tourism on sub-Saharan village life. The discipline, in short, accommodates a wide range of research methods and topics all united by the axiom that everything happens somewhere, that all human and natural phenomena have, well, a geography.

In McCone Hall's basement is the earth sciences library, featuring discipline-specific books and journals; it houses an extensive map collection as well, in a back room filled with flat files. The library's collection also includes an archive of United States Geological Survey (USGS) aerial images, all neatly indexed in an old-fashioned card catalog.

I've spent a lot of time looking at those aerial images. Years before Google Earth went online, I was using the archive to research prisons. With the onset of the "war on drugs" in the early 1980s, California had embarked on the largest prison-building project in the history of the world. The state had built thirty-three prisons in just a few decades. Over the previous 132 years, California had built just twelve. The aerial images helped me to understand where prisons were, why they were there, and what made California's newest prisons different from those of the past.

California's new prisons had little resemblance to their older cousins like Folsom and San Quentin, now immortalized in the songs of Johnny Cash. The new prisons were marvels of engineering, dense prefabricated cities of razor wire and white concrete that could go up at almost a moment's notice. Unlike earlier penitentiaries like Alcatraz, located prominently in the public view as a haunting visual reminder not to break the law, California's new industrial prisons were built far away from urban centers in the poorest and remotest regions of the state, out of sight and, to most of California's population, out of mind. From time to time, stories of torture and extreme violence make their way into the news. At Pelican Bay, California's premier "super-max" prison in the forest near the Oregon border, guards boiled a man named Vaughn Dortch alive. In a 1995 ruling stemming from abuse at the prison, federal judge Thelton Henderson wrote that "dry words on paper cannot adequately capture the senseless suffering and sometimes wretched misery that Pelican Bay State Prison's unconstitutional practices leave in their wake."

At Corcoran State Prison in California's Central Valley, guards staged "gladiator days," sending prisoners who were known enemies into a small yard and betting on which prisoner might prevail in the ensuing mayhem. When fights got out of control, guards trained their weapons on the prisoners. Gunfire was a daily occurrence. In the eight years after Corcoran opened, eight prisoners had been shot dead and fifty wounded. The guards nicknamed Warden George Smith "Mushroom George" because "mushrooms like being kept in the dark and fed shit."

I hypothesized that the prison's physical distance from urban centers translated into a kind of cultural distance: Their geography translated into secrecy. Few outsiders regularly visited the prisons in California's hinterlands. Volunteer-led programming was at a minimum. Visits by family members, journalists, and academics were few and far between. It seemed to me that there was a strong connection between geography, secrecy, and extralegal violence at the prisons.

To understand these prison geographies, I started collecting aerial and satellite images of these "next generation" prisons from all over the Southwest: California, Nevada, Arizona, and New Mexico. I wanted to see what these places looked like from the God's-eye view that aerial images uniquely afforded. How close were they to other institutions? How did they change over time? How was the land being used before the prisons came? As I continued exploring Berkeley's image archive, my focus started to wander. I took to pursuing images for their own sake, indulging myself in the spindly landscape aesthetics of fluvial fans, the circular shapes of desert agriculture, and the fading footprints of abandoned settlements and ghost towns.

As I worked my way through the archive, I noticed that vast swaths of land, particularly in the Nevada desert, were missing from the imagery collections. I assumed that my own ineptitude with the image archive's antiquated filing system was to blame. I expanded my search to the entire USGS archive, plugging longitudes and latitudes into a government search engine to retrieve image previews. When I did that, I stumbled across a series of images that left me flabbergasted: black plates with stenciled white letters reading simply FRAMES EDITED FROM ORIGINAL NEGATIVE. Someone, somewhere, in some official capacity, had deliberately removed these plates from the archives. I was startled to find blank spots on the official map, an image that hearkened back to an earlier age.

Blank spots on maps were a hallmark of Renaissance cartography. Early modern geographers like Henricus Martellus, having rediscovered works of ancient Greek geography such as Ptolemy's *Geography*, used ancient Greek cartographic projections to depict the earth's known surface. Martellus's maps from 1489 updated the ancient Greek projections to include data from Marco Polo's journeys and Portuguese voyages down Africa's coast. His maps portray Africa as a long, distorted, and featureless swath of land, and Southeast Asia as a contiguous landmass extending far into the Southern Hemisphere. Australia is missing entirely. After Columbus and Portuguese explorers began charting the New World, vast new blank spots appeared on contemporary maps. The Cantino planisphere, one of the earliest surviving maps to the New World, shows fragments of North and South American coastlines. Beyond them, the world is vast, empty, and unexplored.

It was hard for me to believe that here, at the dawn of the twenty-first century, there could be such a thing as an unmapped space. Our world has maps for just about everything imaginable: With GPS-enabled navigation systems, it is impossible for modern ship captains to get lost at sea. Real-time weather satellites transmit up-to-the-minute atmospheric conditions to anyone connected to the Internet or with access to a shortwave radio. Google Earth provides detailed, scalable satellite images of nearly every inch of the world's surface. Maps from the United States Geological Survey contain precise topographic and elevation data for the world's landforms. There are maps for the ocean's deepest trenches and maps of the outer planets; cosmological maps describe the large-scale structures of the universe itself, while maps of the human genome chart human life's most basic building blocks. The world, in short, has been elaborately and meticulously mapped. The images I was looking for were missing, not because the desert hadn't been mapped, but because what they showed was secret.

As it turns out, this also had a historical precedent. During the age of exploration there were two kinds of maps: Some were intended for general consumption, others were tightly held state secrets. The maps Magellan used to circumnavigate the globe, for example, were of the latter sort. Although Magellan's maps were rife with blank spots showing the limits of Spanish exploration, they contained far more detail than the public maps. The Portuguese and Spanish empires' secret maps revealed landforms and trade routes the rival empires sought to hide from one another. Other, deliberately inaccurate, maps were produced and "leaked" from one empire to another in elaborate disinformation and deception campaigns. The "real" maps were the empires' greatest secrets, documents so sensitive that an unauthorized person caught with them could be put to death. The maps themselves, and control over the information they depicted, were instruments of imperial power. As author Miles Harvey put it, "The Portuguese controlled the Indies because the Portuguese controlled the maps."

I didn't tell my fellow geographers about my growing fascination with places that had been erased from the public record, although I did locate an old Soviet reconnaissance photo of the black site near Groom Lake, which I posted on my office door as an inside joke to myself. In my free time, I started consuming everything I could on the topic of secret places. Sifting through stories of secret aircraft and black military operations, I realized that I already knew something about this world. As the son of an Air

Force doctor, I'd grown up on military bases all over the world, and like so many other people who grow up in the military, I had always assumed that I'd end up in the service as well, hopefully as a fighter pilot. It was the only world I knew. I was fascinated by aircraft like the SR-71, whose engines seemed to split open the sky itself when its black cobra-like airframe swooped down over annual base air shows. I knew that its performance characteristics were highly classified—almost no one really knew how fast or how high it could fly. When my father fixed up some of the pilots, he was invited to Beale Air Force Base to see the aircraft up close. I remember him arriving home that evening and saying that the plane could go a lot faster than what it said in *The Guinness Book of World Records*. Later on, as a teenager, I'd drink tequila with guys returning from Special Forces missions, who could never say where they'd been or what they'd been doing after returning home. My high school friends and I agreed that the SF guys all had a few screws loose but we were happy to take advantage of their alcohol ration cards.

As I started to research black sites in earnest, I was surprised by the lack of serious literature about them. To be sure, I could find plenty of soft documentaries about places like Groom Lake; the UFO literature abounded with references to "secret bases" like Area 51 and Hangar 18 at Wright-Patterson Air Force Base in Ohio. There were a handful of articles in more legitimate magazines like *Popular Science*. References to the black sites near Groom Lake and Tonopah showed up from time to time in defense industry publications like *Aviation Week & Space Technology*, mostly in articles speculating about new, still classified, warplanes. A few notable books had taken up the subject of secret airplanes or the psychology of UFOs, but the more I looked, the more I discovered another blank spot of sorts: There was very little scholarship on black sites. In other words, there was a blank spot in the literature.

There aren't a lot of things that someone, somewhere in the

halls of academia, hasn't dedicated their life to exploring. The halls of universities play home to people studying some of the most obscure phenomena imaginable, from the life cycles of Siberian slime molds to the geologic makeup of Pluto's moons, and from the question of whether there's something objectively good about eating chocolate to the historical lineage of a particular line in a James Joyce novel. No doubt, at this very moment a handful of scholars are engaged in passionate, even vicious debates on those very topics at conferences and in the pages of peer-reviewed journals. That's one of the wonderful things about academia: Someone, somewhere, is studying just about anything and sharing their theories and findings with a cast of international colleagues. With this in mind, the fact that I couldn't find a serious body of literature on black sites puzzled me. But it wasn't entirely surprising, either: Tales of hidden air bases and secret weapons tend to be so entwined with conspiracy theories and other sorts of fringe vernacular myths that the average academic would have a hard time acknowledging that sort of research to their colleagues, much less get funding to support the work.

At the same time, however, black sites were taking on a different cultural meaning. Not only were they real, they were deadly serious. In an October 12, 2001, memo, Attorney General John Ashcroft instructed all federal agencies and departments to err on the side of secrecy when processing Freedom of Information Act requests, ending the Clinton era's "presumption of disclosure." A few months later, the CIA was interrogating terror suspect Abu Zubaida at an "undisclosed location" after his early 2002 capture in Pakistan. In the Office of Legal Counsel, my colleague John Yoo was writing legal briefs authorizing the creation of "ghost prisoners" and other opinions that would become collectively known as the "torture memos." By 2003, classified military spending equaled the Cold War highs of the Reagan era. Vice President Dick Cheney's frequent jaunts to "undisclosed" or "secure" locations became the stuff of comedy. His comments about having to work on the "dark side" in the war on terror would become emblematic of what Alberto Gonzales called the "new paradigm." Blank spots on maps were coming to define the twenty-first-century United States, just as they have defined empires of the past.

Most social scientists who've studied secrecy have done so by developing Max Weber's pithy comments on the subject from his posthumously published *Wirtschaft und Gesellschaft (Economy and Society)*. These oft-quoted lines are from his chapter on bureaucracy:

> Every bureaucracy seeks to increase the superiority of the professionally informed by keeping their knowledge and intentions secret. Bureaucratic administration always tends to be an administration of "secret sessions": in so far as it can, it hides its knowledge and action from criticism . . . The concept of the "official secret" is the specific invention of bureaucracy.

The Weberian thesis applies to bureaucracies in general: The DMV, or your Parent-Teacher Association, or your Rotary Club, or your local softball league is just as unlikely to disclose its mistakes as the CIA. In the Weberian scheme secrecy is little more than an unintended effect of modern bureaucratic organization.

But the CIA isn't your softball league, and this is where the Weberian thesis falls short. State secrecy is a form of executive power. It is the power to unilaterally and legitimately conceal events, actions, budgets, programs, and plans from the legislature and public at large—the people who are paying for it. State secrecy is a form of monarchical power that contemporary states have inherited from the kingdoms of yesteryear. In our American system, state secrecy is the provenance of the executive branch; it has little statutory basis. It is a tool of kings.

And so, while this book is about state secrecy, it is, more importantly, a book about democracy; it is about how the United States has become dependent on spaces created through secrecy, spaces that lie outside the rule of law, outside the Constitution, outside the democratic ideals of equal rights, transparent government, and informed consent.

It seems to me that when we think about secrecy, it's helpful to think about it in terms of geography, to think about the spaces, landscapes, and practices of secrecy. We live in a world that can often seem supremely abstract, ungrounded, and confusing, especially when it comes to matters of politics and notions of democracy. I think that trying to understand secrecy through geography helps make the subject more real. Thinking about secrecy in terms of concrete spaces and practices helps us to see how secrecy happens and helps to explain how secrecy grows and expands.

State secrecy is an amalgam of logics and practices with a common intent: to conceal "facts on the ground," to make things disappear, and to plausibly deny their existence. To accomplish this, military and intelligence officials create "secure" facilities in military bases and in research institutions, clandestine outposts in the corners of vast deserts, and develop elaborate cover stories and false identities to disguise surreptitious programs. State secrecy means pulling satellite photographs out of public archives, instituting security clearances, compartmentalizing information, and forbidding workers to speak about what it is that they do. But geography theory tells us that it really isn't possible to make things disappear, to render things nonexistent. Geography tells us that secrecy, in other words, is always bound to fail, and because secrecy is always bound to fail, perhaps counterintuitively, it tends to grow ever stronger.

Geography tells us that it's impossible to take something that exists and make it nonexistent at the same time. "Geography," my friend and colleague Allan Pred used to say before he passed away, is "an inescapable existential reality. Everybody has a body, nobody can escape from their body, and consequently all human activity—every form of individual and collective practice—is a situated practice and thereby geographical." What this means is that secrecy can only work as a Band-Aid, a way to cover something up. But just as a Band-Aid announces the fact that it conceals a wound, blank spots on maps and blacked-out documents announce the fact that there's something hidden. Secrets, in other words, often inevitably announce their own existence. For example, when the government takes satellite photos out of public archives, it practically broadcasts the locations of classified facilities. Blank spots on maps outline the things they seek to conceal. To truly keep something secret, then, those outlines also have to be made secret. And then those outlines, and so on. In this way, secrecy's geographic contradictions (the fact that you can't make something disappear completely) quickly give rise to political contradictions between the secret state and the "normal" state. In order to contain those political contradictions, new ways of practicing secrecy are created and deployed. This is one of the reasons why secrecy reproduces itself, why it tends to sculpt the world around it in its own image.

Since the Second World War the secret world has grown dramatically. Covert operations and classified programs have placed new forms of sovereign power in the hands of the executive branch, institutionalized dishonesty and disinformation, and thoroughly militarized the national economy. Secret programs, and the social, cultural, legal, and economic blank spots that they represent, have transformed and continue to transform the United States in their own image.

More often than not, their outlines are in plain view.

It was the weekend, and campus was relatively quiet. No throngs of students meandering to morning classes, no activists handing

out flyers for one thing or another, no overtaxed professors rush-
ing around from meeting to meeting, quietly hoping not to bump
into their graduate students en route. As I stepped into McCone
Hall and turned down the corridor to face my office, I noticed
someone standing outside my door. The well-groomed man, who
must have been in his late thirties, sported casual J. Crew–style
clothes and held himself with the disciplined poise of a military
officer. From his appearance, I knew a few things about him: He
was too old to be an undergraduate, too well-dressed to be a professor, and his posture was too good for him to be a graduate student. I hung back watching, trying to figure out what he was doing
outside my office.

After a few moments, he crouched down to stare at the photograph I'd put in a plastic frame outside my door, the Soviet satellite photo of the base at Groom Lake that was the redacted image
from the archive. The man stared long and hard at the image,
which intrigued me because it depicted something rather esoteric.
As I continued standing at the end of the hallway watching, the
man started opening the frame to take my photograph out. It was
time for an intervention. I ran up and asked him why the hell he
was trying to steal my picture.

The stunned man apologized, stammering that he was only
interested in the photo because he'd never seen such a clear picture of the site. He just wanted a closer look.

"Do you know what that place is?" I asked.

"Yes; do you know what that place is?" came the reply.

"Yes."

After a long pause, he said, "I used to be a fighter pilot."

Back when he flew F-15s, he explained, they'd have big war
games out in the Nevada desert, learning how to dogfight and fly
combat missions in the Air Force's version of *Top Gun*, called Red
Flag. They had a huge amount of airspace for these war games, he
explained, but there was one place, in the middle of the range,

they weren't supposed to fly into—the place in the photo. He said it was called "the Box." You weren't allowed to fly anywhere near the Box, he explained. Even if you were running out of gas and needed an emergency landing strip, you were supposed to bail out rather than land on the runway in the Box.

Eventually, the man let out that one of his buddies from the fighter squadron had actually landed there. Running out of fuel over the Nevada desert, the man's friend had decided to spare the taxpayers the $30 million cost of the warplane, and perhaps his own life, by declining to pull the F-15's ejection seat. Instead, he landed in the Box. When the wayward pilot returned to his squadron more than a week later, his fellow pilots laid into him: He'd flown into the Box; he wasn't supposed to do that under any circumstances; what happened? The pilot just shrugged his shoulders; he couldn't say.

Pointing to the satellite photo outside my door, the pilot said, "That place is part of the black world."

2

A Guy in the Classified World
An Air Force Base in California

Outside the visitors' center at Vandenberg Air Force Base on the California coast near San Luis Obispo, I met my escort, Lieutenant Stewart. The morning fog had lifted surprisingly early from Vandenberg's home atop Burton Mesa, and the warm sun on my jacket reminded me of the California dream and all the hopefulness so many Americans have carried out west. Stewart was also enjoying the surf and sun: He'd been in-state for just two weeks but was already working on his surfing technique in his downtime at the coastal beaches. An easygoing guy with brown shaved hair and glasses, Stewart already had an advanced degree in chemical engineering and was scheduled to begin missile school in a few months. It was a good deal, he figured: a guaranteed salary, health care, school paid for, and when he finished his service he'd have a Top Secret clearance. Stewart calculated that he'd be able to work in whatever sector of the government or private industry he wanted. He was probably right.

"I'd go if they told me to; that's what you signed up for," said Stewart, bringing up the ongoing wars in Iraq and Afghanistan, "but I'm not much of a shot," he continued. He pointed to the Air Force regulation glasses resting on his nose, often called BCGs, "birth control glasses," on account of their unflattering look.

As a prospective missileer, Stewart reckoned that he was far more likely to end up at the bottom of a silo in Nebraska or Wyoming with his finger on a nuclear launch button than he was to find himself on the back of a Humvee in what he called "the desert."

But the beginning of missile school was still months away. In the meantime, Stewart was stuck in the Public Affairs Office babysitting visitors like me. I was there to learn about spy satellites.

One of the contradictory things about the United States is that an incredible amount of the government is dedicated to doing things in secret. At the same time, it's one of the world's most open governments. Where I was standing was a case in point. I wanted to learn something about the secret world, so I called up the public affairs officer at a military base almost entirely dedicated to black projects. They offered me a tour. I could walk right in through the front door. But, of course, they weren't going to let me see everything I wanted to.

"Are we going to be able to go visit the tracking station?" I asked. I figured it was a long shot, but I wanted to see where and how the people at the Vandenberg detachment of U.S. Space Command communicated with the launch vehicles and spacecraft under their control. I knew that there were a number of tracking stations on the base, the most well-known being the Cooke Tracking Station, also known as "Big Sky Ranch."

Stewart chuckled nervously at the question. "Ummm . . . not

this time," he said with a smile. "You need security clearances and stuff to go over there," he explained. I wasn't going to fight about it, but I did point out that a lot of that data was freely available from the United States Strategic Command (USSTRATCOM) in the form of a publicly accessible database called Space Track. Surely there couldn't be too many secrets. "Maybe they're just nervous about people having sticky fingers around all those computers," he offered up as a kind of rhetorical compromise. Instead, we'd get a nice view of the base Burger King, see a couple of launch pads from afar, and take a quick tour of the base museum.

I came to Vandenberg because I wanted to see a top-secret base up close. Vandenberg fit the bill. The base is the nation's "other" gateway to space, the fog-enshrouded doppelgänger of Cape Canaveral along California's craggy coastline. When we think of "the Cape," as locals call it, we may think of Mercury and Apollo astronauts lifting off toward the heavens against the backdrop of Florida's sunny azure coastline and pearl-white beaches. Countless reels of news footage shot at the Cape show expectant astronauts holding press conferences and televised countdowns spearheaded by black-tied NASA launch controllers and engineers. There is far less publicity surrounding the operations at Vandenberg. Although Vandenberg also sits along the beach, the gray waves perpetually crashing into the Pacific's jagged coastline and the fog so thick that you can almost hold it in your hands are a far cry from the postcard-picture beaches of Florida. And the space operations at Vandenberg are decidedly less advertised. The base's geographical location lends itself to putting spacecraft into what's known as a polar orbit, the preferred orbit for photographic reconnaissance satellites. Vandenberg's main tenant, the 30th Space Wing, is responsible for everything from launching experimental Minuteman ICBMs over the Pacific Ocean to putting billion-dollar classified satellites in orbit on behalf of an agency called the National Reconnaissance Office.

The NRO is one of those "riddle, wrapped in a mystery, inside an enigma" sorts of institutions. It is to NASA what Vandenberg is to Cape Canaveral. It is the United States' "other" space agency. For most of its history, the NRO was black: Formed in 1961, its existence remained secret until 1992. For years, it was illegal for Vandenberg-based missileers to even utter the words "National Reconnaissance Office" in public. To this day, the agency's budget, as well as almost everything it does, is classified. If NASA's public mission could be symbolized by the Hubble Space Telescope, quietly orbiting Earth with its electronic eyes peering into the deepest depths of the visible universe for the benefit of us all, then the National Reconnaissance Office's mission is symbolized by the fact that it controls dozens of satellites similar in design to the Hubble Space Telescope, labeled with code names like ONYX, IKON, IMPROVED CRYSTAL, and ZIRCONIC. But in contrast to the Hubble Space Telescope, the NRO's electronic eyes are not interested in the universe's furthest and most ancient mysteries. Instead, their lenses point directly down at Earth. Vandenberg, with its constant schedule of space launches, is the NRO's gateway to the heavens.

This base holds plenty of secrets, and plenty of cover stories designed to hide those secrets. On the afternoon of December 14, 2006, a Delta II rocket, by a joint venture between Lockheed Martin and Boeing called the United Launch Alliance, lifted off from Vandenberg's Space Launch Complex 2. The purpose and payload of the launch, known only by the name NRO L-21, was highly classified, although the spacecraft was suspected of being a prototype synthetic aperture radar imaging satellite for a next-generation series of spacecraft, part of the Future Imagery Architecture (FIA) program.

A month after the launch, journalists would learn that the National Reconnaissance Office lost communication with the mysterious satellite. The spacecraft, called USA 193, was beginning to look like a "comprehensive failure." A year later, USA 193 would appear in newspaper headlines as it tumbled uncontrollably down toward the earth. After its initial launch, USA 193 was in a 349 x 365 km orbit (a typical satellite orbit isn't circular, but oval), crossing Earth's equator at a 58.48 degree angle. On February 11, 2008, its orbit had decayed to 255 x 268 km. Eight days later, it was in a 244 x 261 km orbit. USA 193 was falling from the sky at an increasing rate. The Pentagon decided to shoot the malfunctioning satellite down, but its explanation for the action looked like a cover story.

The shoot-down was necessary, explained the Pentagon, "to rupture the fuel tank to dissipate the approximately 1,000 pounds (453 kg) of hydrazine, a hazardous fuel which could pose a danger to people on earth, before it entered the earth's atmosphere." The official explanation made little sense to defense industry analysts. Writing for *Newsweek*, John Barry pointed out that three quarters of the earth's surface is water and 95 percent of the earth's surface is uninhabited. The odds of the satellite hitting a person were "literally millions to one." In the half century that satellites have been in the sky, about seventeen thousand objects have fallen back to earth. None have ever hit a person. The danger posed by hydrazine was also a dubious claim: It was exceptionally unlikely that the fuel tank would survive reentry. If it somehow did, the fuel would create a gas cloud the size of two football fields and would dissipate within a few minutes. How toxic was the gas? About as dangerous to people as ammonia or chlorine: The National Fire Protection Association's NFPA 704 standard characterizes the health risks of hydrazine as a three on a scale of one to four: "Short exposure could cause serious temporary or moderate residual injury." "The claim there was a danger from the fuel is not the most preposterous thing the Pentagon has ever said. But it seemed to be a bit of a stretch," said defense analyst John Pike.

On February 21, the USS *Lake Erie* successfully shot down the spacecraft with an SM-3 missile over the Pacific Ocean. The Pentagon stuck to its story that the reason for the shoot-down was the dangerous fuel tank, and perhaps they were being sincere. Few foreign countries, however, were convinced. The Russian government claimed that the fuel-tank story was an excuse to test an antisatellite weapons system (ASAT), which the Pentagon denied. Nonetheless, six days after the shoot-down, Defense Secretary Robert Gates said that the shoot-down proved the potential of controversial missile-defense systems. If the fuel-tank explanation for the USA 193 shoot-down was in fact a cover story, it was just the latest in a history of misinformation and outright deception that has gone hand in hand with the history of reconnaissance satellites.

As our white school bus lumbered along a small road toward the museum at Vandenberg's northern end, an old-timer named John acted as tour guide, telling stories through a microphone from the front of the bus. The retired missileer told us that when Khrushchev had come to the United States in 1959, the Soviet premier had wanted to visit Disneyland but the American State Department told him it was too insecure. As a consolation, they put him on a train ride up the California coast, a route that took him right through this part of Vandenberg. Looking out the window of his train, said John, Khrushchev spied three Atlas missiles towering on the horizon, spewing thick white fog from the liquid oxygen in their fuel tanks. "Those missiles are pointed at the Soviet Union," an American representative is said to have told the premier. "Yes, we have many more pointed at you, too," came the reply. "If he looked out the other side of the window," John offered up, "he would have seen a Titan rocket on the launchpad. That was for the Discoverer program that was declassified in the 1980s. It was actually the CORONA program," he said, referring to the United States' first spy satellites. The cover story held it was a research program called Discoverer, when in fact the satellite was code-named CORONA and was designed to take detailed pictures of the Soviet interior. "We knew from CORONA that the Russians only had two missiles on pads and that only one of them worked."

I knew that John's story could not have been true. Khrushchev had indeed come to the United States in the fall of 1959, but the first successful CORONA mission hadn't occurred until nearly a year later. There may have been an Atlas on the launchpad that day—there was a long series of unsuccessful launches throughout 1959 and 1960 before the first success—but the United States certainly didn't have a spy satellite in orbit yet.

Ostensibly an Air Force project to conduct biomedical experiments in space, Discoverer's true purpose was to explain away the new launchpad at Vandenberg Air Force Base and to hide—in plain sight—all of the attention-grabbing activities that go into putting a satellite in orbit. General Electric, which was building the camera capsule for CORONA, went as far as publishing a pamphlet on the Discoverer program, explaining how the satellite would ride an Agena rocket into space and how its capsule containing "scientific data" would be recovered. But it would be a while before the satellite made it into orbit.

On January 21, 1959, Discoverer 1 aborted on the launchpad. Thirty-eight days later, the satellite reached orbit before its stabilization system failed and it spun out of control. Discoverer 2, launched on April 13 without a camera, achieved polar orbit, but its prototype capsule ejected prematurely. The CIA believed it landed somewhere on the island of Spitsbergen, north of Norway. Coal miners in the community of Longyearbyen reported seeing a "starburst" in the sky, followed by a descending parachute. In public, the Pentagon announced that it was not looking to recover the capsule, not knowing whether it had ejected or not. In private, they dispatched a search team to the Arctic island, looking for a gold sphere lying in the snow. The Air Force leader of the expedition, Lieutenant Colonel Charles Mathison, wasn't cleared to know about CORONA, so he didn't know exactly what it was that he was looking for. Mathison ended the search on April 22, wondering if tracks he'd seen near a likely landing site meant that the Soviets had gotten to the capsule first. Another story about the missing Discoverer 2 capsule says that in the winter of 1960–61, a pair of Russian loggers stumbled on the metal globe north of Moscow and split it open with an ax but found it empty.

Eleven subsequent Discoverer launches all failed over the following year. Discoverers 3 and 4 didn't make it into orbit. Number five made it into orbit and ejected its capsule at the correct time, but when the capsule's rocket kicked in it fired in the wrong direction, sending the capsule into a much higher, unrecoverable orbit. When Discoverer 6 deployed its capsule, the radio beacon malfunctioned and C-119 recovery crews failed to locate the payload. Discoverer 7 tumbled out of control after launch. The eighth flew into the wrong orbit. The Thor rocket booster on Discoverer 9 burned out prematurely, sending the satellite back to the ground. On the tenth launch, the booster rocket veered off course at twenty thousand feet, forcing mission controllers to blow the rocket up with a self-destruct button. The next mission, launched April 10, 1960, went into a perfect orbit. Then the capsule disappeared after being ejected. Discoverer 12 almost made it into orbit before an electrical problem on the Agena's altitude control system sent the spacecraft and rocket hurtling back down to Earth.

Discoverer 13, launched on August 10, 1960, was a success. When the CORONA team learned of the victory, they were overjoyed—pictures taken that night show the engineers, cigars in hand, prancing around in the middle of a swimming pool wearing their suits and ties.

Bolstered by the achievement, the CIA's Richard Bissell got to work on the next launch, set for August 18. On this mission, Discoverer would carry a camera and film. It would be a bona fide reconnaissance mission over the Soviet Union. The Agena rocket thundered off the launchpad at Vandenberg, achieved a polar orbit, and began silently photographing swaths of the Soviet Union on each successive orbit. During the satellite's seventeenth revolution, exactly as planned, the satellite ejected its film capsule, the heat shield and parachute worked, and an Air Force captain named Harold Mitchell hooked the capsule from a C-119 in midair.

A remarkable trio of stories came together on the front page of *The New York Times* the next morning; behind all three of them was Richard Bissell's unseen hand. On the top-left, the headline read SPACE CAPSULE IS CAUGHT IN MID-AIR BY U.S. PLANE ON REENTRY FROM ORBIT. An illustrated diagram recounting Mitchell's successful recovery of the capsule accompanied the article, which made no reference to the satellite's actual mission. A subarticle read RUSSIANS ORBIT A SATELLITE CARRYING 2 DOGS AND TV.

On the top-right of the page, another secretly related headline read POWERS GETS A TEN YEAR SENTENCE; SOVIETS ASSERT PENALTY IS MILD, BUT EISENHOWER FINDS IT SEVERE. In an ironic twist of history, the first successful reconnaissance satellite images arrived on the same day that Francis Gary Powers, the U-2 pilot shot down near Sverdlosk, received a prison sentence for spying. The 3,600 feet of film from the CORONA mission covered more than 1.5 million square miles of the Soviet Union, returning, in Bissell's words, "more coverage than all the pictures of that country taken during the entire U-2 program."

I'd wanted to visit Vandenberg for a long time. Like so many other boys fascinated by space as a child, I joined the Young Astronauts and collected newspaper clippings about shuttle launches. When they stopped class in sixth grade and brought in a TV so we could watch the news of the Challenger explosion, I sat in stunned silence. I remember how relieved I felt two years later as I listened live on the radio when the next space shuttle mission came back to Earth unharmed. Driving down Highway 101 the night before on the way to Vandenberg, I couldn't help but keep looking through the sunroof of my car at the night sky, catching glances of the Milky Way, Jupiter, and the star Antares in the Southern Hemisphere. Approaching the Air Force base brought back that sense of wonder about space that has inspired so much human culture and science. For a few hours, I remained in awe of the fact that humans were able to travel into space at all, and, moreover, that it had become relatively commonplace. Vandenberg was a gateway between Earth and the night sky itself.

Vandenberg's museum wasn't much more than a few models and displays thrown together in a dilapidated old one-story barracks. At minimum, I hoped that the museum would feature photos from all the space launches since the base's opening. If that was the case, I'd be able to learn something about their payloads from the size of the rockets' fairings. Instead, we got dioramas of astronauts, a model military weather satellite, and a rather terrifying display showing how the ironically named Peacekeeper missile can drop multiple nuclear warheads at different targets once it's launched.

"In the early days of the missile programs," said John as we huddled in Vandenberg's bare-bones museum, "there was a problem with missiles corroding on the launchpad. They were made out of stainless steel, but not every part was." Water condensation could corrode parts of the rockets, leading to potentially devastating mishaps. "So the Air Force put out a request for someone to develop a water dispersion formula that would keep water off the missile. It would have to weigh less than paint," he explained, "because paint is heavy and can alter the performance of the rocket. . . . An outfit in San Diego got the contract and tried formula after formula, thirty-six, thirty-seven, thirty-eight, thirty-nine, until they finally got it. And from then until the last Titan Four I worked on," he said, "we'd wipe those things down with WD-40."

On the bus ride back to the visitors' center, John mused that a few years ago, it was illegal for missileers to say the words "National Reconnaissance Office." Now the NRO had a sign outside their facility in the old space shuttle launch complex. We passed right by.

Looking out the bus window, I could see the distant towers of the launchpads rising above the Pacific Ocean's deep blue horizon. To my left, the golf-ball architecture of Vandenberg's space-tracking facilities sat like overgrown mushrooms on California's green coastal hills. I was in the middle of a top-secret base, but the black world seemed as far away as if I were on a remote mountaintop looking through a telescope. I'd hoped to catch a glimpse of something unexpected, something I couldn't find in books, in Vandenberg's published launch schedules, in NASA archives, or in articles in *Aviation Week & Space Technology*. It was nowhere to be found.

I should have known that if I wanted a glimpse of the Pentagon's secret world, I'd never get one by going through the front door. My tour of Vandenberg was like GE's little pamphlet on the notional Discoverer program or the Pentagon's story about the incredible dangers of a falling fuel tank. The NRO's gateway to the stars was as opaque as the surface of Venus. There was, quite simply, nothing to see.

I was disappointed, but did I really think that Lieutenant Stewart or John would bend the rules and haul me up to a secure tracking station? That they'd let me into the room with the "big screen" and say "Hi, Trevor, let's take a look at some black satellites! Over there are the Lacrosse/ONYX radar-imaging satellites over North Korea, and there's USA 186 over there! Want to see some real-time images from one of them? How about we show you the camp in the Iraqi desert where we're secretly training Sunni extremists to go after Iraqi Shiites sympathetic to Iran? Oh, and by the way, do you want to see the real orbit of MISTY, our stealth satellite? Everyone thinks that it's in a 64.3 degree Molniya-type orbit, but that's just a decoy; the real satellite is in a 58.6 degree low Earth orbit. Look, it's over Albuquerque right now!"

No. The closest thing I'd see to the big screen would be a window display advertising a one-dollar Whopper Jr. at the base Burger King. If I wanted to see into the secret world, I'd have to try the back door.

3

Unexplored Territory
Downtown Las Vegas

From more than a hundred miles away, the neon signs and street-lights of Las Vegas glow deep pink on the desert horizon like a distant twilight that grows and grows the closer you get. Before pulling over the last set of mountains in the Mojave desert on the drive from California, you're engulfed with the sky's red glow as it pulls a bright veil over the star-filled darkness of the desert. Vegas is truly dazzling. On the Strip, neon billboards and JumboTrons pound the streets with flashing, multicolored brilliance. At the corner of Las Vegas Boulevard and Tropicana Avenue is a mock New York City, complete with faux Statue of Liberty, Brooklyn Bridge, and a roller coaster plunging through fake buildings. Across the street, the Excalibur Hotel: a casino castle replete with staged tournaments and jousting as family entertainment. The

Strip beams with incandescent tributes to Paris, Rome, Venice, ancient Egypt, and the Caribbean. Las Vegas advertises itself as a landscape of seduction, oversized rum cocktails served in plastic footballs, and endless partying. A city whose greatest export is its own image, a vision of excess. But Las Vegas is also home to another, far less illuminated landscape that becomes visible from some of the casinos' higher floors. I chose the eighteenth floor of the Tropicana. Oddly enough, it's one of the best vantage points for catching a glimpse of the Pentagon's black world.

From a hotel perch high up in the Tropicana's Island Tower, my view toward the southeast looked unremarkable. It's a view of McCarran Airport. Exactly the panorama I wanted. I was spending the week looking for airplanes.

With Las Vegas's airport spread out below me, I could spend each day watching plane after plane line up on the crowded runway, barrel down the tarmac, and disappear into the sky. Most of the aircraft wear the same bold colors of the Vegas Strip: Southwest Airlines' bright blue, red, and brown scheme; the green and orange of America West; Frontier Airlines, with the name "Frontier" painted in large block letters across the fuselage; the chrome-silver of Northwest Airlines; and an Air Canada jet, draped entirely in the red maple leaf of the Canadian flag. I was looking for airplanes, to be sure, but in contrast to the bright colors of the commercial carriers, the planes I spotted were remarkable only for their blandness. I went to Las Vegas to chart the movements of a small fleet of 737s and King Airs, unmarked save for an inoffensive white or blue stripe painted down the length of their dry-white airframes. These planes, known by the call sign they use in civilian airspace—Janet—are shuttles to and from the black world. Each day, they bus people to work at a handful of secret military installations in the deep desert to the north. Their home is a small, secure facility on the airport's northwestern side, far away from McCarran's vast commercial terminals. This secure and unassuming building lay almost directly below my hotel room.

My goal for the week was to begin mapping these aircrafts' movements. If I could trace the plane routes, understand their schedules, see where they go and how they get there, I could begin to describe the secret geography their routes represent. By cataloging the places they visited, I could begin pointing to places on the map and be certain that, wherever the destinations might be, they were somehow a part of the black world.

But mapping aircraft routes is far easier said than done, particularly with this wily fleet of planes, which, it turns out, engages in all sorts of high jinks to prevent someone like me from doing exactly what I'd set out to do. My hotel room overflowed with the equipment I'd need for the job: a high-powered telescope, eyepieces, a tripod, and a camera. With these I'd be able to see and record people getting on and off the planes as they made their way to and from work each day. I'd be able to read and record the tail numbers on the aircraft, then use the numbers to look up each airplane's Federal Aviation Administration file, making use of the open information to fill in my map. Another crucial piece of equipment was a RadioShack military-band-capable radio scanner, meticulously programmed with McCarran Airport's communication frequencies. The scanner allowed me to listen to the exchanges between pilots and air traffic controllers, and to overhear controllers' directions to the pilots. A DO NOT DISTURB sign hung from my door.

I awoke to the bell-like monotones of my cell phone alarm. As the predawn light lit up the thin film of grime on the window facing the airport, I saw the parking lot at the Janet terminal begin to fill up. A steady procession of cars moved through a guard gate at the far end of the compound before pulling into their places in the sprawling parking lot. These were the workers. Like many others, they call Las Vegas's expansive suburbs home, but instead of dealing blackjack, working the convention center floor, or filling any of the innumerable services a typical city requires, these men and women spend their days working in the defense industry's deepest recesses. One after another, they walked past a *USA Today* newspaper dispenser into the nondescript terminal. Through the eyepiece of my telescope, I spied them idling in the waiting area under cold-blue fluorescent lights. In time, a security officer on the far end of the room opened up a door to the runway and the workers filed through, across the tarmac, and up a mobile staircase. A stewardess in a dark blue uniform stood there to greet each one of them just before they disappeared into the plane's fuselage. It was 4:10 A.M., the first flight of the day.

A search through Federal Aviation Administration records shows that the Janet fleet is owned by a division of the Department of the Air Force housed at Box 1504 in Layton, Utah, just outside Air Force Materiel Command's Hill Air Force Base. But Air Force pilots don't fly these aircraft: The fleet is operated by the Special Projects Division of Edgerton, Germeshausen, and Grier, or EG&G for short. Their headquarters is just south of the airport at 821 Grier Drive, an address named after one of the company's founders. EG&G's history is synonymous with the history of nuclear weapons testing and classified military activities. Harold "Doc" Edgerton was the inventor of stroboscopic photography, the man who gave us images of bullets passing through apples, the intricate splash of a falling drop of milk, and the indentation on a football at the moment of a punt. Edgerton's images revealed the intricacies of the world faster than the human eye could see. The military ended up hiring his company to take high-speed photographs of nuclear weapons, first at Eniwetok Atoll in the Pacific, then at the Nevada Test Site. Before long, EG&G was developing specialized equipment for other parts of nuclear testing—everything from blast doors to detonators—and providing more mundane kinds of logistical support to the Atomic Energy Commission and military alike. From time to time, EG&G advertises jobs for pilots and flight attendants in the Las Vegas area. The jobs require Top Secret clearances.

The assumption underlying my long week in the Vegas room was one of geography's axioms: that the black world, like the rest of the world, is inescapably spatial. It must exist in the same way that shopping malls, fire stations, casinos, state capitals—indeed everything—must. It had to be composed of the same stuff as the rest of the world. This geographic axiom may seem obvious, but it is why I thought I could learn a lot about secrecy by looking through a telescope, by listening in on air traffic controllers, and by paying close attention to the daily flight patterns of the white 737s on the northwestern side of McCarran Airport. With these instruments, I would be able to see and hear the secret world breathing with life each day as people came and went, reproducing and reinvigorating this hidden world with their movements. Insisting on the black world's materiality is my starting point.

The aircraft on the tarmac below me, now loaded with the day's first batch of commuters, rifled down the runway and into the sky. My scanner crackled to life on 125.90 MHz, the Las Vegas Departure Control frequency. "Janet three-o-one: Climb and maintain four thousand five hundred." Leaving the domain of Las Vegas Departure controllers, the aircraft would start talking to Nellis Control, which manages the larger airspace around southern Nevada on 126.6500 MHz.

"Nellis, Janet three-o-one, good day," announces the plane's pilot on the new frequency.

"Janet three-o-one. Nellis Control. You're loud and clear. Nellis altimeter two-niner-eight-eight."

The aircraft headed northwest out of Las Vegas, making a beeline for the nondirectional beacon (NDB) at Mercury, Nevada, and the southernmost region of the nation's nuclear-weapons testing range at the Nevada Test Site. A few short minutes later, the aircraft entered the restricted military airspace above the Nevada Test Site, sixty miles northwest of Las Vegas. Nellis Control crackled over the radio, "Janet three-o-one, frequency change approved." It's a telling moment: Nellis Control just told the Janet that it's being handed off to another controller, but Nellis doesn't indicate the new frequency. The civilian air traffic controller trusts that the pilot knows which frequency he should tune in to for the new, anonymous controller. "Janet three-o-one. Good day," says the pilot. The Janet enters the restricted airspace of the Nellis Range Complex, a 3.1-million-acre tract of land covered by an even greater twelve thousand-square-mile swath of military airspace, an area the size of Switzerland. With the flick of a switch, the aircraft disappears and my scanner goes dead.

The enormous military range of the Nellis Complex is a landscape of extremes—parched dry lakes, sun-bleached sands, and mountains of craggy bedrock whose jagged outcroppings have been blunted and pulverized by eons of wind and erosion across the Basin and Range. A scant five inches of average annual rainfall nourish seemingly endless fields of gnarled sage and creosote, whose brittle, dry tendrils lay like bleached skeletons across the desert sand. In the summer, the horizon glimmers with mirages and convection waves as the desert bakes in one-hundred-plus-degree heat. Come winter, a thin layer of snow turns the desert into a frozen no-man's-land. From its inception as a bombing range during the Second World War, the Nellis Complex has been a place where the government does whatever it wants. When it created the Nellis Range (originally called the Las Vegas Range), the Army Air Corps explained that the land "wasn't much good for anything but gunnery practice—you could bomb it into oblivion and never notice the difference."

On the southern end of the restricted area is the company town for the Nevada Test Site, Mercury, and the small airfield adjacent to it, the Desert Rock Airstrip (DRA). Just north of Mercury and the DRA, blinding lights from atmospheric nuclear explosions lit the skies throughout the 1950s and '60s, creating the ultimate spectacle for Las Vegas partygoers to the south while raining the invisible death of nuclear fallout on small-town "downwinders" to the northeast. Nuclear detonations left the desert so scarred with pockmarks and craters that astronauts in training eventually used it to simulate the surface of the moon. To the east of the test site, a mock city called Terror Town holds counterterrorism training exercises. On the southern border lies Creech Air Force Base, home to squadrons of unmanned Predator and Reaper drones. The Predator "pilots" stationed at Creech control their aircraft all over the world via satellite uplink from anonymous computer terminals here in the Nellis Complex. Just north of Mercury, squarely in the middle of the Nevada Test Site, a recently constructed secret base takes shape on the east side of Yucca Dry Lake. Lockheed Martin tested an experimental unmanned aerial vehicle nicknamed "Polecat" here in late 2004; new hangars at the base undoubtedly house some of the company's most recent black offerings.

Northeast of the Nevada Test Site, just past Pahute Mesa, is a base called the Tolicha Peak Electronic Combat Range (TPECR), two miles north of Quartz Mountain. A sprawling facility, the TPECR is home to top-secret electronic warfare applications. Military documents suggest that Nellis Air Force Base in northern Las Vegas controls the facility, and that the TPECR plays a role in simulating threats, monitoring activities during Red Flag war games, and conducting acceptance testing for various electronic warfare capabilities. But much about the TPECR remains obscure. According to a research project conducted by the Center for Land Use Interpretation (in cooperation with the U.S. Air Force), "facilities at Tolicha Peak are . . . considered by the Air Force to be too sensitive to discuss."

Just past Mount Helen, near the northern border of the Nellis Complex, stands the Tonopah Test Range (TTR). The TTR is a kind of a "gray" base: Its existence is public, and like other conventional military bases and airports it has an international airport designation (TNX). A sign outside a guard shack on the northern edge of the base welcomes personnel to the installation. The Tonopah Test Range began its life in the early 1950s when Sandia Labs built the facility to experiment with test shapes for nuclear weapons. It was a counterpart to the Nevada Test Site. While the Department of Energy (then the Atomic Energy Commission) lit the skies with mushroom clouds to the south, engineers at Tonopah devised rockets, bombs, and other shapes to deliver those nuclear payloads.

For the last thirty years, however, the Department of Energy facilities at the TTR have taken a backseat to classified Air Force activities. The Air Force laid the groundwork for the base's newer incarnation in the late 1970s, when the 4477th Test and Evaluation Squadron funded improvements to the airstrip and added hangars, taxiways, support facilities, and other structures adjacent to the older Sandia facilities. Known by their nickname, the Red Eagles, the 4477th had an unusual mission: Under the code name CONSTANT PEG, they flew a small squadron of pilfered Soviet fighters, developed dogfighting tactics against the foreign aircraft, and trained a generation of pilots to fight against them. Other classified squadrons followed the Red Eagles to the TTR.

In 1981, the newly created 4450th Tactical Group set up shop at the TTR, building more hangars and funding more improvements to the clandestine Air Force base. The 4450th's mission was to fly an aircraft that would become one of the largest secret programs since the Manhattan Project: the F-117A Nighthawk stealth fighter. As the stealth fighters became operational, they joined the ranks of the other black aircraft at Tonopah, flying secret training missions each night over the American West—missions that surreptitiously continued for almost a decade before the Air Force acknowledged the stealth fighter's existence on November 10, 1988. Thirteen months later, the planes took off from Tonopah to spearhead the December 1989 invasion of Panama. In 1990, the black planes deployed to King Khalid Air Base in Saudi Arabia to lead the first Gulf War. Stealth crews took to calling King Khalid Air Base "Tonopah East." When the stealth fighters returned home to the United States, the Air Force transferred the fighters to Holloman Air Force Base in New Mexico. But the base at Tonopah stayed open for business, its new mission obscure.

Sixty miles southeast of the Tonopah Test Range, nested in the Emigrant Valley between the Papoose Range and the Jumbled Hills, is a place former U-2 pilot Francis Gary Powers once called "one of those 'you can't get there from here' places." If the Tonopah Test Range is a sort of "gray" facility, the base adjacent to a dry lakebed called Groom Lake is a black site through and through. Though the aerospace complex has been operational for more than half a century, the Air Force has said almost nothing about it. Before a series of lawsuits during the 1990s forced the Air Force to admit that it has an "operating location near Groom Lake," the Air Force denied its very existence.

Over the course of its history, the site at Groom Lake has been known by many names. Working under a contract from the Central Intelligence Agency, Lockheed built the base in 1955 to test and train pilots for the U-2 spy plane, known then by the code name AQUATONE. Upon its completion, Lockheed's legendary aerospace engineer Kelly Johnson, who was in charge of the U-2, called the desolate site "Paradise Ranch." In CIA documents, the base went by the name "Watertown," perhaps in reference to the birthplace of CIA director Allen Dulles. In 1958, President Eisenhower issued Public Land Order 1662, withdrawing much of the land around Watertown from public access and designating the surrounding land "Area 51," a name that has stuck in the public imagination ever since. Although former workers simply call it "the Area," "the remote location," or "the test site," on patches, coffee mugs, paperweights, and other souvenirs from classified programs at the base, the site is referred to as "Detachment 3, Air Force Flight Test Center." Not that the "DET 3" name has appeared on any official documents: Air Force officials always claim the site either has no name or has a classified name. The base, nonetheless, remains a state-of-the-art flight test center, home to billions of dollars' worth of black military and intelligence projects.

As my stay on the eighteenth floor of the Tropicana wore on and I started to worry about the bill I was racking up, I discovered that the aircraft maintain consistent flight patterns. The first flight of the day is Janet 301 at approximately 4:10 A.M., followed by Janets 312 and 323, both departing around five A.M. Over the next four hours eight more depart, culminating in Janet 391 just before nine A.M. All the aircraft file flight plans with the FAA indicating that their destination is the Tonopah Test Range. I knew, however, that for some of the flights, the pilots were using Tonopah as a cover story for an actual flight to Groom Lake. By listening to the pilots' interactions with Nellis Control, it became relatively easy to tell which aircraft were going where. Because the Tonopah Test Range has an actual airport code (KTNX), when Nellis Control handed the Janet plane off to military controllers in the Nellis Complex, they'd acknowledge the plane was handed off to the Tonopah Tower on 134.1000 MHz or Tonopah Approach on 127.2500 MHz. On the flights where Nellis Control passed the Janet off to an unnamed control, the plane's actual destination was Groom Lake.

It isn't just 737s that make up the Janet fleet. Just south of the terminal were the propeller-driven King Airs, whose fuselages were adorned with blue stripes. Unlike their 737 counterparts, the King Airs fly using visual flight rules (VFR), meaning that the pilots don't have to take continuous instructions from air traffic controllers. Nor are they required to report their flight plans to the FAA, although they do on occasion. The King Airs didn't keep regular schedules, often flying late at night and on weekends. Regardless, I was able to track enough of them to get a general idea of how they operated. By plugging their tail numbers into an FAA database, I found some of the places that they had filed flight plans to. Like their 737 counterparts, the King Airs' flight paths served as a guide to the black world's geography. Their routes revealed how the black world's contours extended far beyond the restricted borders of the Nellis Range to places that, on their face, are far more familiar.

The King Airs' most consistent destination is North Base, a restricted enclave at Edwards Air Force Base in Southern California's Antelope Valley. A flight from Las Vegas to North Base follows a westward route over Death Valley. En route, the aircraft pass Fort Irwin National Training Center, where the Army trains soldiers in counterinsurgency operations on a vast desert landscape replete with mock Iraqi villages and actors hired to play the roles of civilians and insurgents. As the King Airs make their way to Edwards, they pass by other restricted military ranges whose sizes come close to rivaling the Nellis Complex in Nevada. The China Lake Naval Air Weapons Station in the California desert, for example, is the Navy's counterpart to the Nellis Range. To its south is the vast expanse of the Marine Corps Air Ground Combat Center at Twentynine Palms.

Edwards North Base houses the Air Force's Electronic Warfare Directorate and other units associated with black projects, whose personnel commute to the "remote locations" in the Nellis Complex on the King Airs when conducting black operations and projects. Other King Air destinations include the Air Force's Plant 42 in Palmdale, just south of Edwards Air Force Base, an Air Force–funded industrial plant built in the early 1950s composed of towering aircraft hangars, giant runways, and mammoth buildings, and home to much of the black world's industrial base. At Plant 42, aerospace contractors such as Northrop, Boeing, Rockwell, and the Advanced Development Projects division of Lockheed Martin (the Skunk Works) design and manufacture black airframes and other advanced technologies.

The King Airs' routes show how a place like Edwards North Base connects to the Tonopah Test Range, which in turn connects to Groom Lake, which connects to the secured terminal at the Las Vegas airport. The Janet flights showed how disparate places throughout the Southwest are connected to one another, each place forming one part in a larger geography of military secrecy. They were a kind of map.

By paying attention to flight routes, I began to see what the arch-agitator Karl Marx famously called the "annihilation of space by time." In the emerging world of fast-moving trains, telegraphs, and tourism, the notoriously cantankerous philosopher saw transportation and communication technologies helping to form vast non-Euclidean geographies. Spaces that were distant and disparate in terms of the absolute number of miles between them were becoming connected, even becoming indistinguishable from one another. The same was true for this secret world. Even though I was in the Southwest, through Marx's space-time annihilation, I was also surprisingly close to some of the "war on terror"'s more hidden episodes.

If one way to map classified geographies is by tracking the aircraft acting as its transportation system, a different approach involves studying airports instead of aircraft: Rather than following the tail numbers and call signs of "interesting" airplanes, airport codes can be used to log the comings and goings of all aircraft in and out of specific airfields. This is the "fishing" method, using an "interesting" airfield code to locate aircraft that may prove equally "interesting." A plane going in or out of a place like the Tonopah Test Range, for example, would qualify as "interesting." The Desert Rock Airstrip (DRA), the airfield at the Nevada Test Site, is an excellent subject for this sort of fishing. DRA can be a cover story for a flight whose actual destination is Groom Lake, but flights to DRA hint at other unusual goings-on. In late 2002, a series of flights to DRA opened a window onto some of the more bizarre, even frightening, episodes in recent history. The "interesting" aircraft landing at DRA revealed another way that the Southwest's classified geographies extend to the entire world.

The landings began on October 20, 2002, when a white Lockheed Hercules model L382 (a civilian version of a C-130) touched down at DRA. The plane, a turboprop designed to carry heavy cargo and with the ability to land on short unpaved airfields, was owned by a company called Rapid Air Trans and operated by another company called Tepper Aviation. It bore the tail number N8183J on its white fuselage. The landing was curious because most of the flights to DRA are aircraft operated by the Department of Energy (which controls the test site) or known to use DRA as a cover story for other destinations in the Nellis Range. The Hercules didn't fit into either category. Before long, other obscure aircraft followed. On October 27, a Beechcraft numbered N4489A, owned by Aviation Specialties, filed a plan to the airstrip. That plane was in turn followed by another Aviation Specialties Beechcraft: N5139A. In early December, the little-used airstrip received even more guests: a Cessna (N403VP) owned by One Leasing arrived from El Paso, Texas, on December 3. The Hercules, too, returned that day. On December 5, a Boeing 737 with the tail number N313P (owned by Premier Executive Transport Services) touched down at the test site, followed two days later by a Gulfstream IV sporting the registration number N85VM. The latter two aircraft arrived from Andrews Air Force Base, just outside Washington, D.C.

The purpose of these landings was unclear, but some bizarre details about the planes were immediately apparent. First the Gulfstream IV (N85VM): The plane's owner was a man named Phillip H. Morse, a Florida millionaire who, of all things, was part owner of the Boston Red Sox. But it was the Hercules that provided a clue to the flights' purposes: A quick search through the LexisNexis database brought up some very interesting references to Tepper Aviation.

Tepper Aviation had made news when one of its planes crashed at a remote airfield near Jamba, Angola, back in November 1989. The plane was hauling a load of weapons and supplies to Jonas Savimbi's UNITA faction of Angolan rebels. At the time, Savimbi's outfit was one of a handful of rebel groups around the world covertly supported and supplied by the CIA; others included the mujahideen in Afghanistan and the Contras in Nicaragua. Tepper Aviation was a CIA front company. The CIA created Tepper Aviation in the 1980s as an alternative to another proprietary called St. Lucia Airways when the latter company's name attracted unwanted attention after transporting Oliver North (and HAWK missiles, among other things) to and from Iran in what would become known as the Iran-Contra Affair. When the name "Tepper Aviation" became public after the Angola crash, the CIA failed to create a new front company, as was the custom when the names of proprietaries became a matter of public record. Somewhere, somebody slipped up by keeping the name and, in doing so, left a dangling thread that future researchers would be able to tug upon.

Another secret geography emerged from tracking the Hercules' and the other planes' movements after they had left the DRA. Flight plans showed the aircraft traveling to places like Libya, Afghanistan, Sudan, Poland, Romania, Morocco, Iraq, and Pakistan. There were numerous flights to Guantánamo Bay, Cuba. These planes, it would turn out, were the workhorses of what Dick

Cheney famously called the "dark side" of the so-called global war on terror. Their routes suggested unacknowledged collaborations between the CIA and some of the world's ghastliest dictators and regimes. But the planes would become more famous for their involvement in the CIA's extraordinary rendition program: The CIA was using these aircraft to kidnap terror suspects from around the world and quietly transporting them to a network of secret, agency-run prisons, where "harsh interrogation" and torture had become the norm. The aircraft were being used to disappear people. They would eventually acquire a collective nickname: the "torture taxis." Their movements connected the normally sleepy airstrip in the Nellis Range to the global geography of a largely secret war.

The extraordinary rendition program, however, didn't explain why so many CIA aircraft visited the Nevada Test Site back in 2002. The question nagged at me for years, but I contented myself with assuming that the CIA was doing some kind of counterterrorist training at the Nevada Test Site, maybe an exercise at the test site's faux Middle Eastern Terror Town. It wasn't until 2006 that reporters Michael Isikoff and David Corn would expose the true activities that went on at the Desert Rock Airstrip that autumn. The DRA landings, it would turn out, were no conventional training exercise. They were part of one of the most outlandish and secretive programs set up before the invasion of Iraq: a covert project code-named ANABASIS.

According to Isikoff and Corn, two CIA officers in the Iraq Operations Group at the CIA's Directorate of Operations conceived the Anabasis project in the fall of 2001. The idea was to install a team of covert operatives inside Iraq whose mission would be to create chaos inside the country in the run-up to the anticipated invasion. Composed of Iraqi exiles working for the CIA, the team would bribe and recruit Iraqi military officers, feed disinformation to the Saddam regime, sabotage railroad lines and communications towers, and even assassinate key Iraqi officials. Finally, the Anabasis plan called for the team to stage an incident like a terrorist bombing that would provoke a brutal reaction from Saddam Hussein that could, in turn, justify an American intervention. On February 16, 2002, President Bush signed a classified directive authorizing various parts of the project, and CIA officers in the Directorate of Operations went to work.

By the fall of 2002 (when the rendition planes began landing at DRA), the CIA had established a secret training base at the Nevada Test Site to prepare for the operation. According to Isikoff and Corn, "the existence of the camp was one of the most tightly held secrets in the government." In the fall of 2002, the CIA brought about eighty Iraqi fighters to the secret site in Nevada to train for their upcoming clandestine invasion of their former country. Despite all the expense and effort of this special training, by the time the United States was ready to invade Iraq, General Tommy Franks scrapped the idea of using the Iraqi fighters to stage a war-triggering incident, and the team was used instead to provide more conventional support to the U.S. military over the course of the invasion.

Once again, a close look at the Southwest's secret geographies showed that these spaces were remarkably close to, indeed a part of, a larger geography of secret projects spanning the globe.

The DO NOT DISTURB sign still hung on the door handle outside my hotel room. Damp towels had taken over every chair back, the trash cans overflowed, and dirty clothes piled up in the corner. Each morning before dawn, I watched the red-striped 737s load up with passengers for flights into the Nellis Range. Some of the morning flights brought bleary-eyed workers home after they worked graveyard shifts at one of the clandestine sites to the north. At midday, there was a lull in the Janet traffic at the terminal below my window. The desert sun sent heat waves shimmering throughout the asphalt runways. Between noon and three P.M., when the Janets started to return at the end of the workday, I would go swimming in the faux lagoon at the center of the Tropicana's casino complex in the ironic middle of a territory whose parched history was defined by the absence of water.

It was time to go.

4

Wastelands
Basin and Range

I first heard the silence just before dawn in central Nevada's Railroad Valley. I'd driven all night after an evening seminar at Berkeley on a three-day trip to circumnavigate the Nellis Range in my battered Acura hatchback. Pulling over to the side of Highway 375 to relieve myself, I shut the car door and heard it. Nothing. Nothing at all. No wind rustling clumps of dry sage, no insects buzzing to and fro, no cars in the distance or birds fluttering across the valley's dry desert dust. It was as if the world had simply stopped, and I had been left in the vacuum of Earth's aftermath. The absolute silence engulfed me, imparting to me that I was alone like I had never been alone before.

Although I didn't know it at the time, I wasn't the first person to hear this. Physicist Freeman Dyson had heard the same silence when he arrived in Nevada in the early days of nuclear weapons. "It is a soul-shattering silence . . . ," he wrote. Echoing Hebraic prophets wandering the deserts outside Jerusalem, Dyson described it as the silence of "being alone with God." The absolute stillness tore at something inside the physicist: "There in that white flat silence I began for the first time to feel a slight sense of shame for what we were proposing to do. Did we really intend to invade this silence with our trucks and bulldozers and after a few years leave it a radioactive junkyard?"

The Basin and Range is a place that is at once so still, so vast, and so unfamiliar that it seems to transcend space and time itself, like a vision of the world after the world itself is no more. But it is also violently alive.

From the sky, the rocky mountains of the Basin and Range look like a set of tidal waves flowing from Salt Lake City to the west. Some of the ranges crash into the eastern Sierras; others lose their energy and flow harmlessly into the Mojave Desert like ankle-sized swells lapping onto a sandy beach. Each mountain range can span more than a hundred miles on a roughly north-south axis and reach heights well over ten thousand feet. They're the product of a world that is literally being torn apart. As the North American plate stretches from east to west, Nevada's mountains hurtle toward the sky, riding the planet's molten mantle just below. Nevada's topography, hundreds of miles of basins, faults, and ranges, is the swells, scars, and stretch marks of a geologic upheaval unfolding over eons.

The Sierra Nevada in Eastern California is a blockade to rain and water coming from the Pacific Ocean, stopping eastbound moisture in its tracks and creating a desert out of Nevada's mountains and valleys. Most of the little water Nevada receives comes in the form of winter snowfall, the bulk of which evaporates as soon as it begins to melt. The water that manages to trickle down the ranges forms small seasonal streams, which collect in shallow dry lakes. When desert winds blow across the shallow lakes, the surface ripples spread and condense the underlying sediment like a work crew smoothing concrete on a new sidewalk. The end result is a landscape marked by endless dry lakes, smooth and hard enough to land an airplane on.

For those who haven't spent their lives in the Basin and Range, the landscape is as inscrutable as it is vast. It is filled with illusions, deceptions, and redirections. Distances are notoriously difficult to judge. The weather changes instantaneously from blazing to frigid, from clear skies to lightning storm, and from bone-dry to impassable flash floods that are gone again in the blink of an eye. Then there are the mirages, the reflective horizons that promise water and sometimes deliver. But it's almost impossible to tell the difference between what's really there and one of the desert's cruel tricks.

On a map from 1863 I found in the Berkeley library, created after Nevada joined the union, the region surrounding most of the state's interior was marked by the simple words UNEXPLORED TERRITORY, a precursor to the FRAMES EDITED FROM THE ORIGINAL NEGATIVE that I had found years earlier. The Southwest was one of the United States' original blank spots on the map.

For settlers trekking across the desert in the mid-nineteenth century, lured by the promise of gold on the other side of the Sierras, Nevada was an unknown and terrifying space, a space where European folk did not want to go. The Basin and Range was synonymous with pestilence and death. The settlers' main route through the "wastelands" was a thin path along the Humboldt River, about where present-day Highway 80 traverses the desert. And those souls who, guided by the promise of a better future, made the journey though the desert described what they saw in their diaries: As they traversed the Great Basin's jagged cliffs, vast dry lakes, and lonely waterless valleys, they described a nightmarish world of heat, thirst, violence, and horror. Lacking words for the western landforms so unlike anything in Europe, the settlers drew upon what they did have a language to describe: Hell.

"Here, on the Humboldt," wrote Horace Greeley of his 1859 journey, "famine sits enthroned, and waves his scepter over a dominion expressly made for him." Reuben Cole Shaw explained in his diary,

> The reader should not imagine the Humboldt to be a rapid mountain stream, with its cool and limpid waters rushing down the rocks of steep inclines, with here and there beautiful cascades and shady pools under mountain evergreens, where the sun never intrudes and where the speckled trout loves to sport. While the water of such a stream is fit for the gods, that of the Humboldt is not good for man or beast. With the exception of a short distance near its source, it has the least perceptible current. There is not a fish nor any other living thing to be found in its waters, and there is not timber enough in three hundred miles of its desolate valley to make a snuff-box, or sufficient vegetation along its banks to shade a rabbit, while its waters contain the alkali to make soap for a nation, and, after winding its sluggish way through a desert within a desert, it sinks, disappears, and leaves inquisitive man to ask how, why, when and where?

Horace Belknap was more succinct: "meanest and muddiest, filthiest stream. Most cordially I hate you."

Nor was the Humboldt Sink the crystal-clear oasis the forty-niners might have imagined. Shaw writes,

> On arriving at the sink of the Humboldt, a great disappointment awaited us. We had known nothing of the nature of that great wonder except what we had been told by those who knew no more about it than ourselves. In place of a great rent in the earth, into which the water of the river plunged with a

terrible roar (as pictured in our imagination), there was found a mud lake ten miles long and four or five miles wide, a veritable sea of slime, a "slough of despond," an ocean of ooze, a bottomless bed of alkaline poison, which emitted a nauseous odor and presented the appearance of utter desolation. The croaking frogs would have been a redeeming feature of the place, but no living thing disturbed the silence and solitude of the lonely region. There were mysteries and wonders hovering over and around the sink of Humboldt, but there was neither beauty nor grandeur in connection with it, for a more dreary or desolate spot could not be found on the face of the earth.

Of his camp near the Humboldt Sink, Vincent Geiger described a space of death, where "the most obnoxious, hideous gases perfumed our camp . . . arising from the many dead animals around."

Past the river's terminus at the Humboldt Sink lay sixty miles of desert emigrants had to pass, a trek that spanned days without water or shade before reaching the Truckee River. One emigrant described the landscape as having "large rocks and deposits of lava and the whole surface appear'd cover'd with ashes looking like the effects of some earthquake or volcano, the stones appearing to have melted and run together." The stretch was littered with death and wreckage: "Where we started this morning," wrote Charles Glass Gray, "there was a lot of dead oxen, broken wagons, wheels and lots of iron fixtures scatter'd in every direction. I counted 160 oxen, dead and dying and wandering about scarce able to stand up—being left here to die!" Later that day, "seventy dead animals were counted in the last 25 miles. Pieces of wagons also, the irons in particular—the wood part having been burnt—were also strewn along. An ox-yoke, [a] wheel and a dead ox, yoke, and wheel; and a wheel, dead ox, and a yoke, was the order of the day, every hundred or two hundred yards." Milus Gay wrote that "such destruction of property as I saw across the Desert I have never seen I should think I passed the carcasses of 1200 head of cattle and horses and a great many waggons Harnesses-cooking utensils-tools water casks etc. etc. at a moderate estimate the amount I would think the property cost in the U.S. $50,000. We also see many men on the point of starvation begging for bread."

Upon completing the trip, one emigrant wrote that "until one has crossed a barren desert, without food or water, under a burning tropical sun, at three miles an hour, one can form no conception of what misery is." Forty-niner Alonzo Delano wrote that "any man who makes a trip by land to California, deserves to find a fortune," after making the journey himself.

And that route was north of the present-day test sites. It was the "easy" route to California.

Few traveled through the regions of the present-day Nellis Complex, and the few who haphazardly braved the southern desert barely escaped with their lives, if they escaped at all. When William Lewis Manly decided to take a "shortcut" to California via the "Southern Route" in 1849, the result was catastrophic. Climbing mountains alongside his party's chosen route, Manly later wrote, "I saw that the land west of us looked more and more barren." When Manly finally emerged from the desert starving and dehydrated, he described a landscape of "dreadful sands and shadows . . . exhausting phantoms, salt columns, bitter lakes, and wild, dreary, sunken desolation . . ."

Twenty years after Manly narrowly escaped death on a trek that took his party near Groom Lake and onward through Death Valley, Lieutenant George Montague Wheeler was charged by the Army Corps of Engineers with undertaking a "reconnaissance" mission through the same territory, a region Wheeler described as "hitherto unexplored." Wheeler's objective in mapping out "one of the most desolate regions upon the face of the earth" was to describe the physical features of the landscape, survey potential mining sites, note potential routes for future roads and railroad lines, describe the "numbers, habits, and disposition of the Indians who may live in this section," and, tellingly, to identify and select sites "as may be of use to future military operations."

"All the tribes, without exception, belong to that wild, roving breed known as 'Mountain Indians.' Their lawless and migratory life has carried them beyond the notion of anything like order, even among their own people," wrote Wheeler of the native peoples, but he conceded that "it is almost impossible to obtain white guides who have any accurate knowledge of regions sensibly new, while hardly any nook or corner can be found not well known to the Indian." The "unexplored" land Wheeler's reconnaissance mission was to chart had after all been well-explored for many generations. Wheeler possessed little sympathy for Nevada's natives. Although "they are quite intelligent, and were very friendly," he wrote, "Virtue is almost unknown among them, and syphilitic diseases very common." Per his own estimation, Wheeler's mission gave him ample "opportunity for studying the Indian character," but his dealing with them "has in no way produced a sympathy with that class of well-intentioned but ill-informed citizens who claim that the Indians are a much-abused race." Despite his disdain for the indigenous peoples, Wheeler found one praiseworthy attribute: "They have . . . a wonderful regard for superior force." After the "Indian difficulty is settled" and the railroads came, he remarked, the development of the Southwest could proceed.

Development spelled ruin for native peoples. Mines poisoned the land with mercury and cyanide; whites cut down trees for fuel. Cattle devoured the plants native peoples relied on for food. Local game was frightened away. The brutality was not merely environmental. Invading settlers raped mothers in front of their children, attacked Western Shoshone women, and slaughtered native peoples indiscriminately. In the 1860s and '70s, Nevada's main newspaper, aptly titled *Territorial Enterprise*, advocated "exterminating the whole race." Decades later, those words would echo through the mouth of a deranged Mr. Kurtz in Joseph Conrad's novel about colonialism's heart of darkness: "Exterminate all the brutes."

"History doesn't repeat itself, but it does rhyme," said Mark Twain, who spent his fair share of time traversing the West. So too with human geographies. Landscapes are built upon the foundations of what came before. "Nothing disappears completely . . . ," wrote Henri Lefebvre. "In space, what came earlier continues to underpin what follows. . . . Pre-existing space underpins not only durable spatial arrangements but also representational spaces and their attendant imagery and mythic narratives." For the French geographer, it wasn't just that landscapes were built on foundations laid in the past, but that the way we see a particular place is also guided by what others before us saw. What we see strongly guides what we do: To an extent, we enact what we imagine. When early explorers and settlers first came to the Basin and Range, they saw a wasteland. Then they laid waste to it.

Beginning in the early 1960s, history began to rhyme once again when the Department of Energy and the military began setting off nuclear weapons in the desert. Mushroom clouds lit the skies, and fallout fell like snow. The explosions were called tests but were nonetheless full-fledged dress rehearsals for Armageddon, perhaps more. Among the desert's longtime residents, the difference between "nuclear testing" and "nuclear war" was far from self-evident.

One day in October, as the beginnings of winter added a dry chill to the desert wind, I drove along Highway 80 parallel to the Humboldt River in a big white Suburban along roughly the same route the settlers had trekked almost two centuries earlier. In a matter of minutes, I'd blown through the stretch of desert between the Carson Sink and the Truckee River that had once been littered with abandoned wagons and pack-animal corpses, and where so many westbound pioneers met their fate in the unforgiving desert. I turned south near Elko and drove into the Crescent Valley, looking for another base of sorts. This one was only slightly easier to find than the "nonexistent" military facilities two hundred miles south.

Scribbled on a page of paper torn from a spiral notebook, my directions said "white, single wide trailer—first trailer facing the road across the street from the old baseball diamond." When I arrived at a cluster of trailers about a mile past the convenience store, I realized that I had no idea what the directions meant, so I knocked on the first plausible door.

A young woman with long, dark hair named Okaadaka answered and invited me into the dilapidated structure. Unpacked suitcases sat in the corner, fresh with baggage tags marked ELY, the closest airport to the Crescent Valley (several hours away). Files, papers, and pamphlets were piled high on every horizontal surface. Flyers, maps, and pictures were plastered on the far wall. This trailer was home to the Western Shoshone Defense Project, and from this remote location, an elderly Native American woman named Carrie Dann and her staff of two full-timers and two part-timers take on the military, the Bureau of Land Management, mining and defense contractors, and the U.S. government itself. Dann says that the United States has been illegally occupying Western Shoshone land for 150 years and that she has the paperwork to prove it.

As I sat in the unmarked trailer with Dann, Okaadaka, and a human rights lawyer named Julie Fishel, who works with the defense project, Dann explained that their work began in 1992, two decades after the Bureau of Land Management started harassing Dann and other Western Shoshone in the area for "trespassing."

The Shoshone provoked the BLM's ire by refusing to pay grazing fees for allowing their cattle to wander through the Crescent Valley. "I've never seen any documentation that says the Western Shoshone ever gave their land to the United States," said Dann. In her view, the Crescent Valley still rightfully belongs to the Western Shoshone, and it's the United States, not the Native Americans, who are doing the trespassing. The Indian Wars never really ended, she says.

The basis for Dann's argument hangs near a doorway leading to a back room in the trailer. Bound with a red ribbon, the document has a cover page written in calligraphic letters: the Treaty of Ruby Valley.

Signed in 1863 between the United States and the Western Shoshone, the Treaty of Ruby Valley was meant to end an undeclared war that began when thousands of whites arrived in present-day Nevada. As previously mentioned, the emigrant trains destroyed local food sources and indiscriminately killed indigenous peoples, initiating cyclones of violence across the desert. The endgame began in the early 1860s when a colonel named Patrick E. Connor set up a fort in the Ruby Valley. Charged with protecting the mail routes from periodic Shoshone raids, Connor ordered his California Volunteers to "destroy every male Indian whom you may encounter" and to "leave their bodies thus exposed as an example of what evildoers may expect." In January of 1863, Connor ambushed a Shoshone village along the Bear River in present-day Utah. His troops raped many and massacred approximately 250 Shoshone, among them approximately 80 women and children. The event became known as the Bear River Massacre. Later that year, at gunpoint, the Western Shoshone signed the Treaty of Ruby Valley.

Shoshone legend holds that the signing was a grisly affair. As Western Shoshone Council Chief Raymond Yowell tells it:

They had [the Indians] lined up along that ridge, and the troops were standing there ready with their rifles. . . . They fed the Indians first, before signing the treaty. Before they did that they had the Indians turn over a supposedly bad Shoshone to them, who'd maybe killed some white people or something like that. And so they hung him in front of them first, that morning when they were going to sign the treaty. And then, after he was dead, they cut him down and took him away, and they [the Shoshone] didn't know what they did with him. His relatives wanted the body, but they wouldn't give it to them. Later on, they fed [the Shoshone] a meat that they couldn't recognize. Pretty soon, they figured out that they had cooked the Shoshone that they had hung and fed it to them.

It's not clear whether Yowell's story is historically accurate or not. More revealing is that the cannibal story is not entirely implausible. If settlers saw a wasteland on their way out west, the indigenous people saw—experienced—a storm of ultraviolence.

Whatever the circumstances under which the treaty was enacted, the Treaty of Ruby Valley's text declares "peace and friendship" between the United States and the Shoshone and outlines a working relationship toward the lands that the Western Shoshone call Newe Sogobia. In addition to granting the United States certain rights of passage and mining claims in Western Shoshone territory, the Western Shoshone are charged with ensuring that "hostilities and all depredations upon the emigrant trains, the mail and telegraph lines, and upon the citizens of the United States within their country shall cease."

But the Treaty of Ruby Valley was, and is, clear about one thing: The Western Shoshone retain sovereignty over their traditional land. At the time, this was perfectly reasonable: No one in the United States wanted the wasteland anyway. For the same reason, it was one of the few treaties that the United States never bothered to nullify. And, according to Carrie Dann and other traditional Western Shoshone, the treaty remains a singular legal basis for the relationship between the indigenous nations and the United States. The United States, for its part, has not refuted Dann's argument, nor has it offered any documentation showing that the treaty of friendship between the two nations has been abrogated.

In September of 2002, the United States returned. Once again, Dann was being accused of trespassing; once again, Dann rejected the notion that it was possible for her to trespass on land she saw as rightfully belonging to her people. At four A.M. one Sunday, around forty-five armed federal agents, a helicopter, an airplane, and a fleet of ATVs descended on Pine Valley and other places where Dann's herd grazed. Mary Gibson, a Shoshone, was camping in one of the canyons with a group of eleven people, waiting for the raid after being warned to expect it. "We saw a convoy of twenty vehicles with flashing lights roaring up the valley," she recalled. "I could not help but think of how this is how our ancestors felt when they saw the cavalry coming. So many of my people were killed on this land and now it's happening again." The Feds rounded up Dann's cattle and loaded them into trucks to be sold at auction. The ranch was devastated.

As our conversation wound down, I asked Dann what would happen if somehow the Western Shoshone were put in charge of the territory they call Newe Sogobia. What would happen if, say tomorrow, the United States came out and said, "You're right, this land is yours—here it is." What would change?

"I think about that a lot," says Dann. "I couldn't give you an answer, but my personal opinion is that we're willing to sit down with anyone, with the Feds, or whomever. When you sit down and talk, you can work out pretty much any problem. The problem right now is that they're not even willing to sit at the same table with us. I'm sure that there are ways that things could be figured out for the best of everyone who's here."

Julie Fishel chimes in: "There are a couple of things that you can be sure about. If the Shoshone won this tomorrow, there'd be no more testing at the nuclear test site, there'd be no nuclear waste at Yucca Mountain, and there'd be some kind of compensation for the things that are going on now in terms of mining. The Western Shoshone would start thinking about how to repair the land and figuring out how to clean this mess up."

"What's happening right now is a spiritual holocaust," says Carrie. "I don't know what they call it, but that's what's happening."

"When you allow this kind of corruption to fester in a government and you allow it to spread, it legitimizes everything," says Fishel. The United States starts to think, "We killed a bunch of people to get this land in the first place, and it worked then and we didn't get in trouble for it, so let's do it some more. Let's do it in Iraq, let's do it somewhere else, too."

For the collection of activists sitting in an unmarked trailer in the recesses of Nevada's vast valleys, the black world is much more than an array of sites connected to one another through black aircraft, encrypted communications, and classified careers. It is the power to create those geographies, to create places where anything can happen, and to do it with impunity.

5

Classified Résumés
Mojave Desert

In the fall of 2004, I called up the Flight Test Historical Foundation at Edwards Air Force Base, hoping for an invitation to an annual fund-raiser and reunion for the test pilots and aerospace engineers whose industry has long dominated California's Antelope Valley. This year's event promised to be particularly interesting. Entitled "Out of the Black . . . Into the Blue," the ceremony would induct a handful of test pilots into a club of "Eagles," a kind of flight-test hall of fame administered by the Historical Foundation. This year's ceremony was unique because it honored pilots who'd tested previously classified aircraft, all of which had flown at Groom Lake between the late 1970s and the late 1990s. These men had spent much of their lives working in the black world. With the aircraft they piloted now declassified, they were receiving long-overdue credit for their work. After a series of conversations, the Flight Test Historical Foundation's volunteer officers said they'd be happy to have me.

"Out of the Black . . ." took place at a hotel ballroom one hot, dry autumn evening in Lancaster, California, in the westernmost part of the Mojave Desert. To the north, lights from the legendary flight test center at Edwards Air Force Base filled the horizon with a deep orange glow. First built as a remote Army airfield in the run-up to the Second World War, modern-day Edwards (first known as Muroc) came into its own when it became the secret base for the United States' first black aircraft, the XP-59A, which was the original American jet fighter and whose secure hangar at North Base remains home to black aviation projects and units to this day. After the war, Edwards was ground zero for the so-called golden age of test flight. Chuck Yeager broke the sound barrier here in 1947, and Scott Crossfield blazed past Mach 6 in the X-15 rocket plane twenty years later. In 1981, the space shuttle Columbia landed on Edwards's expansive dry lake after its maiden flight into space.

Just to the south of Lancaster, the colossal hangars of Plant 42 and the Lockheed Martin Skunk Works tower above the horizon. The North American aircraft company built the rocket-powered X-15 and the supersonic XB-70 "Valkyrie" bomber here at Plant 42. The Skunk Works performed maintenance and upgrades on the glider-like U-2 spyplane and faster-than-a-speeding-bullet SR-71 in its hangars. Plant 42 is home to the advanced development research projects for aircraft like Northrop's Global Hawk, Lockheed's F-22, and Boeing's venerable B-52. Variations and upgrades to those aircraft are tested just to the north at Edwards. Plant 42 is also home to numerous black aviation projects that fly at "remote locations" in Nevada.

I felt out of place in the Lancaster ballroom, like I'd crashed a party I hadn't been invited to. Stocky old-timers drinking Scotch

on the rocks milled around, laughing and bragging to their erst-
while colleagues. These were the people who'd been at the heart of
the flight test industry: the men who'd built the engines, designed
the airframes, pumped the jet fuel, flown the planes, and occasionally "augured in" when something went wrong.

As I sat down at my assigned table and waited for the ceremony
to start, one of the old-timers came up and introduced himself.
An enormous third-degree burn covered the side of his face. I remembered Chuck Yeager's quip about the true hero among test
pilots being the one who survives. The old-timer said he recognized my face but couldn't place me. Caught off guard, I replied
that my father used to treat SR-71 pilots up at Travis Air Force
Base, but he'd have to have a pretty good memory to remember
me from way back then. He nodded vaguely and strolled away.

The evening commenced with an Air Force honor guard of
young men and women in starched dress uniforms marching an
American flag up to the stage while "The Star-Spangled Banner"
blared through the house PA. I joined everyone in the ballroom
standing at attention with my hand over my heart, remembering
the ritual from my childhood, when military base movie theaters
opened each film with a rendition of the national anthem.

From the podium at the front of the ballroom, Lee Trlica, one
of the Historical Foundation's board members, whom I'd talked
to on the phone, explained that three aircraft would be coming
"out of the black and into the blue" that evening: a Lockheed
stealth prototype from the late 1970s code-named HAVE BLUE, a
Northrop stealth demonstrator from the early 1980s code-named
TACIT BLUE, and a Boeing demonstrator from the late 1990s
nicknamed Bird of Prey.

HAVE BLUE was built in 1977 after engineers at Lockheed's
Skunk Works plant stumbled upon the idea of using angular, faceted shapes to create an aircraft virtually invisible to radar. With
their new approach to "stealth" in hand, the Skunk Works entered

a Defense Advanced Research Projects Agency (DARPA) competition called "Project Harvey." Named after the invisible rabbit from a 1950 movie starring James Stewart, the competition's goal was to develop an aircraft with the lowest possible radar cross-section, a key element in modern-day stealth designs. After beating out Northrop for the prize, the Skunk Works went on to build two stealth demonstrators under the HAVE BLUE program. The two faceted aircraft verified the stealth concept in a series of flights beginning in December 1977. HAVE BLUE 1001, the first prototype, crashed on May 4, 1978, when the landing gear was damaged on a hard impact. Worried that the plane would skid off the Groom Lake runway, test pilot Bill Park took the aircraft back up into the air. When the landing gear failed to extend again, Park ejected and was knocked unconscious. When paramedics found him, his parachute had dragged him across the desert floor and filled his mouth with dirt. The test pilot's heart was not beating. Paramedics were able to resuscitate him, but Park would never fly again. Lockheed buried the classified aircraft's wreckage at Groom Lake.

The HAVE BLUE program ended on July 11, 1979, when the second prototype, HAVE BLUE 1002, crashed near the Tonopah Test Range after a hydraulic line in the aircraft ruptured and set the engine on fire. Pilot Ken Dyson was able to parachute to safety. HAVE BLUE 1002 met the same fate as its older sibling: Its wreckage was buried at Groom Lake. The Flight Test Historical Foundation was now honoring Ken Dyson for his contribution to the program.

The second plane on the agenda was a Northrop's TACIT BLUE. Before its 1996 declassification, TACIT BLUE had been somewhat of an enigma among military aviation journalists, the subject of much "RUMINT" (a joke word meaning "rumor intelligence" that defense industry journalists sometimes use, recalling military designations for various types of intelligence: SIGINT, or "signals intelligence"; HUMINT, or "human intelligence"; PHOTINT, or "photo intelligence"; and so on). RUMINT long held that Northrop developed a plane called "Shamu" or "the Whale" during the 1980s, but the consistency of the intelligence ended there. Some stories described a supersized flying wing, while others told of a vertical takeoff and landing (VTOL) plane. Still others held simply that the Whale was a "funny-looking" electronic warfare platform. Shamu left traces all over the flight test community: During the early 1980s, the offices of Northrop's Advanced Projects Division were filled with images of whales. There were paintings of whales on lobby walls, drawings of whales on letterheads, and whale-adorned company logos stamped on Northrop's office supplies. When the Air Force finally acknowledged the program more than a decade after its first flight, TACIT BLUE was revealed to be long and boxy, with short, stubby wings and a shovel-nosed chine around a uniformly white fuselage. If nothing else, the plane was certainly "funny-looking." At the Gathering of Eagles, I learned that Dick Thomas first flew the Whale in 1982, and the plane was subsequently flown by pilots Ken Dyson, Dan Vanderhorst, Russ Easter, and Don Cornell on 135 sorties, before retiring in 1985.

The last of the three black jets on the evening's agenda was a technology demonstrator originally built by McDonnell Douglas's Phantom Works, an advanced technology group modeled on Lockheed's Skunk Works, and first flown in late 1996. Nicknamed Bird of Prey after a twenty-second-century Romulan starship from the TV series *Star Trek*, the short, tailless plane had a simple, angular shape, drooped wings, and a flat gray paint job. Phantom Works test pilot Rudy Haug first flew the aircraft in the fall of 1996. Over the course of the Bird of Prey's testing regimen, Boeing merged with McDonnell Douglas, absorbing the Phantom Works but continuing funding for the black aircraft. Between Rudy Haug and Joe Felock, both Boeing test pilots, and Air Force

pilot Doug Benjamin, the plane flew thirty-eight missions between 1996 and its retirement in 1999. The aircraft was declassified on October 18, 2002.

The most interesting aspects of the Gathering of Eagles weren't
the introductions or the acceptance speeches. Far more fascinat-
ing were subjects that the community carefully spoke around but
didn't directly address. The audience let out a collective harrumph
when pilot Doug Benjamin mentioned that the Bird of Prey flew
at a "remote location" and pilot Ken Dyson announced his desire
to make some "uncleared" remarks about why the audience
should support George Bush instead of John Kerry in the upcoming election. That remark, perhaps unintentionally, revealed that
everything he said had been vetted by Air Force security officials.
"Out of the Black . . ." was no exercise in free speech or government transparency.

The evening continued with carefully scripted absences and
silences. No one said the words "Groom Lake" even though it was
where all of these aircraft proved themselves. Other remarks were
so filled with roundabout language that the audiences' knowing
nods left me utterly confused. At times, listening to the talks was
like hearing someone read from a heavily redacted document,
filled with the blacking-out of information too sensitive to
include.

As it turned out, the most illuminating parts of the event were
contained in something I could take home with me: the evening's
program notes. On the glossy pages—sandwiched between ads
for Lockheed Martin, Northrop, and a handful of other defense
contractors seeking to curry favor with flight test bigwigs—were
the biographies of the pilots who flew the black jets. The section
on Doug Benjamin (who had flown Bird of Prey for the Air Force)
explained that sometime during the mid-1990s, he "*moved to the
black world* where he flew on and commanded a variety of classified programs" (emphasis added). This locution—Benjamin

"moved to the black world"—echoed the evening's tenor. Keith Beswick's biography added to the intrigue: In 1978, Beswick "was promoted to Director of Flight Test at Lockheed and became responsible for the U-2, SR-71, F-117A, F-22, and *several other classified programs*" (emphasis added).

And then there was Dan Vanderhorst, who "has been the lead pilot on *seven classified aircraft to date*" (emphasis added). In fact, according to his biography, "[Vanderhorst] has made his career in the cockpit of *so many classified aircraft, there is not much that we can say about him, on the record*," and "his work has been outstanding and will probably never be recognized by the general public." Although Vanderhorst was honored that evening, he wasn't able to make it to his own party: He was "working at Edwards AFB on a classified program."

The silences, absences, and unsaid implications in these men's biographies were like blank spots on maps. They were guides to the places where the public record ran out. The carefully constructed blank spots in Vanderhorst's biography alone had remarkable implications. To build a single aircraft is a tremendous financial, industrial, and intellectual undertaking. Building an airplane means spending millions or billions of dollars with dedicated factories, test facilities, and countless workers from janitors to managers, pilots to machinists. Vanderhorst, one pilot, had flown seven. In the first instance, his biography spoke to the scale of the classified flight test industry. It pointed to a hidden geography of finance, research, development, engineering, manufacturing, and testing projects as complicated and industrialized as modern airplanes. Second, his biography spoke to the black world's ability to keep a secret, about not only the physical but the social engineering that goes into building classified aircraft. There's plenty of RUMINT about secret airplanes. The pages of magazines like *Aviation Week & Space Technology* and *Popular Mechanics* are filled with stories of vertical takeoff and landing transports for Special Operations forces, high-speed reconnaissance aircraft, and spaceplanes capable of putting classified satellites into low Earth orbits. But good evidence to corroborate these rumors is thin. Given the number of personnel and the amount of money involved in developing an aircraft, the fact that there aren't more credible leaks, more inadvertently declassified histories or photos, or more disgruntled ex-officers willing to spill the secrets out into the open means that the secrecy enveloping Vanderhorst's biography is a remarkable feat of social engineering. Finally, this pilot's biography says something about the dynamics of secrecy: If Vanderhorst alone piloted seven classified, manned aircraft, and if the three previously classified aircraft at the Gathering of Eagles represent the sum of black aircraft that have made their way "into the blue" since the 1970s, then the declassified record represents an exception to the rule rather than the rule itself. HAVE BLUE, TACIT BLUE, and Bird of Prey are not unusual in that they were secret. They're unusual because they are not secret anymore. Long after their retirement, most black airplanes stay black.

After a dinner of hotel-cooked roast beef and mashed potatoes, I drove through Lancaster's dark desert streets back to my cheap motel room along Highway 14, utterly confused by the fleeting glimpse into the world of classified flight tests that I'd just gotten. The "golden age of flight test" that had made Edwards Air Force Base a modern icon, I realized, never really ended. Instead, the whole thing went black. The modern-day Chuck Yeagers, whoever they were, would "never be recognized by the general public." I wondered how many taxpayer-funded discoveries about aerospace engineering were realized in the black world, never to see the light of day. How many scientists spent their lives working out breakthroughs to cutting-edge engineering problems whose results would never appear in the peer-reviewed literature?

Looking at the résumés from the program notes, I realized that there must be many others like them. If there were pilots flying classified aircraft, then there must be classified support crews, engineers, manufacturers, all of whose résumés might look like that of Dan Vanderhorst. I suspected that I might be able to find other biographies with equally telling blank spots and absences. It could be a new approach toward intelligence gathering: résumé intelligence, or RESUMINT.

I explored military Web sites for keywords I knew to be associated with classified flight-test projects. Several assumptions helped with the search: First, I knew that an Air Force test pilot would probably have attended the Air Force Test Pilot School at Edwards Air Force Base. Second, I imagined the pilots would have been assigned to a squadron known to be associated with black projects subsequent to completing their test pilot education. Squadrons such as the 6513th Flight Test Squadron (the "Red Hats," who flew stolen Soviet aircraft), the 413th Flight Test Squadron (the 6513th's descendant after an early 1990s reorganization), and the "Classified Flight Test Squadron" or the "Special Projects Flight Test Squadron" were all units that fit this assumption. Other phrases, like "data masked," would signal information that had been redacted in an unclassified electronic document. Finally, the phrase "AFFTC, DET. 3" attached to any pilot's biography would also be revealing, based on numerous indications that the black site at Groom Lake is the Third Detachment of the Air Force Flight Test Center (AFFTC).

The search for résumés yielded far more than I had hoped. From these keyword searches I found many more pilots and more black aircraft. A local paper in Bird of Prey pilot Doug Benjamin's hometown of La Crosse, Wisconsin, described a plaque on the pilot's wall that he received upon his retirement from the Air Force in 2000. The plaque showed four aircraft covered in black sheets. His parents told a local journalist that Benjamin couldn't talk about what he had done for the Air Force during the last five years of his military career. Assuming that one of the covered aircraft was the Bird of Prey, that means that between about 1994 and 2000, Benjamin flew three still-classified aircraft.

My friend Peter Merlin, who works at Edwards Air Force Base right next to the secure North Base section, told me about a pilot named Frank T. Birk. In the 1960s, Birk was a "Raven"—a nominally civilian pilot who'd transferred from the Air Force to the CIA to fly secret missions over Laos during the Vietnam War. After the war, Birk attended test pilot school, becoming the Air Force's most highly decorated pilot before retiring. Birk died in 1993 when a Ranger 2000 aircraft trainer he was testing crashed near Manching, Germany. According to Merlin, who attended Birk's funeral, the pilot's eulogy stated that he had made the first flight of a "classified technology demonstrator" in 1985 and had won the Bobby Bond Memorial Aviator Award for his work on that project.

The biography of a man named Colonel Dennis F. Sager stated that he commanded a classified flight test squadron during the early to mid-1990s and that he shepherded a "classified prototype" called the YF-113G from development through first flight.

Then I found the biography of Colonel Joseph A. Lanni, hosted on the Edwards Air Force Base Web site during Lanni's tenure as the commander of the 412th Flight Test Wing. Lanni spent five years in the black world, from August 1992 through June 1997. He first flew for the 6513th Flight Test Squadron (the Red Hats), then the 413th Flight Test Squadron. From July 1995 until June 1997, Lanni commanded the "classified flight test squadron." Lanni's biography stated he flew "numerous classified prototypes," including an unknown aircraft called the YF-24.

As I built up a collection of pilot résumés and biographies, I realized I could use these scraps of information to concoct an analytic problem not unlike the word problems found on college entrance exams: "Dan Vanderhorst flew seven classified aircraft between 1980 and 2004. He *did* fly TACIT BLUE. He did *not* fly

the Bird of Prey. Doug Benjamin flew four classified aircraft between 1994 and 2000. He *did* fly the Bird of Prey but was the *only*
Air Force pilot to do so . . . ," and so on.

The information I had was, of course, incomplete, but when I
solved my word problem, something rather dramatic jumped out
from the fragments: At minimum, the United States has researched, developed, and flown between seven and eleven manned
aircraft between the 1980s and the present, all of which remain
classified. In solving my problem, a few other pieces of information came out as a side effect: Sometime during the late 1980s or
1990s, the Air Force formed at least one unnumbered squadron
dedicated entirely to classified flight testing, the Special Projects
Flight Test Squadron. Another discovery was that at some point in
the 1990s or early 2000s, the Air Force's unacknowledged flight
test infrastructure grew to the size of an entire wing—one of the
largest unit sizes in the Air Force.

Another curious discovery in these searches was that names of
astronauts kept coming up. Three-time spaceflight veteran Donald R. McMonagle, for example, was the "operations officer of the
6513th Test Squadron at Edwards AFB" just prior to becoming an
astronaut in 1987. Carl E. Walz, a four-time space shuttle veteran,
"served as a Flight Test Manager at Detachment 3, Air Force Flight
Test Center," before joining NASA in 1990. Before becoming an
astronaut in 1985, Colonel John N. Casper served as the "Operations Officer and later Commander of the 6513th Test Squadron . . . He was then assigned to Headquarters USAF at the
Pentagon and was Deputy Chief of the Special Projects Office . . ."
It made sense in a way. If astronauts were guys with the "right
stuff," and if the bulk of experimental flight testing went black in
the 1970s and 1980s, then it made sense that a significant number
of astronauts flew classified aircraft just before their selection to
join NASA.

RESUMINT was paying off. Searching specifically for redacted information in résumés was much like hunting for secret bases by looking for missing satellite photos. Searching for the phrase "data masked" brought up a list detailing the reassignments of senior Air Force officers. A man named Colonel Terry Tichenor was being transferred from Hanscom Air Force Base to become the commander of the operations group at a "data masked" location. Colonel Gregory Jaspers, a former stealth fighter pilot from the plane's black days in Nevada, was moving out of his job as the commander of the data masked operations group, replacing Colonel Thomas Masiello as the commander of a data masked wing. Masiello was going on to become the inspector general at Air Force Materiel Command at Wright-Patterson Air Force Base, the major Air Force command responsible for "management, research, acquisition, development, testing and maintenance of existing and future weapons systems and their components." In official Air Force documents, the "data masked" phrase was associated with two types of units: classified flight-test outfits and off-the-books Special Forces units. Because these guys all had flight-test experience (and weren't commandos), the evidence suggested they were some of the commanding officers of the Air Force's black flight-test installations and programs.

It's hard to say what it is, exactly, one learns by collecting and collating the black world's traces and refuse, the weird unit designation here, the data-masked words there, or the code names that aren't associated with any known projects. It's supposed to be that way: The black world is compartmented and cubbyholed, an epistemological maze of special security channels, "need to know" clearances, and obscure code words. Even among those in the highest ranks of the military and intelligence communities, only a few people are allowed to see the whole picture.

Most people are under the impression that security classifications are relatively straightforward: The higher the clearance someone has, the more stuff they get to see. But that's only part of the story. In fact, security classifications are more like a tree. The standard classifications—Restricted, Confidential, Secret, and Top Secret—form a hierarchical trunk. "Above Top Secret," however, the system branches off into thousands of arms, which in turn branch off into even more obscure subcategories. Each branch is known as a "Special Access Program" (SAP), and each has its own specialized security "channels." Every person associated with the program must be "read" into the SAP's specific information compartments. Even then, they only get access to the information they need to know to do their job. An SAP can split into multiple sub-branches within each information channel. If, for example, an engineer on a classified satellite works on a new infrared imaging capability, she might be read into a compartment like "Top Secret-Byeman-Crystal-Dragon," where "Top Secret" is the baseline clearance, "Byeman" indicates a general engineering compartment for spy satellites, "Crystal" is the channel for a specific type of satellite (in this case, a KH-11), and "Dragon" refers to the infrared imaging capability of that satellite. The engineer with the Dragon clearance would not be read into the necessary security compartments to see how other parts of the satellite (its propulsion system, for example) were designed.

The more time I spent trying to understand the relationships between different Air Force units and their classified activities, trying to understand the syntax of code names or the difference between data masked flight-test units and Special Forces units, the more I saw RESUMINT as a form of code-breaking, a necessary tool in the dark world. After all, it was code-breaking that first set the black world in motion.

Born in 1889, Herbert Yardley had an early life that compels writers to invoke the cliché "all-American boy." At his school in Worthington, Indiana, Yardley was class president, editor of the school paper, and captain of the football team. His friends called him "a genius" and "the smartest boy in the country." As a teen-ager, he taught himself how to play poker by dealing hands to himself at home, memorizing the odds of different plays, and learning to fold when the cards were stacked against him. Yardley's father was a railway telegrapher, and Herbert mastered the skill as a youth. When Yardley left Indiana in 1912 to pursue a career as a code clerk and telegrapher at the State Department in Washington, D.C., his combination of skills would come together in the "Black Chamber"—the early prototype of what would become the Pentagon's black world.

As a telegrapher for the State Department, Yardley developed an interest in cryptology—the science of making and breaking codes—and taught himself the art using Captain Parker Hitt's *Manual for the Solution of Military Ciphers*. When work slowed or when he had spare time, Yardley tried to decipher the encrypted messages coming across his desk. After he shared his success, friends started bringing him encrypted diplomatic messages from foreign embassies. One slow night, a communication to President Wilson from Colonel House came over the wire, and Yardley made a copy. "This would be good material to work on," he reasoned, "for surely the President and his trusted agent would be using a difficult code." Yardley was shocked to realize that he was able to decipher the message in less than two hours.

Over the following year, Yardley devoted much of his time to completing a one-hundred-page analysis of the American crypto-graphic system, entitled *Solution of American Diplomatic Codes*, which he dutifully presented to his superiors at the State Department. When Yardley's State Department supervisor David Salmon began reading the young code-breaker's work, he was stunned. Salmon knew that the British employed a team of code-breakers specifically to decrypt diplomatic communications, and when he asked Yardley if he thought that the British were able to read American diplomatic communications as well, Yardley replied with a quote that would become famous in intelligence circles: "I always assume that what is in the power of one man to do is in the power of another."

On April 6, 1917, Congress declared war on the German Empire after the sinking of the *Lusitania* and after the British gave President Wilson a copy of the Zimmerman Telegram that the Royal Navy cryptanalytic group had intercepted. In the telegram, the Germans proposed to Mexico that the two countries join forces to attack the United States and reclaim lands lost in the Mexican-American War.

Yardley saw an opportunity. After collecting letters of recommendation from his State Department supervisor and military officers whom he knew, Yardley approached the Army with the idea of establishing an American cryptanalysis unit. By midsummer, Yardley was the head of MI-8—military intelligence, section 8. In lieu of an office, Yardley received a few feet on a balcony in the Army's War College building and a desk. He was now in charge of the United States' first cryptologic agency. And so began a project that would one day evolve into the National Security Agency.

As the First World War pounded on, Yardley built up MI-8 to include the Code Compilation Subsection, to develop new and more secure code systems; the Communications Subsection, to provide secure communication with military and intelligence operatives overseas; the Shorthand Subsection, to concentrate on understanding foreign shorthand systems; the Secret Ink Subsection; and the Code and Cipher Solution Subsection, designed to decrypt and decipher foreign messages. By the end of the war, MI-8 employed 77 people, had deciphered 10,735 pieces of foreign communication, and had solved about 50 codes and ciphers from a handful of foreign governments.

With the end of World War I, Yardley assumed that he would be out of work and resigned himself to "getting some sort of job with the American Code Company." But there were stirrings of keeping MI-8 around even though its original mission was now over—perhaps it would be useful to maintain such a powerful capacity. Yardley was asked to write a proposal to preserve MI-8 and convert its mission to peacetime purposes, which he readily did. A day later Yardley submitted his proposal, calling for a budget of $100,000 (roughly $1.3 million in today's dollars), $40,000 to be paid by the State Department and $60,000 by the War Department, and retaining a staff of about fifty people. The following day, May 17, 1919, Frank Polk, acting secretary of state, scribbled "OK" on Yardley's proposal. Yardley's Black Chamber—as his outfit would become known—was born.

The budget for Yardley's Black Chamber was probably the first instance of a secret intelligence budget in U.S. history. The War Department's share of the Black Chamber's budget was disguised under the line item "Contingency Military Intelligence Division, General Staff" and was submitted as a "confidential memorandum" not subject to the review of the comptroller general. This early form of the black budget manifested in the space of a four-story brownstone at 3 East Thirty-eighth Street in New York City, whose cover story was the Code Compilation Company.

For the next ten years, Yardley's Black Chamber cracked Japanese diplomatic codes, and supplied the State Department with a stream of messages that inevitably began with the words "We have learned from a source believed reliable that . . ."

The Radio Communication Act of 1912 guaranteed privacy in communications: The law made intercepting cable traffic illegal without a court order. In spite of this, Yardley made a personal visit to Newcomb Carlton, the president of Western Union. After the meeting, "President Carlton seemed anxious to do everything he could for us," said Yardley. This too became a precedent: black agencies operating outside the law.

Nonetheless, the Black Chamber began to wither away, the victim of budget cuts. By 1925, Yardley was compelled to bring his

operation down to a mere seven code-breakers. The final cut to
the Black Chamber came with the incoming Hoover administration in 1929.

When Herbert Hoover took control of the White House and
named Henry L. Stimson secretary of state, the existence of the
Black Chamber remained secret even to the incoming administration. Yardley had asked his liaison at the State Department to
remain quiet about the code-breaking operation, hoping not to
draw undue attention to his project during the first few months of
the government's transition. After a few months had passed, Yardley decided that Stimson had settled in well enough to be informed
and provided the secretary of state with a handful of decrypted
Japanese messages. Stimson didn't take the news of the Black
Chamber as well as Yardley would have hoped. Outraged, he famously exclaimed, "Gentlemen do not read each other's mail,"
and sought to immediately shut down Yardley's operation. On
October 31, 1929, the Black Chamber closed its doors for good. Or
so it seemed. Just as the Black Chamber was shutting down, the
Army tapped William Fredrick Friedman to continue its mission
under the guise of a secret military unit.

Yardley's Black Chamber was not only the precursor to the
National Security Agency, it was a fledgling prototype of what
would swell into an enormous black world over the next sixty
years. It employed specialized workers using a legitimate business
as a cover; its budget—even its existence—was hidden from Congress; and it commanded a small infrastructure composed of in-
nocuous rooms and buildings in New York, and a clandestine
network of relationships to commercial cable companies and selected members of the State and War departments. The capacities
the Black Chamber represented were revived on a tremendous
scale during the next great war, and like the MI-8 group, whose
existence remained in place even after its stated mission during
World War I was over, the black projects of the Second World War

would remain in place at the end of that conflict as well. Ironically, fifteen years later, the same Henry Stimson who had closed the Black Chamber in a fit of indignation would be responsible for a nascent black project of almost infinitely larger proportions: the atomic bomb.

6

Fiat Lux
Alamogordo, New Mexico

The conversation took place in Eugene Wigner's office at Princeton University on the evening of March 16, 1939. That night, Leo Szilard was in town from New York to meet with a handful of eminent physicists assembled on the campus: John Wheeler, Leon Rosenfeld, Niels Bohr, and Edward Teller. The topic of discussion was Szilard and Enrico Fermi's recent discovery of large neutron emissions from a block of beryllium at Fermi's laboratory at Columbia University, an experiment whose results showed the chances of creating a nuclear reaction to be very real. An atomic weapon might be possible.

A dark cloud hung over Wigner's office that evening. The day before, the Nazis had invaded Czechoslovakia, and Hitler had declared on German radio that the country had "ceased to exist!"

The scientists in the room were particularly attuned to the gravity of events unfolding in Europe. Except for Wheeler, they were all from the Continent, having fled to the United States with the rise of German and Italian fascism. They also realized that if they were able to understand how one might go about building an atomic bomb, then the Nazis were similarly capable. The basic research was already in the open literature. The thought of a Third Reich armed with nuclear weapons terrified them to the core.

Szilard sketched out his findings from the Columbia experiment on Wigner's blackboard and put three emphatic proposals to the assembled group: One, that the president of the United States and the American armed forces be immediately informed of their discoveries; two, if additional experiments confirmed the Columbia results, they "must start a campaign" to continue fission research with renewed urgency; and finally, Szilard argued for secrecy: "We must induce all physicists to stop all publicity about fission." His reasoning was clear: By publishing nuclear research in open journals, the physicists would inadvertently assist the Nazis' own atomic aspirations. Their experiments therefore should be secret, "lest the Nazis learn of them and produce nuclear explosions first," remembered Teller.

Niels Bohr alone expressed deep reservations about bringing their research under a shroud of secrecy. The Danish scientist was one of the most esteemed researchers in the world and an elder statesman among Nobel Prize winners. In his home country of Denmark, Bohr was considered a national treasure. His reputation for genius and integrity followed him around the world. All of the other men in the room had been fellows at Bohr's institute for theoretical physics in Copenhagen, which Bohr had used to promote international cooperation among scientists since its founding in 1921. Bohr promoted openness and cosmopolitanism among the visiting international scholars at his institute: The Danish physicist would have nothing to do with the contemporary trend of excluding the Central Powers of the First World War from scientific collaboration and refused to be affiliated with any institutions (such as the International Union of Pure and Applied Physics) that excluded any nations. The atmosphere of cooperation, openness, and humor he cultivated was known as the "Copenhagen Spirit."

As the physicists contemplated the implications of Szilard's research and the Nazi army moving across Europe, Bohr remained adamant in his position: "Secrecy must never be introduced into physics." If science was to progress, absolute openness must prevail. Introducing secrecy into the scientific community, Bohr reasoned, would turn science into a political pursuit, rather than the collaborative, international quest for pure knowledge he had spent much of his career trying to foster. Science conducted in secret would become an instrument of coercion, a power benefiting the selfish, shortsighted, and violent ambitions of whoever controlled its findings, a fact that the rising Nazi state was demonstrating in its own burgeoning secret weapons programs.

Bohr had just as much reason to fear the Nazis as anyone else in the room. He was neither naïve nor a coward. Since 1933, Bohr had been using his institute, his reputation, and the international network of physicists he'd cultivated to help Jewish scientists escape from Hitler and Mussolini. Enrico Fermi, whose experiments with Szilard at Columbia demonstrated the possibility of a bomb, was among them. Moreover, Bohr used his platform as a world-renowned scientist to publicly criticize the Nazi regime. Addressing the International Congress of Anthropological and Ethnological Sciences in 1938, Bohr publicly denounced Nazi notions of Aryan supremacy. "Using the word much as it is used in atomic physics to characterize the relationship between experience obtained by different experimental arrangements and visualized only by mutually exclusive ideas, we may truly say that different human cultures are complementary to each other . . .

each such culture represents a harmonious balance of traditional conventions by means of which latent potentialities of human life can unfold themselves in a way which reveals to us new aspects of its unlimited richness and variety." Bohr argued that cultural diversity was extremely valuable to human knowledge and progress, because different peoples were able to see things differently, creating multiple vantage points that complemented one another in unlocking human potential. Contact between cultures, argued Bohr, contributed immeasurably to human progress. The German delegation walked out on him.

Bohr saw in science a model for what an ideal society might look like. Much more than the pursuit of technical knowledge, science was a way of being, of interacting with others; it was a community. To practice science was also a profoundly democratic enterprise. Practicing science meant uncovering and insisting on certain truths, no matter how politically uncomfortable that might be. The tradition of science had gone hand in hand with democratic ideals, a long history going back to modern science's earliest days.

In the early seventeenth century, Galileo first published his observations of planets and celestial bodies. The early modern astronomer's nighttime observations had as many social implications as scientific ones. Reporting in his *Sidereus Nuncius* that the moon's surface was cragged and pockmarked with canyons and craters, Galileo insisted that the Aristotelian notion of the "perfection of the heavens" was simply wrong. When he wrote that Jupiter exhibited four visible moons in its orbit, the Copernican implications of his observations were self-evident. Galileo's empirical truth was blasphemy, an affront to the Church's geocentric doctrine. But the egalitarian spirit of Galileo's method was even more revolutionary than his observations. His empirical methods implied that anyone, aristocrat or peasant, with a well-crafted telescope could repeat his observations and come to the same radical conclusions: The earth does, in fact, revolve around the sun. The planet Jupiter does indeed have many moons. Truth was no longer the province of the Church, but of everyone.

The promise of science and the promise of democracy were, in the minds of progressive scientists like Bohr, quite the same thing. The principles of scientific inquiry—shared, observable phenomena; the application of reason; and a community of rational thinkers—suggested the principles of liberal democracy, a point made by Giambattista Vico in 1708 when he argued that whoever "intends a career in public life, whether in the courts, the senate, or the pulpit," should "master the art of topics and defend both sides of a controversy, be it on nature, man, or politics, in a freer and brighter style of expression, so he can learn to draw on those arguments which are most probable and have the greatest degree of verisimilitude." Meaning, the ideals of science were the same ideals that one should strive toward in civic life. These notions quickly helped form the political philosophies of Enlightenment political thinkers and gave rise to notions of civil rights and equality. These ideals, in turn, inspired the American Revolution.

Thus, for Bohr, there was much at stake in the idea of introducing secrecy into science. On one hand, there was the very real chance that fission research conducted in the public sphere might encourage the Nazis to undertake their own nuclear weapons program. On the other, conducting science in secret would be a deep betrayal—not only of the most fundamental of scientific conventions, but a betrayal of the polis itself; conducting science in secret meant turning reason into a weapon. The question that evening at Princeton was this: Did the ideals of science and democracy have to be betrayed in the face of Nazism? And if they were betrayed, would the ideals eventually come back, or would that betrayal remain permanent?

As the Princeton meeting ground past midnight and into the cold early hours of the East Coast winter, Bohr, unable to convince his colleagues they should preserve the openness that characterized their field, finally skirted the issue. The whole conversation was moot, he concluded. Separating U-235, the uranium isotope required to sustain a chain reaction, in any quantity suitable for a weapon was simply too much effort. The largest plant capable of separating U-235 from U-238 would take ten days working twenty-four hours a day to separate one thousand-millionth of a gram. Working at that maximum speed, it would take 26,445 years to produce a single gram of U-235. Such an undertaking would be nearly impossible given the resource restrictions in a time of war. According to Edward Teller, Bohr claimed that "it could never be done unless you turn the United States into one huge factory."

The next month, Bohr returned to Copenhagen. Europe was on the brink of destruction. Hitler was threatening Poland. It was only a matter of time before the German Panzer columns rumbled into Bohr's homeland. His colleagues resolutely opposed Bohr's return to Europe, pointing out that the physicist could have almost any academic appointment in the United States that he wanted if only he were to stay. But the elder physicist refused. Bohr felt compelled to return to Europe, to maintain his institute, and to continue helping other scientists escape from the Nazis' ever-growing sphere of domination. For many scientists still in Europe, Bohr's institute was the only means of escape.

Back in Copenhagen, Bohr continued to accept fleeing refugees through the institute, often putting them up in his own home when they arrived in Copenhagen, and used his influence with the Swedish royal family to arrange for refugees to find sanctuary in Sweden. In April of 1940, the Nazis invaded Denmark and the small country capitulated to overwhelming Nazi force with little resistance. Bohr began destroying records of the refugees he'd helped flee Germany and other occupied countries lest they fall into Hitler's hands. Once again, Bohr's American colleagues sent him a flood of cables imploring him to leave Denmark for the relative safety of the United States. Once again, Bohr refused, convinced that his presence in Denmark was needed to resist the Nazi occupation. In late August of 1943, the Danish government resigned rather than accept the latest round of Nazi demands, and the Germans declared martial law throughout the country. Arrests increased. People disappeared. Within a few weeks, Bohr learned the Nazis planned to intern all "undesirable aliens"—Jewish refugees who'd found asylum in Denmark. On September 29, Bohr was told of his own impending arrest. That night, with his family, Bohr fled Denmark in a small motorboat bound for the Swedish coast. Upon his arrival, Bohr immediately used his influence to arrange for the reception of thousands of Jewish refugees who would soon be fleeing Denmark. Over the next few weeks, six thousand Jews were able to find sanctuary in Sweden, crossing from Denmark in clandestine nightly evacuations. On October 6, an unarmed British Mosquito bomber landed in Stockholm to smuggle the physicist out of the country. Bohr crept into the plane's empty bomb bay and escaped to Britain.

In Britain, Bohr, who had been out of the loop while in Denmark, learned of the Manhattan Project—the effort to build an atomic bomb—the project Bohr had so recently dismissed as unfeasible. After two months in Britain, the physicist boarded a ship bound for the United States, accompanied by his son Aage. When the ship arrived in New York, a group of Army security officers received him. The Secret Service had prepared for the physicist's arrival. Bohr's very presence in the United States could signal an American interest in developing nuclear weapons. The physicist was compelled to go undercover. It began with his name. When Bohr set foot on American soil, he became "Nicolas Baker," a sterile identity. His existence became a state secret.

This led to inevitable mishaps: While buying a suit in Washington, "Nicolas Baker" mistakenly left his watch in the shop, a watch engraved with his proper name. When his son Aage went to retrieve it, the younger Bohr explained that he was Mr. Baker, an assistant to Niels Bohr. Realizing that the shop owner didn't believe the story, Aage suggested that they call the Danish foreign minister's office. A secretary at the legation explained that they had no record of a "Mr. Baker," and that Bohr's assistant also held the name Bohr. Aage was forced to explain that he and his father were using the name "Baker" while traveling in the United States. The shopkeeper handed over the watch with a stern reprimand: "In the U.S.A. it is against the law to use a false name."

After finishing their business in Washington, the Bohrs set out for a secret site in New Mexico that Manhattan Project insiders knew simply as "Y." General Leslie Groves, the Army's director of the Manhattan Project, joined Bohr for the long train ride. En route, Groves briefed Bohr on what to expect at the classified research facility. The project, Groves explained, was compartmentalized: A person working on one part of the bomb effort wasn't cleared to know what was happening with the other parts. Groves told Bohr what was permissible to say and what wasn't. It was as if the closer Bohr got to the bomb, the more its secrecy controlled him. The bomb had changed his name, was now adding silences and absences to his speech, and would dictate the research questions he posed.

Built on the site of an old boys' school in the Jemez Mountains, Los Alamos was as remote as it was breathtaking. The location was chosen by Robert Oppenheimer, who famously loved the desert. From the mesa on which the facility sat, evening sunsets turned the Sangre de Cristo Mountains a sublime red. The mountains lived up to their name: Blood of Christ. Although many of the scientists at Los Alamos had spent time in Bohr's Copenhagen institute, the classified facility where they now worked had an entirely different spirit than the one Bohr had fostered in Europe.

Upon his arrival, Bohr found an environment buzzing with

energy: Scientists and engineers worked at breakneck speeds to develop the bomb. He wrote, "What until a few years ago might have been considered a fantastic dream is at the moment being realized in great laboratories erected for secrecy in some of the most solitary regions of the States." But underlying the Manhattan Project was a sense of mounting anger, hostility, and remorse among the scientists. Even as these men worked to generate a light more powerful than a thousand suns, the environment at Los Alamos was diametrically opposed to the "Copenhagen Spirit" that so many of them had come to take for granted. The secrecy was crushing: Colleagues couldn't talk openly with one another about their work—a hallmark of the scientific tradition. Army security officers censored the physicists' incoming and outgoing mail and regulated all contact with outsiders. Even Leo Szilard, who had passionately argued for keeping nuclear fission secret back at Princeton and who had done more than anyone to start the Manhattan Project, was frustrated with life at Los Alamos. He hated working under military leadership. The feeling was mutual: In 1942, General Groves unsuccessfully tried to have Szilard interned for the duration of the war as an "enemy alien." Moreover, the physicists at Los Alamos were haunted by the fact that they were now building, in secret, what they knew would be the most devastating weapon ever devised. They were realizing the gravity of their work. They were unlocking nature's secrets—a cause whose nobility few of them ever had any reason to doubt—so that the U.S. Army could incinerate entire cities in the blink of an eye. Victor Weisskopf later wrote, "In Los Alamos, we were working on something which is perhaps the most questionable, most problematic thing a scientist can be faced with. At that time physics, our beloved science, was pushed into the most cruel part of reality and we had to live it through."

As Bohr learned more about the bomb, he gradually came to realize the true scale and scope of the Manhattan Project, discovering what historian Richard Rhodes called "a separate, secret state with separate sovereignty linked to the public state through the person and by the sole authority of the President." The Manhattan Project had its own bureaucracies, its own Air Force, its own pilots, its own bombing ranges, its own factories, its own industrial workers, its own laws and police, even its own quasi-universities. At its height, the Manhattan Project employed over 130,000 people: It represented an industrial sector equal in size to the entire American auto industry. Bohr came to learn that the Manhattan Project was much, much more than a secret weapon. A secret geography and an attendant mode of sovereign governance had taken hold. In a conversation with Edward Teller, the Danish physicist remembered their exchange back at Princeton: "You see, I told you it couldn't be done without turning the whole country into a factory," said Bohr. "You have done just that."

Perhaps even more remarkable than the scale of the bomb was the fact that, by and large, the bomb actually did remain secret—not necessarily from foreign intelligence agencies, but to the public, to Congress, and to the courts. It was a stunning feat of social engineering and a tremendous exercise in executive power. Roosevelt secretly authorized funding for the bomb in 1941 "from a special source available for such an unusual purpose," but by 1944 the amount of untraceable monies attracted the attention of a certain Senator Harry Truman. Billions of dollars were disappearing into the "Manhattan Engineering District" under line items like "Engineer Service, Army" and "Expediting Production." When Truman discovered the disappearing funds, he was livid. The senator assumed that someone was bilking the government, but as he tried to follow the money trail, he only encountered the bureaucratic labyrinth that served as a cover for the Manhattan Project's financing. Truman eventually confronted Secretary of War Henry L. Stimson about his findings, and Stimson—the man who'd shut down Yardley's

Black Chamber fifteen years prior—found himself on the opposite side of the line separating the black world from its white counterpart. He told Truman that the funds were going toward a project that the president had ordered "most top secret," and that Truman would not be told of its purpose under any circumstance. Truman retreated, but Stimson realized he could not maintain the Manhattan Project's enormous black budget without informing some members of Congress. With an eye toward preserving the bomb's secret funding, Stimson held a meeting on February 18, 1944, to brief top congressional leaders. The assembled congressmen gave their approval and committed themselves to protecting the project—the architects of the Manhattan Project would no longer need to fend off the Appropriations Committee. Except for a small handful of legislators, Congress, including Truman, was kept in the dark about the bomb. The future president would only come to learn the details of the nuclear program after being sworn in in 1945.

The secrecy that went along with the Manhattan Project was also relatively new for the Army. If the Manhattan Project represented a new era in industrialized bomb-making, so did the industry-sized secrecy apparatus joining it. Nine years after the first nuclear explosion, Leslie Groves would testify at the Oppenheimer hearings that he had very little experience with secrecy before the Manhattan Project: "The Army as a whole didn't deal with matters of security until after the atomic bomb burst on the world because it was the first time that the Army really knew there was such a thing, if you want to be perfectly frank about it!"

Trying to break the spell of collective despair plaguing the secret lab at Los Alamos, Bohr took to arguing that atomic power could be put toward the benefit of humanity at the conclusion of the war. The end was by now in sight. Just as the small community of nuclear physicists had taken the lead in advocating for and building the bomb, Bohr looked toward a future in which these same men would become leaders of a postwar nuclear policy that would improve the lives of countless people.

Bohr started preparing for a return to openness in nuclear physics and for international cooperation in preventing nuclear proliferation. Nuclear energy was no longer a theoretical possibility. It was salient fact. Bohr understood that the postwar fate of nuclear energy went hand in hand with the postwar fate of societies in general. If atomic research and development continued to be defined by the logic of its wartime origins, then it spelled an impossibly dangerous future. An international version of Bohr's "Copenhagen Spirit" was the best insurance against human annihilation, an "open world," as Bohr called it.

Bohr aggressively lobbied the American and British governments to develop a postwar nuclear policy defined by openness, international cooperation, and the peaceful use of atomic energy. He traveled to Britain for an audience with Winston Churchill. The notoriously cantankerous prime minister dismissed him outright. In Washington, Bohr was more successful. Meeting with his old friend Supreme Court justice Felix Frankfurter, Bohr described his failed meeting with Churchill and his sense of urgency about postwar nuclear policy. Frankfurter relayed Bohr's concerns to the president, and Roosevelt agreed to see the scientist. In preparation for the meeting, Bohr crafted a memo for the president outlining his arguments: "A weapon of unparalleled power is being created which will completely change all future conditions of warfare. . . . Unless, indeed, some agreement about the control of the use of the new active materials can be obtained in due time, any temporary advantage, however great, may be outweighed by a perpetual menace to human security." For Bohr, the only possible way to prevent an arms race was "an initiative, aiming at forestalling a fateful competition, [that] should serve to uproot any cause of distrust between the powers on whose harmonious collaboration the fact of coming generations will depend." Bohr's memo calling for harmonious international cooperation was stamped "Top Secret."

On August 26, 1944, Bohr arrived at the Oval Office to see Roosevelt. Over the summer, the Allies in Europe had successfully crushed the German army's western front. The war in Europe would soon be over, its scales having tipped decidedly in the Allies' favor. Roosevelt was now in a position to contemplate postwar policy. As Bohr and Roosevelt sat together in the Oval Office, the president explained that he'd read Bohr's memo and that he agreed with the physicist's main points. Roosevelt joked with Bohr about the scientist's failed meeting in London; he had plenty of experience dealing with Churchill's obstinacy. Nonetheless, intimated Roosevelt, the prime minister would eventually come around. The president promised to discuss the matter with Churchill the following month.

The meeting at Hyde Park couldn't have gone worse for Bohr. On Monday, September 19, the two leaders sequestered themselves in one of the smaller rooms of Roosevelt's great estate overlooking the Hudson River. Paris was liberated; the Germans had been driven out of much of France; Allied armies were steadily taking Italy; and there was no indication that Hitler would be able to build the bomb. But as the leaders discussed Bohr's proposal, Churchill remained unyielding. That day in Hyde Park, Roosevelt either capitulated to the prime minister or made it clear that he had never intended to go along with Bohr's proposal in the first place. Churchill was clearly furious with what he perceived as Bohr's political meddling, later growling, "The President and I are worried about Professor Bohr. . . . He is a great advocate of publicity. He made an unauthorized disclosure to Justice Frankfurter who startled the president by telling him all the details. . . . It seems to me that Bohr ought to be confined or at any rate made to see that he is very near the edge of mortal crimes." The meeting ended with a renewed commitment to the bomb's secrecy. Moreover, the leaders agreed, Bohr would be placed under investigation "to ensure that he is responsible for no leakage of information, particularly to the Russians." The very qualities that made Bohr an international treasure before the war—his intellect and his commitment to international cooperation and openness—now made him suspect. The elder scientist was put under surveillance.

One of the grim ironies about the Manhattan Project's secrecy is that by the time of Churchill and Roosevelt's meeting in late 1944, the initial justification for the secrecy was gone: It was clear that Nazi Germany would not be able to develop an atomic weapon, certainly not before the war's end. But the secrecy persisted. What was at the outset a temporary wartime measure had in a few short years become a new normal. For challenging what had become "common sense," Bohr fell under official suspicion.

Just as the Black Chamber stayed open long after its initial justification was gone, when the Second World War finally ended, the "huge factory" Bohr had foreseen didn't go away, nor did the secrecy associated with it. The secrecy didn't end when nuclear weapons incinerated Hiroshima and Nagasaki and newspapers reported on the "secret cities" producing the bomb; it didn't end when Japan surrendered and the war was officially over. Instead, the bomb's secret geography grew. Secrecy had become, in the words of McGeorge Bundy, "a state of mind with a life and meaning of its own."

Building secret weapons during a time of war was nothing new. Building *industrialized* secret weapons, employing hundreds of thousands of workers, the world's top scientists, dedicated factories, and multibillion-dollar budgets hidden from Congress— that was unprecedented. It would become a standard operating procedure.

The Manhattan Project set the black world in motion, established its footprint on the landscape in New Mexico, in the nation's capital, and on elite university campuses just as it brought new powers to the executive branch of the federal government. Hiding phenomenal sums of money from Congress had become a reality, a reality that trumped the clear language of the Constitution's Receipts and Expenditures Clause: "a regular statement and account of receipts and expenditures of *all* public money shall be published from time to time" (emphasis added). The bomb had begun to transform the state in its own image.

As the war came to an end, scores of nuclear scientists joined Bohr in opposing military control over nuclear policy, opposing secrecy, and advocating for international cooperation to avoid a nuclear arms race. Leo Szilard joined other Manhattan Project scientists in 1945 to form the Federation of American Scientists to advocate against arms proliferation and secrecy, and for international cooperation and the development of rational policymaking. In 1946, the federation published *One World or None*, a pamphlet featuring essays by some of the bomb's chief architects, including Leo Szilard, J. R. Oppenheimer, Eugene Wigner, Hans Bethe, and Albert Einstein. In its foreword, Bohr wrote that a new, international spirit of cooperation must take hold to "prevent any use of the new sources of energy that does not serve mankind as a whole." He imagined a new age of worldwide openness when he wrote that "no control can be effective without free access to full scientific information and the granting of the opportunity of international supervision of all undertakings that, unless regulated, might become a source of disaster." This new age would "demand the abolition of barriers hitherto considered necessary to safeguard national interests but now standing in the way of common security against unprecedented dangers." For Bohr, what was at stake in ending the secret weapons research associated with wartime science was not just an abstract commitment to an idea of democracy, it was the survival of the human race itself. The other scientists' essays echoed Bohr's warnings, as did the title of the pamphlet. But the scientists made little headway. The secret state won.

The Manhattan Project was a tremendous undertaking, involving thousands of people, a dedicated industrial base, a black budget of staggering scope, and a network of factories, laboratories, and testing sites, all compartmentalized to ensure maximum secrecy. Although the Manhattan Project reflected the Black Chamber in terms of organization and financing, its sheer scale dwarfed Yardley's team of code-breakers by several orders of magnitude. The Manhattan Project, more than any other program in American history, was not only a blueprint for what would become the black world, it was the black world's foundation.

I decided to make a simple calculation. The Manhattan Project, a project lasting roughly five years from start to finish, had cost $2.3 billion in 1945 dollars. A contemporary sum of about $26.8 billion: a tremendous amount. But here, a startling fact: The budget for the entire Manhattan Project was still billions of dollars less than the present day's annual black budget. Every year, the United States spends more black dollars than it took to build the bomb.

In the few short years it took to build the bomb, and with the ensuing Cold War, the notion of having classified industries, multibillion-dollar secret budgets, legions of security-cleared personnel, and entire branches of science devoted to secret science went from being unthinkable to being so natural that few people even bothered questioning it.

When you train yourself to see secret geographies, the Manhattan Project's legacy, you start to see them everywhere. Back in the Antelope Valley, among the skyscraper-sized hangars built to house classified aerospace development, it had been relatively obvious. The same holds true for much of the southwestern deserts: the Nevada Test Site, the China Lake range in Southern California, the Dugway Proving Ground in Utah, not to mention the launchpads at Vandenberg or restricted parts of Edwards Air Force Base. Closer to home, there were the recruiting letters from the National Geospatial-Intelligence Agency showing up each year at Berkeley's geography department and the office of "torture memo" author John Yoo. I had learned to see secret geographies, but I had yet to see any of the classified machines that so much industry, wealth, secrecy, and ingenuity went into producing. On a high-rise balcony in downtown Toronto, Canada, I'd get the chance.

7

The Other Night Sky
A Few Miles North of the U.S. Frontier

Ted Molczan reaches into the filing cabinet behind his desk and pulls out a faded black notebook. We're sitting in the living room of his Toronto apartment, a small, spartan abode on the twenty-second floor of the downtown high-rise where he's lived for twenty-seven years. His two cats, Rusty and Sparky, lounge around on the hardwood floor. Molczan is a lifelong space buff and an amateur astronomer of sorts. A small bookshelf across the room is neatly stacked with books on two subjects: space and math. There's *Men of the Stars*, *The Sputnik Challenge*, *The Heavens and the Earth*, along with the *Handbook of Mathematical Functions*, and a worn tome with the intimidating title *Celestial Mechanics*.

Molczan knows more than just about anyone (who can talk about it) about the subject of his particular investigations: spy satellites. With little more than a desktop computer, some star charts, a pair of binoculars given to him by a friend, and an eastward-facing balcony, Molczan works with a team of global "observers" to keep tabs on almost two hundred spacecraft that aren't officially there. Next to Molczan's bookshelf is a framed cover of an issue of *Aviation Week & Space Technology* from the late 1980s. He won't tell me its significance. I assume he played some unacknowledged role in the issue. Molczan has lots of stories; many of them are off the record.

Molczan opens the notebook and carefully lays it out next to a neat stack of star atlases on his desk. In the middle is a piece of old, yellowed graph paper with a series of points and dates, and a curve drawn to connect them. The pencil points are a record of Molczan's earliest observations. Little points are scattered from left to right in an arcing pattern. A delicate pencil mark drawn through the dots forms a slowly undulating sine wave. We're looking at a decade's worth of Ted's observations of PAGEOS (Passive Geodetic Satellite), a giant balloon satellite launched in 1966 made mostly out of highly reflective mylar. The craft's large area and relatively light weight meant that the spacecraft was highly susceptible to the effects of solar radiation pressure, an effect James Clerk Maxwell first theorized in 1871 and Pyotr Lebedev proved experimentally in 1901. SRP is pressure exerted on an object in space by solar energy reflecting off its surface. In most cases, it's subtle but nonetheless detectable. Molczan learned about SRP by observing its effects on PAGEOS. Decades later, his ability to calculate its effects would come in very handy as he tried to track a spacecraft that wasn't supposed to exist.

Amateur satellite observing began as a civic institution, a state-sponsored hobby. When artificial satellites began filling the night sky in the 1950s, the dawn of the space race, the American and British governments established satellite prediction services, encouraging amateurs (and training them) to take up satellite observing as a national hobby. In the United States, the Smithsonian Astrophysical Observatory organized Operation Moonwatch, enlisting and training amateur astronomers to observe and track the artificial satellites that were beginning to appear in the night sky. Moonwatch was an exercise in popular public science, but it was also a pseudomilitary institution, an extension of the U.S.'s Ground Observer Corps, which organized Americans to watch the skies for Soviet bombers. In the years before Cray supercomputers and worldwide networks of military satellite-tracking stations, the government could enlist hobbyist observers to help keep tabs on the artificial objects in Earth orbit, a kind of citizen surveillance not unlike the civilians trained to spot Nazi bombers over Britain during the Second World War.

The state-sponsored hobby trained a generation of observers to make highly accurate descriptions and predictions of satellites' orbital characteristics. At the Royal Observatory of Edinburgh, Scottish observer Russell Eberst became one of the field's luminaries. According to the hobby's bible, Desmond King-Hele's 1983 book *Observing Earth Satellites*, Eberst was "the world's leading observer . . . who began observing in 1958 and had made more than 90,000 observations by 1982."

"One way to look at it," Molczan, a tall, thin man with a pale complexion and graying blond hair, tells me in a deep, warm voice, "is that it's a form of science-based investigation. . . . I guess that it's like modern detective work, which is also based on science." The hobby is possible, Ted explains, because no matter how many security classifications and code words the NRO uses to hide its secret satellites, the agency can't classify the laws of Newtonian physics. The tools of satellite observing are so simple that they are almost anachronistic: a good pair of binoculars, some star charts, and a stopwatch. That's it, really. To these tools, Ted adds a computer program called Obsreduce, which he wrote to put his observations into a sharable form. With these modest means, Molczan keeps detailed records about a different night sky than the one most amateur astronomers see once the sun sets each day.

Molczan observed his first satellite by accident one high school summer in the 1960s, a bright, slow-moving object arcing over the night sky in his hometown of Hamilton, Canada. He flips back a few pages in his rumpled black notebook to his first observations from the early 1960s. "8:30, High in the east. 10:20, low in the west." Molczan was having a rough summer. He'd failed all his classes the year before. Math looked like hieroglyphics, auto maintenance class had no appeal whatsoever (to this date, he's never owned a car), and his parents were starting to worry about his performance. But he wanted to know more about Echo-2, the satellite he'd glimpsed by chance. Using the kitchen clock as a timepiece, Molczan would walk out in the backyard at the times he figured the satellite should be visible and take observations. As the summer wore on, he remembered a side exercise in his math textbook that showed how to calculate the speed of a satellite. It had piqued his interest as he'd flipped through the textbook the previous year while ignoring the lesson at hand, but the equations and square-root symbols made his eyes glaze over. When it was time for school to start again, Molczan went to buy some school supplies and picked up an eighty-cent slide rule. He knew from watching *My Three Sons* that engineers used them. That made him think having one might help him learn more about Echo-2. Over the next few weeks, he read through the little instruction manual that had come with the slide rule. By the time school started that year, he'd become enchanted by the power of his new school supply, attempting to regale anyone who'd listen with the fact that he could calculate how long it would take for a ball to drop from his hand using nothing more than the power of the slide rule. "They didn't yet have the word 'geek' back then," he laughs. Echo-2 put Molczan back on track. That year, he got straight A's. He went on to become a technologist, analyzing energy efficiency for companies and eventually starting his own business as an energy consultant.

Molczan started paying attention to classified satellites in the 1980s. Before then, in accordance with international conventions, the United States reported the orbits of all its spacecraft to the United Nations. It didn't identify its satellites beyond their international designation numbers, but the data was public. That changed in the summer of 1983, when the Reagan administration abruptly and inexplicably stopped publishing up-to-date information about the orbital characteristics of its military and intelligence satellites. In the meantime, the Thatcher government was rapidly dismantling Britain's prediction service. The sudden policy reversals on either side of the Atlantic created an unintended challenge for the teams of highly skilled satellite observers whose hobby now seemed to serve no purpose: Could they identify and maintain accurate orbital data for spacecraft that had disappeared from official maps? Molczan, Eberst, and others began mapping the "other night sky"—the mysterious, secret objects in orbit around Earth.

Satellites come in all shapes and sizes, and dwell in all sorts of different orbits, depending on their particular job. The ones in low Earth orbit are visible just after twilight and just before dawn, gliding from north to south or south to north in what's known as a polar orbit. But there are many more that can't be seen with an unaided eye. Perched in stationary orbits 22,241 miles above Earth's surface, the faintest objects in the other night sky are the geosynchronous satellites. From such a high vantage point, a reconnaissance satellite is able to provide coverage of about half the planet. Geosynchronous eavesdropping spacecraft have code names like MAGNUM, MENTOR, ADVANCED ORION, and MERCURY, while data-relay satellites in similar orbits purportedly have code names like NEMESIS and QUASAR. Then there

are the military communication satellites of the MILSTAR constellation, perched on opposite sides of Earth: MILSTAR 5, for example, is parked on the equator over eastern Africa, about halfway
between Nairobi and Mogadishu, while MILSTAR 6 hovers over
the opposite side of the globe near the Galapagos Islands off the
coast of Ecuador. But one of the MILSTAR birds is visible with
binoculars in the Southern Hemisphere as it arcs through the sky.
MILSTAR 3 isn't in a geosynchronous orbit. It is a corpse. The billion-dollar satellite spun into a useless orbit during its 1999 launch
when someone entered the number -0.1992476 into the software
controlling its "roll rate filter constant." The correct number was -
1.992476. The cost of the misplaced decimal point? 800 million
dollars for the satellite and $433 million for the rocket.

Just visible to the unaided eye at an altitude of about 1,100 km
are the Naval Ocean Surveillance Satellites (code-named PARCAE
after Jupiter's three daughters), designed to track naval vessels by
eavesdropping on shortwave and other transmissions. The NOSS
satellites cruise across the night sky in formations of twos and
threes, appearing as points of light moving in a triangular forma-
tion. In other words, they look like a late-generation UFO or
super-secret delta-winged aircraft with a cloaking device. In fact,
they are so easy to mistake for UFOs or black aircraft that UFO
researchers have come to realize that a great deal of "black triangle" sightings can be explained by the PARCAE constellations.

The kings of the other night sky, however, are the imaging satellites. For an hour or two after sunset or in the predawn morning, these low-Earth-orbiting spacecraft appear as some of the
brightest objects in the sky. The size of school buses, their pol-
ished hulls light up like meteors when they reflect sunlight toward
the earth below. There are two basic variations of imaging satellites: those that use photographic imaging methods and those
that use something called "synthetic aperture radar." The primary photographic satellites are the KH series, namely USA 116,

USA 129, USA 161, and USA 186, which circle the globe every couple of hours at altitudes between one hundred and six hundred miles.

Even basic facts about imaging satellites, such as their names, are hard to come by: Are the contemporary "big birds" late-model eleventh-generation KH-class satellites, or do they represent an entirely new generation? If they're updated KH-11s (KH-11Bs), then they probably go by the code names IMPROVED CRYSTAL (or ADVANCED CRYSTAL) and IKON. If they're an entirely new generation, their manufacturer's designation would be KH-12. Among satellite observers, the consensus is that they probably bear the manufacturer's designation KH-11B, but for the purposes of amateur catalogs, it's common to find them described as KH-12s. Though the question itself might be moot: According to historian Jeffrey Richelson, after the KEYHOLE (KH) code name became publicly known, "the NRO decided to abandon such designations and refer to the satellites by a purely random numbering scheme."

The KEYHOLE's cousins in the night sky are the ONYX imaging satellites, sometimes known by the old code name LACROSSE, whose ground controllers and engineers sport mission patches with a pair of owl eyes along with the phrase "We Own the Night." As of this writing, there are four ONYX satellites in low Earth orbits around Earth: ONYX 2, 3, 4, and 5. They appear as majestic points of orange light moving across the sky. But one of these birds is not like the others. ONYX 5 (launched April 30, 2005) has a tinge of white to its color. More interestingly, ONYX 5 has a proclivity for doing what satellite observers call a "disappearing trick," a source of curiosity, if not heated debate, on satellite-observing Listservs. ONYX 5 will often appear at a predicted moment in a predicted place, shine brightly as it moves across the night sky, and then suddenly vanish for no apparent reason, only to reappear on its previous track a few seconds later.

The disappearing trick isn't consistent in any way. Satellite observers have so far failed to predict when it's going to happen, and the amount of time that the spacecraft disappears isn't consistent either.

The ONYX satellites are designed to "see" at night and through cloud cover, hence their controllers' motto. To do this, they use synthetic aperture radar to shoot microwaves down at Earth, measure the reflections, and create a composite image from the result. It's the same basic idea as radar, hence the name. If the Hubble Space Telescope is a white version of a KEYHOLE, then a white version of the ONYX is the Magellan probe, launched on May 4, 1989, from the space shuttle Atlantis (five months earlier, Atlantis had deployed ONYX 1). Its mission was to map the surface of Venus, using its SAR to see through the dense clouds covering the totality of the planet.

As far as spy satellites are concerned, these are only the beginning. The National Reconnaissance Office's still-classified files overflow with the code names and security compartments associated with secret spacecraft. There are the TRUMPET/ADVANCED JUMPSEAT satellites, designed to intercept signals from radars, surface-to-air missiles, and other electronic devices. The MERCURY/ADVANCED VORTEX constellation of near-geosynchronous satellites conduct eavesdropping operations, while the MAGNUM/ADVANCED ORION and MENTOR spacecraft pluck other wayward signals emanating from the ground. The QUASAR constellation acts as a data relay system between ground controllers and other satellites. And then there are the MISTY/ZIRCONIC spacecraft, a class of stealth satellites that have proven just as adept at hiding from amateur satellite observers as they have from congressional oversight committees. In sum, the "other night sky" is a mind-boggling collection of colorful and highly classified spacecraft.

The other night sky extends down to the earth. For every satellite in Earth orbit, there are giant corporations like Lockheed,

Boeing, and Northrop with contracts to research, develop, and deploy the spacecraft. There are legions of soldiers and contractors whose job it is to operate the spacecraft from a global network of control facilities and downlinks, from the Pine Gap facility in Australia's outback to Onizuka Air Force Station in the heart of California's Silicon Valley, and from Thule Air Base, near the North Pole, to Diego Garcia, the restricted island in the Indian Ocean. The sole purpose of agencies like the National Reconnaissance Office and U.S. Space Command, not to mention the satellite arms of the Navy and the National Security Agency, is to coordinate, organize, and oversee all of these spacecraft. Although most classified satellites are invisible to the unaided eye, their earthly footprint is tremendous.

More than fifty years of black spacecraft design has also meant creating a vast bureaucratic, cultural, and social architecture of secrecy and deception. Building secret satellites means creating enormous black budgets, hidden factories and obscure contracts to task their development, ultraclassified security compartments to protect the "product," and a history of disinformation and outright lying to protect their secrets. "Overhead assets," as the National Reconnaissance Office and Pentagon call them, are not only technological marvels but social and cultural things.

The first problem with identifying black satellites in the night sky is learning how to tell the difference between something interesting, such as an ONYX spacecraft, from something more quotidian, like a DirecTV satellite. The place to start is an online catalog called space-track.org. Produced and maintained by U.S. Strategic Command (USSTRATCOM), Space Track is a collection of data describing the motion and location of all the satellites and significant pieces of space debris that the Department of Defense keeps active tabs on. Classified satellites, however, do not appear in the catalog.

The Space Track catalog is a map to the unclassified night sky, the "known knowns" in Earth orbit. If something appears in the night sky and it's not in the catalog, that's a strong indication that the unknown object is a classified spacecraft.

Using Space Track is a little creepy. First of all, the domain name is registered through a company called Domainsbyproxy. com, whose business is to anonymously register Internet addresses. To access the data on Space Track, a user has to create an account with the Defense Department, promise not to distribute the information anywhere else, and submit to a policy that includes the following:

> WARNING! This web site contains data and information provided by the U.S. Government. If you are not authorized to access this system, disconnect now. You should have no expectation of privacy. By continuing, you consent to your keystrokes and data content being monitored.

A Space Track account gives access to lines of data sometimes called "Keplerian elements," more commonly known by the acronym "TLEs," for "two-line elements." A TLE is a series of numbers that looks like this:

ISS (ZARYA)

1 25544U   98067A 04236.56031392 .00020137 00000-0 16538-3 0 5135

2 25544   51.6335 341.7760 0007976 126.2523 325.9359
            15.70406856328903

To the uninitiated, a TLE looks like a mysterious code. The top line (ISS) designates the catalog or common name of the orbital element. In this case, ISS stands for "international space station," often the brightest thing in the night sky besides the moon. The first entry on both subsequent lines, 25544, is the United States Space Command's satellite catalog number for the object—the

military designation for the satellite (00001 was Sputnik). The letter "U" after the number means that the object is unclassified.
The second number, 98067A, denotes the object's international
designation, also known as its COSPAR (Committee on Space Research) number. In this case, the ISS was launched in 1998 (98), it
was the sixty-seventh successful launch that year (067), and it is
the first object from that launch tracked, so its COSPAR number
is 98067A.

From here, things get complicated as the numbers begin describing the object's orbital characteristics. One number describes
the last observed south-north equatorial crossing of the satellite,
others the inclinations, eccentricities, perigee, mean anomalies
and motions for the object, and so forth.

The Space Track resource is amazing, a testament to what
Niels Bohr meant with his notion of an "open world." The Space
Track catalog, like much else in the satellite-observing hobby, is a
holdover from the Moonwatch days. Back when civilian observers
acted as a de facto satellite-tracking service, NASA's Goddard
Space Flight Center provided observers with known orbital elements, enabling the amateurs to check their accuracy and to identify any satellites the government had no records for. Once the
military developed tracking systems far more advanced than
teams of volunteer hobbyists, there was no reason per se to keep
making the tracking data public, but the tradition of making the
elements public remained intact. Nonetheless, the Space Track
catalog is constantly under threat of becoming classified: There
are plenty of people in the Air Force and NRO who don't at all like
the idea of an average civilian with a Web browser having access
to the same data that they do.

Ted Molczan uses the Space Track catalog as a backdrop to process his observations and those of other satellite hobbyists like
Russell Eberst and Mike McCants (who post regular reports to a

Listserv called SeeSat-L). When his colleagues observe an "unknown" object, Molczan compares the sighting to the catalog. If there are no obvious correlations, he tries to match the data to a classified object in his own catalog. When he finds one, he updates the TLE files he maintains for the black spacecraft. Using these methods, Molczan generates phenomenally accurate records.

"In addition to accurate positional data, [some observers] estimate visual magnitude," he explains. In other words, some observers will describe the brightness of a witnessed satellite using a scale derived from astronomy, where Jupiter is about mag -1, the stars in the Big Dipper are around mag 2, and the faintest visible star on a moonless night might be around mag 5.5. For Molczan, these observations reveal even more: "We try to develop a 'standard magnitude' by normalizing data as if they're all at a thousand kilometers from the observer. Brightness follows the inverse-square law. We can take mag observations amassed over time and recompute them as if they're at one-thousand-kilometer range. Satellites show phases just like the moon and planets." If Molczan can determine a standard brightness from multiple observations, he can use that data to estimate the size of an object: Larger objects are intrinsically brighter than smaller ones, because they have more surface area to reflect light. Another variable is the payload capacity of the rockets used to launch spy satellites: Molczan estimates the size and mass of an object by studying the performance characteristics of rockets like the Titan IV (published for the benefit of commercial companies launching satellites).

Using these methods, Molczan and his colleagues figured out that a new generation of KH reconnaissance satellites took to the skies in 1992: The newer reconnaissance birds were larger than their forebears but were simultaneously about a magnitude dimmer. By paying close attention to the perturbations of an orbit due to atmospheric drag and solar radiation pressure, Molczan can calculate the area-to-mass ratio: He can learn how dense an object is and how much it weighs. A skilled observer can derive a surprising amount of information from nothing more than little streaks in the night sky.

The bulk of this work happens on a Listserv for satellite observers called SeeSat-L. Although anyone can join the forums, it's a tough place to be a newbie. Most posts contain nothing more than strings of numbers, mathematical descriptions of the previous evening's sightings.

When he has some spare time, a satellite observer in Texas named Mike McCants compiles SeeSat observations into a simple text file he calls "classfd.tle." The file contains only twenty kilobytes, about the size of an e-mail, but it serves as a near-complete map to the other night sky. With classfd.tle, anyone with access to a computer can generate predictions of reconnaissance satellite overpasses for any location in the world. The data is usually accurate to within a fraction of a second.

Import the classfd.tle file into a freeware application like Orbitron, and the information blossoms with details of almost two hundred secret orbits. At the top of the list is a leftover piece of debris from a Japanese spy satellite named Information Gathering Satellite 4A (IGS 4A). The list ends with an entry for XSS-11r, the rocket booster left over from a joint Lockheed/Air Force Research Laboratory project called the Experimental Small Satellite, a "micro-satellite" that could rendezvous with other spacecraft for "inspection" (a mission widely understood to mean that the XSS was, in fact, designed to intercept and destroy other satellites).

"It's a good night for observing satellites," says Molczan as he loads up the Obsreduce software he developed to process observations on his desktop computer. He also uses the software to make predictions about where a satellite will be in the sky, then plots its path with a dry-erase marker on a laminated page in his star atlas. We're going to focus on three objects this evening: First up is an object the observers call 05683A. The number is a "pseudo-international designation," Molczan explains. The object doesn't appear in the Space Track catalog, meaning that it's a classified object. Like a few other objects in orbit, the observers don't know where it came from or what launch it's associated with. They invented the "pseudo-international designation" as a naming scheme for objects like this one: "05" represents the year of the first sighting, and "683" is the day of year it was first sighted plus five hundred (because there are far fewer than five hundred satellites launched each year, the extra numbers prevent an amateur pseudo-international designation from being confused with an official designation). So object 05683A is an unidentified classified object first documented on the 183rd day of 2005. It seems to be lurking in a geosynchronous transfer orbit; it's probably a spent rocket body. The second object we're planning to look at is USA 129, a KEYHOLE-class imaging satellite, one of the NRO's "crown jewels," as Molczan puts it. The last object is a special request. I've asked to look at an object called 9928C, also known as USA 144deb. Molczan humors me: He spent the evening observing it a few days ago, and its elements are up-to-date. Observing USA 144deb tonight will have little value in terms of the data collected. But I get the impression that he welcomes my interest in it. If Molczan has a trademark satellite, it is USA 144deb. The only problem is that USA 144deb isn't, strictly speaking, a spacecraft. It's probably a decoy, meant to disguise a spacecraft Molczan can't track.

Even with access to the U.S. Strategic Command's exhaustive unclassified catalog, coupled with the highly accurate map of the secret night sky compiled from decades of collective observation, there remains a small class of objects that continues to baffle the world's most proficient amateur observers. A class of stealth satellites code-named MISTY continually thwarts Molczan. After more than fifteen years of trying to track the black spacecraft, Molczan has come to the conclusion that it's personal.

Molczan's cat and mouse game with the MISTY program began on February 28, 1990, with the launch of space shuttle Atlantis Mission STS-36. The shuttle's pilot for the classified mission was a man named John N. Casper, whose name I'd first encountered doing RESUMINT on astronauts. Casper's NASA biography explains that after attending the USAF Test Pilot School at Edwards Air Force Base, he joined and later commanded the 6513th Flight Test Squadron. Translation: Casper was a Red Hat—he flew Soviet MiGs at Area 51 before going on to become deputy chief of the Special Projects Office at the Pentagon; Casper spent his career in the world of classified research, development, and procurement.

A blurb in *Aviation Week & Space Technology* piqued Molczan's interest in the mission. The trade magazine reported the project's designation as AFP-731 (for Air Force Project 731), an "advanced reconnaissance satellite to be used by the Central Intelligence Agency and the National Security Agency," and that it was "a 'combination' spacecraft carrying both digital imaging reconnaissance cameras and signal intelligence receivers." Molczan's trained eye noticed another unusual fact about the mission: the shuttle would fly into a 62-degree inclination, the steepest shuttle orbit before or since.

Molczan assumed that STS-36 was another KEYHOLE-class object and that he'd eventually be able to track it, "but being impatient and wanting as much data as I could get, knowing launch date and time, it was easy to determine that it wasn't going to be in range of most active observers. We were out of luck for weeks." The mission wouldn't be visible from his Toronto balcony, so, he said, "I needed to find observers in the north." So with a bit of "inspired phone-calling," Molczan recruited teams of agreeable amateur astronomers at Yellowknife in the Northwest Territories, at Whitehorse in the Yukon, and a third team in Alaska, then held a series of informal training sessions to teach the astronomers the basics of satellite observing. As the launch approached, Molczan calculated "look angles" for each of the teams, predicting where they could expect to see the object in the sky.

"Things went really well," Molczan explains, "It went into the orbit that it was supposed to be in from *Aviation Week*. The whole idea of tracking it was to refine the estimated orbits that I'd predicted. That all worked like a charm." The observers in Whitehorse and Yellowknife supplied useful data. In the United Kingdom, Russell Eberst made some very precise observations. "A few days of this, and the guys up north asked if I had all the data I needed. Remember that it was about forty degrees below outside." Molczan concluded that he did, even though it would be weeks before he'd actually be able to see the object from his home. Then something unexpected happened: "About a week goes by and a press release comes out from the Soviets saying that the satellite may have blown up." An article in *Aviation Week* explained that the "apparent failure of the $500-million AFP-731 imaging reconnaissance satellite launched by the space shuttle Atlantis Feb. 28 is a serious setback in the U.S. strategic intelligence program," and that "the apparent failure of the AFP-731 imaging spacecraft was the third in a series of major Western space failures in the last month." Responding to the Soviet press release, the U. S. Defense Department issued a statement that "Shuttle Mission 36 achieved its goal associated with a classified Defense Dept. program. Hardware elements associated with the mission are expected to reenter the Earth's atmosphere." Molczan, like everyone else, assumed that the mission had been another billion-dollar boondoggle. He was in for a surprise.

That November, eight months after AFP-731's apparent explosion, Molczan remembers, "I get this message from Russell Eberst in Scotland, and others, and I realize we've seen precise unknowns on the same nights." The European observers saw an especially bright object that none of them could identify. "Russell refined the orbits, and we expected it to match something already up there," Molczan says. Assuming that the unknown object was a wayward rocket body or a forgotten Soviet spacecraft, Molczan checked the numbers against the Space Track data and his own records of classified orbits. He couldn't ID it, so he turned to another set of records: objects that they'd tracked and subsequently lost. Using the observations of the unknown object, Molczan precessed the orbits back in time and "lo and behold, they lined up on the seventh of March, the day the Russians said that the satellite exploded." The satellite "had been exceedingly bright and was still bright, especially considering its height of about eight hundred kilometers." Molczan, Eberst, and other observers continued tracking the object for several weeks, reporting their sightings to one another on a BBS board, the precursor to the World Wide Web. From time to time, the press snooped in on the BBS conversations, and a reporter named Todd Halvorson at *Florida Today*, the local paper for Cape Canaveral, wrote up an article about the sightings. Pretty soon, the wires picked up the story. *The New York Times* eventually wrote that "amateur satellite trackers in Canada and Europe reported they had spotted the spy satellite in a higher orbit than anyone suspected, an indication that the craft was not only working but also highly maneuverable."

"Soon after it became public in the press it vanished again," Molczan recounts. "We had a hunch that it was going to make some adjustment, but I fully expected it to be no challenge to think of." Molczan assumed that the spacecraft had made a simple adjustment and that a straightforward search of the known orbital plane would recover the object. That didn't happen. "It was just gone."

Over the following years, theories abounded in online conversations about what had happened to AFP-731. One theory was that the satellite went into a different orbit to support the first Gulf War. A rumor circulated that the bird had been "sacrificed" for the war. When he heard the word "sacrifice," Molczan thought that it was transferred into a lower orbit where it could take higher-resolution images. By doing so, he thought, it had probably entered an orbit that induced a lot of drag and that it had depleted its propellant in the maneuver. It would be "sacrificed" because the lower orbit guaranteed that it would burn up in Earth's atmosphere far sooner than intended. Another theory held that the National Reconnaissance Office put the bird into a higher orbit, which would provide longer dwell times over Iraq but compromise its longer-term mission. Another form of "sacrifice." Molczan and the other observers conducted planar searches for both hypothesized orbits but came up empty-handed. AFP-731 was gone. A decade later, Molczan realized what probably happened.

Right around Christmastime in 2000, work was slow at Molczan's energy consulting business and he took some time to go through Russell Eberst's records of unknown sightings: things that the arch-observer had seen in the sky but that no one had yet identified. "We have lots of these going back to the 1980s," Molczan explains about the list of unknowns. He resolved to spend the holiday downtime trying to make sense of Eberst's unknowns, objects Eberst had seen but no one bothered to ID. "I had one February 1997 observation of a 66.1 degree inclination," he says. Having only two data points for the object, Molczan made the standard assumption that the object would be in a circular orbit, which put it at an altitude of 730 km. "I see this and think, 'What could that be?' Lo and behold, I find the same orbit and the same unknown in October of that same year." Eberst had seen the same object in February of 1997 and again in October. "I thought, 'That's a lot like the orbit of AFP-731,' " Molczan recalls. The problem was that Eberst's records showed that the unknown object he'd seen was exceedingly faint, and Molczan knew that AFP-

731 should be one of the brightest things in the sky. Nonetheless,
on a hunch, Molczan precessed the orbit all the way back to October 1990, when AFP-731 had disappeared for the second time. It
fit like a glove. There had been no "sacrifice": "All it did was drop
altitude by sixty to seventy kilometers."

But that didn't explain why the observers had lost AFP-731 in
the first place. Such a bright object should have been child's play
to track. AFP-731 had most certainly disappeared, and Eberst's
chance "unknown" sightings were of an exceptionally faint object. It didn't make sense. And then it dawned on him: AFP-731
wasn't just randomly hiding. *It was hiding from him*: "Once we
unmasked the orbit [back in 1990] we were added to the list of detection threats."

Discussions with John Pike, an analyst at Globalsecurity.org,
and Allen Thompson, a former CIA analyst who'd also become
fascinated by the AFP-731 story, revealed a plausible account of
what had happened, one that supported Molczan's view. The story
goes like this: AFP-731 was the first object in a planned constellation of stealth satellites—spacecraft designed to take advantage of
the stealth revolution in weapons design that was pioneered with
the A-12 and SR-71 spy planes and reached maturity in the late
1970s and early 1980s with the HAVE BLUE aircraft and F-117A
stealth fighter. A series of patent applications for stealth satellites
had shown up in the "white" world (perhaps accidentally), lending
credence to the notion that the United States had an active stealth
satellite program. Allen Thompson uncovered old CIA documents
showing that the intelligence community had spent decades trying
to figure out how to make satellites "disappear." It made perfect
sense that the NRO would have a stealth satellite program.

According to John Pike, the AFP-731 "explosion" back in
March of 1990 was clearly some kind of subterfuge. The explosion
explanation had never made sense. Paying attention to the "body
language" of the Russians and Americans surrounding the "ex-

plosion," Pike told me, it just didn't add up. "The Russians weren't normally in the habit of commenting on American satellite operations, and the Russians demonstrated some fairly serious consternation" over AFP-731. "If there were problems with American satellites, the Russians would act like nothing had happened," said Pike.

In Pike's reasoning, the Russian reaction to the launch was another layer of deception: The Russians, pretending to have been fooled by the explosion charade, were trying to convince the Americans that they'd been duped when they knew full well what was going on. On the American side, the "body language" also didn't add up to an explosion. "I guarantee you that if a billion-dollar satellite blew up one day, whatever consternation that was coming out of Moscow would be nothing compared to what would come out of Washington," said Pike. "While most of what goes on in the NRO doesn't see the light of day, something of this magnitude would. But the dog did not bark . . . the dog did not bark." It would be impossible to keep such a catastrophic failure secret: "This town don't work that way," said Pike. The explosion reminded Pike of an old submarine tactic from World War II. When a sub came under attack, its crew would load up the torpedo tubes with flotsam and shoot it out, hoping that when antisubmarine ships on the surface saw pools of oil, life rafts, and maritime debris, they'd assume that the sub was sunk, allowing the embattled ship time to slip away.

A stealthy satellite program would entail multiple layers of deception. First, try to convince an adversary that there is nothing to look for. The NRO couldn't hide a rocket or space shuttle launch, but if a payload "exploded" it might convince potential onlookers to strike the spacecraft from their watch list. A second layer of deception would involve hiding the object from radar. This is a relatively straightforward engineering challenge: Weapons manufacturers like Lockheed and Northrop had already worked out stealth designs for everything from jet fighters to air-craft carriers. The last part of making a satellite "stealthy" would involve reducing its optical signature—making it invisible to the human eye. In the case of a stealth satellite, engineers could meet this goal by attaching a large mirror or other reflective surface to the spacecraft and positioning the mirror in such a way that it reflects the blackness of space to the earth below. The problem with this would be that the optical stealthiness would be highly directional. Ground controllers would have to dial specific ground-based "detection threats" into the satellites' operating instructions.

Molczan's hypothesis, which Pike and Thompson consider quite plausible, is that AFP-731 was indeed a stealth satellite. Initially, the National Reconnaissance Office assumed that the only "detection threats" were Russian and Chinese military tracking stations. When newspapers published the amateurs' AFP-731 sightings in the fall of 1990, the theory goes, the NRO looked up Molczan's address in Toronto and Eberst's address in Scotland, and added their houses to the satellite's list of "detection threats." When the spacecraft flew over their observing sites, AFP-731 would be camouflaged against the night sky. "If those guys with binoculars were giving away the store," Pike told me, "that theory is entirely plausible." But, he added, "I've thought enough about how these things work that I understand that I don't understand it."

Molczan's balcony is as threadbare as his apartment. There are no chairs, no barbecue, no tables, and none of the junk that tends to accumulate when urban balconies end up serving as makeshift outdoor storage spaces. As Molczan sets up his binoculars, I look out past the Toronto skyline to Lake Ontario. The sun is setting behind us and the evening lights are beginning to come to life. Below, floodlights illuminate a downtown tennis club. A building a few blocks away sports an illuminated sign: MAPLE LEAF FOODS. That's where Molczan worked before going into business for himself.

With the tripod set up, Molczan pulls out a tattered piece of foam and places it in front of the tripod. He's found that the most comfortable position for observing is kneeling on the pad in front of his mounted binoculars. He's chosen a faint pair of stars in the eastern sky to serve as guideposts for his observation. He'll try to find the satellite along its predicted path, then press his stopwatch at the precise time the satellite bisects an invisible line between the two stars. He'll then note where the object was in relation to the prediction he's made and update his database accordingly. "I've got it," he says, "I'm tracking it.... One third down ..." Molczan walks inside to record his observation on the computer. It'll be another hour or so before USA 144deb becomes visible.

"I can't speak for everyone involved in this hobby," Molczan says about his pastime, "but for me, this is about democracy. There are elements out there who want to keep everything secret. I try to put pressure in the other direction. I try to put checks on that power. When people ask me about what gives me the right to make these decisions, I say, 'Citizenship in a democracy gives me the right to make these decisions.' I don't break in, I don't steal stuff. I assert my right to study the things that are in orbit around the earth and study them with the belief that space belongs to all of us. I exercise my right to know what's there."

Before meeting Molczan, I'd spent years hanging around the plane spotters, amateur radio engineers, and Freedom of Information Act–filing citizen-historians whose hobbies, often by chance, involved collecting data that described the black world's outlines. Most of the people I met did the work for the thrill of the chase. I'd rarely heard people explicitly connect what they were doing to any kind of larger democratic project.

Over our series of conversations, I couldn't help but think of Molczan as a kind of latter-day Galileo, insisting on empirical truths in the face of official orthodoxies. In George Orwell's *1984*, the protagonist, Winston Smith, echoed the relationship between empiricism and democracy when he wrote in his diary: "Freedom is the freedom to say that two plus two make four. If that is granted, all else will follow."

Molczan's observations and calculations described a space where the black world ran up against immutable laws of nature: No matter how secret a particular satellite was, it had to obey the same laws of physics as the rest of the solar system. A few data points could not only describe the motion of a body in Earth orbit but could allow accurate predictions about where it would be in the future. Tracking the NRO's classified moons was really no different at all from tracking the moons of Jupiter. They were there for all to see.

Molczan and the other satellite observers use telescopes and binoculars to look at secret spacecraft in the night sky. Many of those spacecraft are themselves essentially telescopes. It's a tension that has characterized the telescope since its invention in the early seventeenth century, a tension between the use of telescopes as instruments of reason in the service of the public good and as instruments of reason in the service of domination.

Legend holds that the telescope appeared in 1608 when a spectacle maker named Hans Lipperhey presented Prince Maurice of Nassau of the Netherlands with a crude scope that he thought would give the Netherlands an important strategic advantage over the Spanish, with whom they were at war. The story of Lipperhey might be little more than historical anecdote, but the fact is that telescopes appeared all over at almost exactly the same time. For his part, Lipperhey saw the advantages a telescope, or spyglass, would confer upon military strategists. But early scientists like Jacob Metius saw something else: a device one could use to peer into the depths of reality itself. In a patent application Metius filed in October 1608, he wrote that he was interested in "some hidden knowledge which may have been attained by certain ancients through the use of glass."

Fast-forward 450 years. On October 4, 1957, the Soviet Union launched the world's first artificial satellite, Sputnik, to the horror of many Americans. Democratic senators railed against Eisenhower. Henry Jackson called Sputnik "a devastating blow to the prestige of the United States as the leader of the scientific and technical world." His colleague Stuart Symington claimed the satellite was "but more proof of growing Communist superiority in the all-important missile field." James Killian, the MIT president who had worked on the U-2 program, saw what many in the military and intelligence services understood. Sputnik was much more than a preliminary research craft: "The capacity to lift a satellite ninety or a hundred miles above the surface of the earth, and place it in orbit, ominously suggested a capacity to lift a nuclear bomb into the upper atmosphere and send it hurtling down upon its target of choice."

For his part, Eisenhower played down the achievement. White House press secretary James Hagerty tried to quell reporters'—and Americans'—fears, responding to the news of the Soviet satellite by explaining, "We never thought of our program as one which was a race with the Soviets." Secretary of Defense Charles Wilson called the satellite "a nice scientific trick," while White House aide Maxwell Rabb described Sputnik as "without military significance."

Then, on November 2, the Soviets launched Sputnik 2, carrying a payload six times heavier than the first. On board was a small dog named Laika. Washington reeled.

On January 22, 1958, the National Security Council issued Action Memorandum 1846, making the development of a reconnaissance satellite the nation's highest technical intelligence priority. In the meantime, Allen Dulles became convinced that the CIA, not the Air Force, should be in charge of any space-based reconnaissance systems, as they were with the U-2. Eisenhower agreed. A few weeks after the NSC issued its memo, Allen Dulles called Richard Bissell into his office and put him in charge of the CORONA program—the nation's first spy satellite. CORONA would be a tremendous undertaking, one costing billions of dollars and entailing the creation of its own global geography. And like the other overhead reconnaissance programs, CORONA would be a deep black project. But with the inherent visibility associated with the United States launching its first satellite into orbit, CORONA required an elaborate cover story.

Since 1955, the Air Force had been working on a satellite reconnaissance system code-named PIED PIPER but had made little headway. One of the many problems with PIED PIPER was how to get reconnaissance images down from space. The Air Force wanted to relay a television signal from the satellite down to Earth, broadcasting the reconnaissance "take" in real time down to ground-based interpreters. But the idea was far ahead of its time—in August 1957, RCA (the company responsible for the system) informed the Air Force that the television signal would provide such poor resolution that it wasn't worth the effort to design and develop. The alternative was an ejectable film payload. When the satellite had exposed a requisite number of images, it would drop a film canister that could be recovered as it parachuted down to the earth. To the Air Force, the idea of scurrying around trying to snatch film canisters from midair was ridiculous. It chose not to pursue the idea.

After Sputnik, U.S. space reconnaissance programs went black. Eisenhower publicly canceled the PIED PIPER program, unleashing a torrent of anger from congressmen who interpreted the move as Eisenhower pinching pennies where the nation could least afford it. "We of course couldn't tell anyone that the Air Force program was being replaced by a bigger one," Richard Bissell would later recall. The point of "canceling" the programs was to hoodwink both the Soviet Union and the American media into thinking that the United States had given up on the idea of space-based reconnaissance. Of course, the Air Force programs weren't canceled at all— they were given to the CIA. The agency's new space reconnaissance program would hide under the cover story of Discoverer.

Spyglasses, as Lipperhey called telescopes, whether they're in the form of spotting scopes, spy planes, or reconnaissance satellites, are more than simple instruments or tools. They beget infrastructures and geographies. Building secret aircraft or classified spacecraft means building new bureaucracies in the halls of government, new offices, new positions, and new budgets. Like the effort to build the bomb, it means building secret laboratories to conduct the basic research, classified design shops to engineer the hardware, and hidden factories to manufacture the instruments. Deploying spy satellites meant developing elaborate cover stories and security clearances, secure air bases and launch facilities. Just as maintaining a lie means creating more lies, or keeping secrets means creating more secrets, undertaking secret projects means producing ever-expanding black geographies. This was a central paradox of the U-2 and CORONA programs: The more effort the Air Force and CIA put into charting the Soviet Union's blank spots on maps, the more the United States itself became secret.

When the photographs from covert missions began returning home, secret geographies continued to expand. Not only did the technical secrets of spy satellites need to be protected, now their "product" also needed secrecy. To control the clandestine photographs, the CIA created new security compartments and "special access programs," above-top-secret designations. TALENT KEYHOLE was the new compartment for CORONA imagery. The new security channel descended from a compartment called TALENT, created for overhead U-2 imagery. "KEYHOLE" referred to the newly created reconnaissance satellites. The security compartment allowed for the dissemination of reconnaissance imagery without revealing to the public the fact that the capabilities existed in the first place.

On August 26, 1960, Eisenhower formally signed the new security channel into existence. The agency drew up security oaths for employees to sign: "I do solemnly swear or affirm that I will never divulge, publish, or reveal either by word, conduct, or by any other means any classified information, intelligence, or knowledge relevant to 'Talent' material or the nature of 'Talent' sources (KEYHOLE) except in the performance of my official duties and in accordance with the requirements set forth in the 'Talent' control system manual, unless specifically authorized in each case by the Director of Central Intelligence or his designee."

TALENT KEYHOLE was just half of the elaborate new secrecy mechanisms that were put in place around spy satellites. Another, entirely separate, channel granted access to engineering data associated with overhead reconnaissance. Created in 1960, its code name was BYEMAN: "a man who toils underground."

The CIA's Photographic Interpretation Division at the Steuert Building on Fifth and K Street N.W. grew from 13 people in 1953 to 150 people in 1956. In 1961, Eisenhower merged all of the intelligence community's photo interpreters into the National Photographic Interpretation Center (NPIC). The NPIC grew like mushrooms in a dank basement. In 1996, NPIC merged with the Defense Mapping Agency and other parts of the intelligence community to become NIMA, the National Imagery and Mapping Agency. More than four thousand of its employees worked in the Washington metro area alone, headquartered in a collection of windowless brick buildings in Bethesda. In 2003, NIMA became the National Geospatial-Intelligence Agency, taking a place alongside the CIA, the NRO, and the NSA as a full-fledged intelligence agency. The NGA probably employs around nine thousand people in the Washington area and in St. Louis, Missouri. Essentially, the

NGA is the Pentagon's geography department. They sponsor professional geography meetings and conferences. They recruit at universities. The people who work for the NGA often have the same training I have.

It wasn't just the new armies of photo interpreters that grew to agency size. Throughout the U-2, CORONA, and OXCART projects, the Air Force and the CIA had an uneasy relationship. The Air Force, which provided much of the logistical work for the programs—from launching rockets at Vandenberg Air Force Base to maintaining the bases where the U-2s flew—felt like it was being asked to serve as the CIA's water boys. The agency set the intelligence collection targets and maintained control over the photographic "product." For its part, the CIA thought the Air Force was doing exactly what it was supposed to be doing: The CIA, not the Air Force, was the nation's intelligence agency. With the number of reconnaissance flights increasing, the number of spy satellites on classified drawing boards and in night skies flourishing, and the venom between the Air Force and the CIA over control of it all getting ever more poisonous, President Eisenhower created a new secret agency to formalize the CIA/Air Force relationship in 1960. At first, this was the National Reconnaissance Program. In 1961 it became the National Reconnaissance Office. NASA was the public face of the "space race" against the Soviet Union, with its astronaut heroes like John Glenn and Alan Shepard, with Neil Armstrong walking on the moon, and with the Voyager expeditions to the outer reaches of the solar system. Meanwhile the National Reconnaissance Office, NASA's black twin, would conduct the dark space race. By the time the NRO's existence was made public in 1992, it had become, budget-wise, the largest agency in the intelligence community.

After observing USA 129, a KEYHOLE-class satellite, from his threadbare balcony, Molczan and I sat back down at his living room computer to get an accurate prediction of where our next object, USA 144deb, would be in the sky. On one hand, the vigilant observations made by Molczan, Eberst, and the other satellite spotters had produced an astoundingly accurate map of the other night sky. But the Keplerian elements and TLEs they produced were only part of the story. The other night sky wasn't a simple system guided through passive inertia. The observers found themselves in an elaborate epistemological ballet with the spacecraft gliding through the night skies above them. When Molczan looked up, the sky looked back; when Molczan made a move, the sky made a countermove. To observe the other night sky was to become a part of it, to change it. The other night sky could tell the truth, but it was just as capable of lying and deceit. A few minutes later, we'd spot a decoy in the sky created to fool both professional and amateur satellite trackers alike. For years, Molczan had been fooled by the USA 144deb object, seduced by looking into the sky and seeing what he wanted to see.

8

The Observer Effect
3,000 km Altitude, 63.4 Degrees Inclination

"So it should be about sixty percent down from this star to the next," I say. Molczan and I are doing the final calculations for the USA 144deb overpass, which should be visible in a few minutes. Molczan's just shown me how to hold the stopwatch—press the wrong button and all your data for the evening is useless. "Try to forget that number," he says. "You don't want to bias your observation." He's trying to teach me how to see. To get accurate data, he explains, you have to see what's there, not what you want or expect to see. Getting good data means being as objective as possible; it means trying to see what's actually there in spite of one's own disposition. It requires a tremendous amount of self-discipline. Richard Feynman, the renowned physicist (and Manhattan Project scientist), once said that science's first principle is that "you must not fool yourself, and you are the easiest person to fool."

Minutes later, I'm kneeling on a foam pad out on the balcony with my right eye up against the binocular's eyepiece. A point of light enters my field of view, glittering like a diamond against a black sky. I click the stopwatch as it bisects the guidepost stars Molczan has chosen for me. It looks like it's about 60 percent down. I can't tell whether it actually was there or if I'd only seen it there because I'd remembered the number. I continue tracking it for a while by guiding the binoculars along the object's path. USA 144deb brightens and fades over long intervals as it glides through the sky. Then I lose it.

I didn't get any useful data from my observation of USA 144deb, but the attempt to accurately observe it reminded me of two things: first, the necessity of an objective observation; second, the impossibility of a truly objective observation. But there was something else underlying Molczan's study of the USA 144deb object, another pitfall of seeing, something called the "observer effect." It's a principle that holds true for the natural sciences as much as the social sciences: When you observe something you tend to change it. In the sciences, the idea goes back to the early days of quantum physics: To "see" an electron, you have to make it interact with a photon. But the interaction with the photon changes the electron's path. A more mundane example is the fact that if you want to measure the voltage in a circuit with a multi-meter, you have to apply its tips to the circuit you want to measure. But applying the tips changes the circuit's electrical properties. The observer effect in the human sciences is quite straightforward: People act differently when they know they're being observed. The observer effect questions the easy distinction between observer and observed: To observe something is to become a part of the thing one is observing.

There's a corollary to the observer effect that comes from looking too closely at the secret world. The more you look at it, the more you learn to see. At some point you see it all around you and realize that you've somehow become a part of it. As the arch-spy Robert Baer once put it, "Involvement is the first step towards understanding."

With more than two decades of watching black spacecraft from his balcony under his belt, Molczan has accumulated a lot of knowledge he isn't supposed to have. He's developed sources and methods. He's learned to see things that are meant to be hidden. Over the course of his hobby, Molczan has become involved.

On May 22, 1999, the National Reconnaissance Office launched a classified satellite on board a Titan IVB rocket from Vandenberg Air Force Base. Two days before the launch, Molczan reported that he thought the spacecraft would be another member of the ONYX constellation, specifically ONYX 4. On the day of the launch, however, several facts put that theory in doubt. First, the rocket would use a fifty-foot fairing, where previous imaging satellites had used fifty-six-foot and sixty-foot fairings (the ONYX satellites typically used a sixty-six-foot fairing). *Florida Today* speculated that the payload contained either some kind of next-generation PARCAE constellation or a " 'super-secret-who-knows-what' satellite," pointing out, "The Air Force has never flown this Titan 4 configuration before and it is believed by military watchers that the NRO has a few new test platforms floating around."

When it started to become clear that USA 144 wasn't going to be an ONYX-class spacecraft, Molczan turned his attention to another program rumored to be active; something code-named "8X." Supposedly, the 8X concept came out of battlefield commanders' complaints. "One of the biggest criticisms [of the intelligence community] during the Gulf War," an unnamed source told the *Los Angeles Times*, "was the lack of broad-area photographic coverage—the military wanted to be able to look at all of

Iraq at the same time." The KEYHOLEs could take high-resolution photos of specific sites, but they had a narrow field of view. Looking through a KEYHOLE was too much like looking through, well, a keyhole, or a large-aperture astronomical telescope: good for a close examination of Jupiter's great red spot, but bad for a broad view of the Milky Way. The 8X program was supposed to provide a big-picture look at an operational theater. To Molczan and other independent analysts like Allen Thompson, USA 144 was starting to look a lot like what 8X was supposed to look like.

About two weeks after the launch, something interesting showed up in the Space Track catalog. Although the military did not publish the requisite TLEs for USA 144, a search for its common name turned up ten international catalog numbers, beginning with 1999-208A and ending with 1999-208L. The line items implied that the launch had generated a cloud of debris that was now in orbit along, presumably, with the "A" object: the spacecraft itself. Watching USA 144 through a pair of binoculars from his balcony, Molczan suspected that something was wrong. The object was dim; he expected something far brighter. USA 144 also seemed to "flash" as if it were tumbling through space, its rotating hull sending flashes of reflected sunlight toward Earth below.

By the end of June, Molczan and the other observers had found an unknown object in a coplanar orbit to where USA 144 was supposed to have been and decided that it was probably the "A" object, the missing spacecraft. In Molczan's classified spacecraft catalog, he changed the designation of unknown object 99099A to 99028A, USA 144. The object had settled into a relatively circular 63.4 degree orbit at an altitude of 2,700 to 3,100 kilometers. At that altitude, a standard KEYHOLE satellite would provide a resolution of about 1.5 meters. It seemed to be exactly what the generals had ordered. "USA 144 is the first object in an 8X constellation," thought Molczan. Mystery solved, but not without some reservations.

It took almost three years for Molczan to conclude that something was terribly wrong with the object he'd designated USA 144. Listserv murmurings held that it was "something else" or "something really weird." The problem was that the object didn't appear to be part of any existing constellation—if it were an imaging satellite like 8X, one would expect it to operate in tandem with others in a similar orbit. There was no other object like it and nothing on the launch manifest pointing to a sister object.

Something else wasn't right about USA 144. "One of the things that bugged me," Molczan confesses, was that "the object had a drag term that seemed too high, about ten times too big. It does have a nice small drag term, except it needed to be about ten times smaller." It took Molczan years to come around to doing the calculations. He wanted to believe that the object he'd found was USA 144, in spite of visual observations indicating that something wasn't quite right with it. Its orbit seemed far too affected by perturbations in the upper atmosphere and the surrounding space. "It took a while before my curiosity drove me to do the calculations."

One Sunday afternoon in the late summer of 2002, Molczan decided to start digging into USA 144's subtle anomalies. Sitting at the desk in his apartment, he hypothesized that the strange drag term might be caused by solar radiation pressure, the effect he'd first learned to calculate from observing the PAGEOS satellite in the 1970s. "Once you set your mind to testing it, it's not difficult. I exploited the fact that objects affected by SRP experience the effects in a predictable cycle: There are periods when there's a net gain, there are neutral periods, and there are negative periods. One period follows another. You can even predict the dates when the transition occurs for the different modes," Molczan says. With three years of observations now in hand, Molczan put the historical observations into an SRP equation. When he ran the numbers, they "matched like a glove": USA 144 was being affected by SRP. Once he knew the effect of SRP on the mysterious object, Molczan could calculate the object's other characteristics.

"One neat thing that pops out of this," Molczan explains. "A by-product of an orbit with measurable SRP is that you can figure out the area-to-mass ratio." From the observational data, he said, "You have intrinsic brightness; you know other objects with similar intrinsic brightness, if reflective area is a proxy for cross-sectional area, which is true. So you can get mass." When he ran these numbers, USA 144 got even weirder: "It's less dense than a rocket body. It's a light object as far as objects go. It's about one tenth the mass of a payload. At the upper limit its mass is about a thousand kilograms, and at the lower limit it is a hundred kilograms. We know that the Titan IV could have put far greater mass at that altitude. This tells you conclusively that this can't be the primary object." Molczan realized that what the observers were actually seeing was something else. They were seeing what they were supposed to be seeing. The thing they were calling USA 144 wasn't the real satellite at all: The National Reconnaissance Office had placed something, probably a decoy, in a plausible orbit. Whatever the real USA 144 was, it had vanished.

Using the SRP analysis to learn about USA 144 was a triumph for Molczan, but it came with a dose of self-criticism. For more than two years, he'd ignored evidence of SRP affecting the object. He could have learned about the deception far earlier if he'd been able to be a more objective observer. "So strong was my belief that the object was USA 144, that I was not open to contrary evidence," he said. "That made it easy to ignore or explain away inconvenient facts, like the high rate of decay and the slow rotation." Molczan had allowed his observations to become biased by what he wanted to see.

But he was now confident that what the observers had been tracking could not be the primary payload and that whatever was going on was some sort of deception, Molczan saw the present rhyming with the past. In a Listserv post, he wrote:

This mission reminds me of Misty, aka AFP-731, aka 90019B. It was shuttle-deployed into a low 62 deg orbit. A week later, Russia reported that it had vanished, leaving behind only debris. Speculation was that it had exploded. Seven months later, Russell Eberst, Daniel Karcher and Pierre Neirinck found it in a 65 deg, 800 km orbit. Soon after, in early Nov 1990, it disappeared again. . . .

   USA 144 remains more mysterious than ever.

And so, Molczan started to strongly suspect something that he'd probably never be able to prove: the object he assumed was USA 144 was actually a decoy; its designation should be USA 144deb instead of USA 144. The real USA 144 was AFP-731's younger, possibly more advanced, sister. Both spacecraft were part of the same stealth satellite program going by the code name MISTY. AFP-731 was MISTY-1; USA 144, wherever it was, was MISTY-2. Once again, the other night sky wasn't just hiding. It was hiding from him.

As he thought about the 8X rumors and the MISTY program, something else dawned on Molczan: Perhaps the whole "8X" thing was an elaborate cover story for the MISTY program, a cultural analogue to MISTY's propensity to hide under debris clouds, to exhibit an exceedingly small signal-to-noise ratio, to "blind them with bullshit," as the saying goes. "Now, this is pure speculation," he says, "but given the widespread rumors and almost open acknowledgment of the 8X program in the late 1990s, I wonder whether the Russians might have been fed some disinformation along the lines that the 8X would orbit at a nearly three-thousand kilometer altitude, sixty-three point four degrees." The point of the ruse would be to "[condition] them to accept the eventual MISTY 2 decoy orbit. Makes me wonder whether or not 8X was purely deception to provide a cover for MISTY 2," he explains, but admits that he can't go nearly that far with the available evidence: "I make no great claim for this hunch."

The secrecy surrounding the spacecraft is difficult enough to peel away. When coupled to the possibility of disinformation, studying the other night sky becomes an epistemological hall of mirrors.

That was the crux of it: The black architecture of spy satellites—machines designed to be all-seeing, to serve as the ultimate instruments of rationality, to count Cold War missiles and tanks just as Galileo had counted Jupiter's moons—those orbiting telescopes, spyglasses, had helped to create a world where one's own eyes and own ears could not be trusted. Eisenhower had lied about the true purpose of the U-2 in the aftermath of Gary Powers's fateful flight in 1960. The Discoverer program had been a massive exercise in disinformation. The lies had persisted, grown, become institutionalized. And along with them, a tremendous bureaucracy arose to keep the secrets safe, to keep the lies plausible. It was as if the Pentagon and National Reconnaissance Office had created a world in which two plus two could equal five after all.

The endless equations from Newtonian mechanics Ted Molczan diligently solved to bring a measure of light to the other night sky were rife with the unknown variables of a new kind of physics. The only constant was the fact that the world was not quite what the Pentagon said it was. Beyond that, Molczan couldn't really say.

Retired CIA analyst Allen Thompson puts his training to use trying to understand some of the more secretive episodes in American history. He's spent years compiling and updating a document called "A Stealth Satellite Sourcebook," a 174-page compendium of declassified documents, patent applications, news articles, and e-mail exchanges he made available through the Federation of

American Scientists (the same organization that Niels Bohr, Leo Szilard, and the other architects of the Manhattan Project had helped form after World War II).

For Thompson, the 8X cover story hypothesis went too far. "I saw enough and heard enough about 8X that the idea of it being a cover story gets into a conspiracy so vast that I don't believe it. . . . I think there really was supposed to be an 8X program. 8X was alive as late as 1996 or 1997." His conclusion: "I am of the fairly strong opinion that 8X was real." But there was another far-reaching part of the MISTY story that he did subscribe to.

Before 1983, the Goddard Space Flight Center published regular tracking data of known satellite orbits and maneuvers, including those for KH-11 imaging satellites, although it did not name them as such. A researcher named Anthony Kenden had used this data set to virtuosic effect, writing articles and publishing detailed accounts of reconnaissance satellite activities, including a classic February 1983 article about whether a KH-11 had photographed the space shuttle Columbia's underbelly to check for damage on a 1981 flight.

In June of 1983, the Goddard Space Flight Center abruptly stopped publishing that data set. At the time, the move was widely seen as a response to Kenden's work. As aerospace historian Curtis Peebles put it, "Apparently, NORAD [North American Aerospace Defense Command] realized just how much could be learned from the data . . . although the Soviets have their own tracking network, it was decided not to give them the data 'for free.' "

Years later, once the MISTY hypothesis sounded more and more plausible, another theory emerged: that the Reagan administration had stopped publishing the data set to create a "new normal" of increased secrecy. Removing the tracking data from the public record would have other benefits: It would get the Soviets used to the idea of finding—and losing—satellites (the United

States knew that the Soviets weren't as good at tracking satellites as NORAD was). Thus, when the first MISTY spacecraft went up a few years later, its disappearing act wouldn't seem out of the ordinary. The Soviets would assume that when the object vanished, the most likely cause was their own tracking error. If the Soviets did pick up the actual stealthy payload at some point on radar, its signature would look like an uninteresting piece of debris. According to Thompson, that theory was right: The 1983 classification wasn't about Kenden, it was about the upcoming MISTY program.

In late 2004, the MISTY program made a brief public appearance when *The Washington Post* reported the program's cost had swelled from $5 billion to $9.5 billion, and that it had probably become the largest single line item in the vast intelligence budget. MISTY was consuming so much money, said one official, that "you could build a whole new CIA." The Senate Select Committee had tried to kill the program twice in the past, only to have the stealth satellite resurrected by the Senate and House appropriations committees and by the House Intelligence Committee, chaired at the time by future CIA director Porter Goss. Senator John D. Rockefeller IV joined other Democratic senators in refusing to sign the "conference sheets" that the committee uses to develop the intelligence authorization bill. Rockefeller took his protest to the Senate floor itself, explaining, "My decision . . . is based on my strenuous objection—shared by many in our committee—to a particular major funding acquisition program that I believe is totally unjustified and very wasteful and dangerous to national security." Rightwingers went for Rockefeller's throat, accusing him of divulging classified information. Under the black world's bureaucratic cover, MISTY had become so stealthy that the Senate committee charged with overseeing it lacked the power to cancel it.

In the summer of 2007, MISTY's glint once again flashed in

the public sphere. At a briefing, newly appointed director of national intelligence Mike McConnell joked that he'd been advised to "kill a multibillion-dollar" program to show that he had the cojones for the new job, and, he added, he "did just that." Newspapers and blogs spread the news that MISTY was now, definitively, dead. After McConnell's statement, other unnamed intelligence officials confirmed that the program on the DNI's chopping block was indeed MISTY. It later came out that former NRO director Donald M. Kerr had recommended canceling not one but two major classified satellite programs. The programs, said Kerr, "represented significant new acquisitions undertaken by the NRO and they were touted by NRO as examples of excellence and industry ingenuity—and both of them failed." Again, MISTY was supposed to be one of them. The identity of the other program was unclear.

But was MISTY actually canceled? At Globalsecurity.org, John Pike thought that McConnell's statement could quite plausibly be a bureaucratic equivalent to the USA 144deb decoy Molczan had spotted in a 63.4 degree orbit. The director of national intelligence, said Pike, "was under no obligation to tell the truth, the whole truth, and nothing but the truth." The DNI is a spy, not a Boy Scout. The purported cancellation could be another piece of disinformation: "If I was gonna build me a stealth satellite constellation, I'd try to persuade the Chinese that I had canceled it."

As Pike and I chatted about the MISTY program, he mentioned the continuing threats to classify the Space Track catalog. I had another question on the tip of my tongue when he stopped me. "That just went right by you, didn't it?" he chided. If I wanted to divine MISTY's future, he was telling me, I'd be smart to pay close attention to the fate of the Space Track catalog. Remember that the Space Track catalog is useful in that it provides a guide to the night sky's "known knowns," the other night sky's negative outlines. Pike recalled the recent threats to classify the Space

Track data. "It's very real that they're trying to pull that," said Pike. The justification? "It's probably because they say bin Laden would find the data useful." But Pike saw a potentially much deeper subterfuge at work, something recalling the 1983 end of the Goddard elements: "The objective of MISTY follow-on," if there were such a program, he reminded me, would be "to make the spacecraft look like space debris. The object of MISTY follow-on is to have spacecraft disappear into debris populations." There are different "families" of space debris, said Pike, everything from missing astronaut gloves, to spent rocket bodies, to shards of satellites blown apart by antisatellite weapon tests. The Americans, he said, had put a huge amount of work into tracking all of this debris, far more than any other country. "Based on ballistic coefficients and orbits, if I had a gigantic bank of computers, I could run my data on all this space debris on those computers and run it through signal processors and categorize every piece of space debris into different families. It would seem to me that if the Red Chinese did this, they'd determine that there were three to four pieces of debris that were in a family by themselves and that they were exhibiting attributes that were un-debris-like. They'd conclude that these were the American stealth satellites." Having access to the Space Track data set, in other words, would vastly simplify the job of anyone wanting to find stealth satellites.

And so, like so many other black satellites, the key to MISTY's future might be in a debris cloud hidden in plain sight: "If they stop publishing this report," Pike concluded, "then I'd guess MISTY follow-on is still alive."

9

Blank Spots in the Law
Berkeley and Las Vegas Revisited

One afternoon at a café in Berkeley, I sat down for lunch with Lee Tien, senior staff attorney at the Electronic Frontier Foundation. Tien was one of the lead attorneys working on the *Hepting v. AT&T* case, a class-action lawsuit charging the telecom with illegally collaborating with the National Security Agency to spy on Americans. Attempting to quash the lawsuit, telecom and Department of Justice lawyers invoked a once-obscure "state secrets privilege," arguing that the case could not proceed because by doing so, the state would be forced to publicly disclose information sensitive enough to endanger national security. The case revolved around a black site in my own backyard.

In January 2003, Mark Klein, a veteran technician at AT&T, noticed unfamiliar workers constructing a new room in downtown San Francisco's SBC Communications building at 611 Folsom Street. Klein recognized the man in charge of the new construction. The previous year, AT&T's site manager told Klein to be on the lookout for someone from the National Security Agency, who'd be interviewing a high-level technician for a special job. That technician was now installing equipment in room 641A, right next to the company's 4ESS switch room, where public phone calls are routed. Once the construction finished, none of the building's employees were given access to 641A. It was a secret. Later that year, AT&T put Klein in charge of the Worldnet Internet room, home to racks of routers and modems connecting AT&T customers to the Internet. Klein noticed that fiber-optic cables in the Worldnet room were being diverted into room 641A. From internal technical documents, Klein learned the secret room housed a Narus STA 6400, a "semantic traffic analyzer" that, its manufacturer claims, "captures comprehensive customer usage data . . . and transforms it into actionable information . . . [providing] complete visibility for all [I]nternet applications." Klein knew intelligence agencies use the Narus STA for filtering huge amounts of data. To the veteran technician, the evidence led to an obvious conclusion: The National Security Agency was piggybacking on AT&T's communication infrastructure, vacuuming up Americans' Internet use in an elaborate surveillance program. In conversation with another technician at a different AT&T site, Klein learned of similar rooms under construction in Seattle, San Jose, Los Angeles, and San Diego.

After ordering ham and cheese sandwiches, Tien and I discussed the EFF's case against AT&T. Although the Bush administration publicly acknowledged the existence of what it called a "terrorist surveillance program," it was arguing to throw the EFF's case out on "state secrets" grounds. The phone companies, argued Department of Justice lawyers, couldn't defend themselves without revealing classified information. In the vast majority of post-

9/11 cases where the Bush administration invoked "state secrets," said Tien, "the court made the case disappear."

Tien's case, however, was different. Federal district court judge Walker wasn't going along with the Bush administration's wishes. Tien paraphrased the judge's rationale: "No, I'm not going to make the case disappear. You haven't proven that the surveillance program is a state secret. In fact, a lot of what you're arguing isn't a secret at all because the government admitted that it's partici- pated in the so-called 'terrorist surveillance program,' and AT&T has said that it does what the government tells it to do." Judge Walker wrote, "The compromise between liberty and security re- mains a difficult one. But dismissing this case at the outset would sacrifice liberty for no apparent enhancement of security." In re- sponse, the Justice Department appealed to the higher Ninth Circuit.

At first glance, geography and the law might seem to have little to do with one another. But the legal system is inextricably woven into the ways that spaces are created and is often, in turn, strongly sculpted by existing facts on the ground. Zoning policies create possibilities and constraints for urban development just as rent- control laws dramatically affect the social makeup of cities. But black sites are a peculiar case: They are designed to exist outside the law. The history of secret geographies shows that when they do come into contact with the legal system, the legal system tends to change in order to accommodate them. When the secret state wins, as it usually does, blank spots on maps create blank spots in the legal system.

As Tien and I sat around our table at the sidewalk café, I couldn't help pointing out that we were, quite literally, sitting in the shadow of John Yoo's office at Berkeley's law school. Yoo was a young law professor who worked with Alberto Gonzales at the Office of Legal Counsel in the early years of the second Bush ad- ministration, as I mentioned in the first chapter. A proponent of the unitary executive theory of presidential power, Yoo was famously responsible for declaring the Geneva Conventions irrelevant to the war on terror, for giving the president the legal go-ahead to torture terror suspects at Guantánamo Bay and at CIA black sites, and for authoring a classified legal opinion arguing for the NSA domestic surveillance program.

Returning to a teaching position at Berkeley after leaving the Bush administration, Yoo became a public advocate for the administration's most controversial policies. On the subject of the NSA case, Yoo told Fox News, "There is, I think, two lawsuits that were just filed against the NSA program. But, I think, they're going to fail because you need to show standing, which means that you have to show that the plaintiffs in those cases actually suffered a harm or were actually surveilled by this program. And they don't appear to have anyone who knows or can show that that happened."

"I don't understand why that guy hates America so much," said Tien when I mentioned Yoo's shadow over our lunch.

"Have you spent any time looking into Area 51?" Tien asked, seemingly out of the blue.

After a moment, I saw where the affable lawyer was going. "I just talked to Stella Kasza a few weeks ago," I replied.

At this, Tien chuckled and said, "Imagine my surprise when I learned that a serious precedent for this case went to Area 51."

As it turned out, I had spent far more time "looking into" Area 51 than Tien might have imagined. "Looking into" the black site near Groom Lake means driving deep into the Nevada desert and climbing a mountain named Tikaboo Peak. I'd made the trek many times.

Getting to the base of Tikaboo Peak means finding the dirt road located at mile marker 32.2 off U.S. Highway 93, just between the Upper and Lower Pahranagat lakes near the small town of Alamo,

Nevada. From this easy-to-miss highway turnoff to the mountain base, the route is a twenty-mile dirt road through valleys filled with Joshua trees, sage, fine desert dust, and dry heat. Along the approach, cacti give way to juniper pines surviving on a few inches of annual winter snowfall. Near a cattle watering hole called Badger Springs, the road deteriorates completely.

The hike isn't at all bad at first. A trail marked with bits of yellow caution tape that a friend of mine puts up every year serves as a guide. Before long, a small hill gives way to a clearing littered with nylon sheets from shredded tents, a fire pit filled with Bud Light cans, and a pair of faded blue sweatpants that have been hanging from the same tree for at least three years.

From this point, the trail gets harder to follow. I usually lose it, but the only way to go is up. There aren't any switchbacks or official routes. Although this is public land, this isn't a national park. Toward the summit, the side of the mountain turns into a river of pulverized shale. Small landslides career down the mountain with each step.

The steep stretch of shale peaks with a spectacular panoramic view of Nevada's Tikaboo Valley. This is the false summit. Up to the right, the true peak towers in the distance.

From here, the route leads down a ridge and to the left of a large rock outcropping and down to a saddle where previous climbers have left another charred firepit filled with burned leftover cans of Vienna sausages. The next ascent involves a bit of climbing to navigate through the boulders and red rock of the mountain's face. This section of the mountain leads to a second false summit. The peak, however, is just in sight.

After a final scramble, Tikaboo Peak offers a breathtaking view of Nevada's Basin and Range. A brass USGS medallion cemented into a boulder on the mountaintop reads ELEV. 8000 FT. ABOVE SEA LEVEL. Scratched into the wood on a railroad tie, 1990s-inspired graffiti speaks to the black site twenty-six miles to the west: THE TRUTH IS OUT THERE. On an exceptionally clear day, it's just possible to make out a building at the base of the Papoose Mountain Range beyond the Jumbled Hills in the foreground. The black site lies so far in the distance that it's all but invisible to the unaided eye.

Through the eyepiece of a telescope, the dot of the building is clearly part of an entire secret city far to the west. Shimmering through the convection waves of desert heat and blurred by miles of thick airborne dust, rows of hangars, runways, radar dishes, and a red-and-white checkered water tower make up the site at Groom Lake. At the south end of the base, a small quarry carved into the mountainside provides the raw materials for the base's continual expansion. A few miles to the north, dozens of dormitory, operations, and administrative buildings form a dense "downtown" in front of a massive loading area where scores of semitrucks line up to deliver cargo. On the northern end of the base's five-mile backbone, the spindly shapes of oversized radio towers and antennae crisscross the desert floor. If the day is exceptionally clear, it's just possible to see two black outlines on the tarmac: the base's Black Hawk security helicopters.

As I've returned to this mountaintop year after year, I've never failed to notice new constructions rising from the desert floor at the black site in the distant west. One year, a titanic blue tower appeared among the radar dishes and antennae on the base's northern edge. On another occasion, I noticed a handful of new hangars in the south and the deep black lines of freshly laid tarmac for a new taxiway. More recently, a colossal new hangar the size of a city block rose from the dust in the base's southern section.

It's unclear what all of this means. Like desert-crossing forty-niners tricked by mirages because they wanted to see water, it's easy to see what one wants to see when staring into the distant landscape. Professional intelligence analysts learn about the dangers of placing too much trust in images, as anonymous visual data tends to support whatever truths the observer is predisposed toward. In 1962, Adlai Stevenson made dramatic use of overhead imagery at the United Nations during the Cuban Missile Crisis. More recently, Colin Powell attempted an equally dramatic presentation to the U.N. in the run-up to the U.S. invasion of Iraq. Powell claimed that the satellite photos he presented to the international community showed proof of prohibited Iraqi biological weapons programs. One of Powell's own aides, State Department intelligence analyst Greg Thielmann, later said, "My understanding is that these particular vehicles were simply fire trucks." "Satellites and intercepts can't see into someone's head," complained former CIA operative Robert Baer about the intelligence community's love affair with glossy, high-technology satellite photos. When the famous operative arrived home for a stint at CIA headquarters in the early 1990s, he lamented that "satellites, not agents, became the touchstones of truth in Washington. Few things are more satisfying for a policymaker than to hold in his hand a clean, glossy, black-and-white satellite photo, examine it with his very own 3-D viewer, and decide for himself what it means." For Baer, satellite photos were a recipe for ignorance.

Watching the black site at Groom Lake grow larger year after year, it's tempting to hypothesize correlations between rumored aerospace programs and different buildings. No doubt, there probably are some unconfirmable correlations. But after watching the black site grow over time, the most I'd venture to say is that the site's expansion is a microcosm of the black world's continuing expansion. Not just behind the restricted borders and no-fly zones in the Nevada desert, but in the United States' most fundamental civic institutions.

Lee Tien learned Stella Kasza's name trying to sue AT&T for helping the NSA spy on its customers. Wherever there were lawsuits involving the black world, her name inevitably appeared on government briefs and motions to dismiss on the grounds of "state secrets." Kasza's name adorned the pages of *El-Masri v. Tenet*, brought against the government by Khaled El-Masri, whom the CIA kidnapped in Macedonia and spent months torturing in a secret prison outside Kabul before deciding he was the wrong guy. When they finished, the CIA dumped him on the side of a country road in Albania. Stella Kasza's name surfaced in government motions in the *Arar v. Ashcroft* case, filed by a Canadian victim of the CIA's "extraordinary rendition" program after Americans shipped him to a gravelike prison in Syria. After a year of torture, the Syrians shipped him back to Canada.

After Lee Tien filed suit in the AT&T case, Kasza's name adorned the Justice Department's motion to dismiss. In short, in every case alleging disappeared people, black world malfeasance, and state secrets, government attorneys used the words *"Kasza v. Browner"* to argue that some things lie outside the purview of the law.

I found Stella Kasza in the Las Vegas white pages and drove to the city's outskirts to meet her.

The sweltering summer day reminded me of the journals forty-niners had kept during their brutal ordeals through Nevada's parched landscape. Mirages were indistinguishable from the asphalt; the "check engine" warning light on my car flashed on and off in a silent but persistent protest. Reaching the city's outermost developments, I turned into the trailer park where I'd arranged to meet the woman whose name echoed through the nation's halls of justice.

I knocked, then stood waiting in the sun. Nobody answered. Wondering whether I'd found the right place, I double-checked the address. As I turned to leave, the door cracked open. A small, thin, aging woman in a blue blouse studied me for a long, silent moment. "Uh . . . I'm Trevor," I said. She stared uncomprehendingly until I was certain of my mistake, then she broke into a smile and said, "I'm Stella."

Sitting down at the kitchen table with Stella Kasza and her daughter, Nancy, I explained my interest in the case they'd been involved in during the 1990s, when the government had, in effect, told Stella that her husband, a sheet metal worker named Walter, didn't exist. "He did exist!" Nancy protested.

Stella was nervous about my recording of the interview. She confessed a tendency to swear a lot when she talks about the circumstances of her husband's death. "Sons of bitches!" she hissed when we first spoke on the phone. "They can do whatever they want." In an ironic twist, Stella Kasza's name was now used by the government to do to other people what they did to her husband. Her husband, Walter, had, in a sense, been killed by secrecy. He'd been sacrificed to keep Groom Lake black.

Walter Kasza didn't have a lot of control over where he worked, Stella told me. "Back then," in the 1980s, "if you were a sheet metal worker, you joined the union, and the union assigned you to different job sites." One day, Wally came home with news that he'd been assigned to a particularly strange job site, one he wasn't supposed to talk about: a military base so deep in the Nevada desert that he had to take an unmarked plane to get to work each day. When the plane landed, he told his family, it was met by a column of armed soldiers he had to pass through on the way to his job. They told him not to look anywhere but straight ahead. An easygoing guy, Wally wasn't fazed, but he did find the whole thing bizarre. He did as he was told, though, looking down when they told him some strange new plane was flying overhead, and rarely spoke about what went on at the secret base. The new job made his daughter, Nancy, nervous. "I told him that I didn't like him working in a place like that," she said, "something could happen."

Wally laughed off his daughter's concerns and kept up his work at the black site plying his sheet metal trade. The 1980s were boom times for the black world. The Reagan administration's unprecedented peacetime military buildup meant Wally had plenty of work. Government watchdog groups estimated that during the Reagan administration, 34 percent of the Air Force research budget went black and 39 percent of its procurement was secret. The pages of public accounting documents started looking like Dadaist sound-poems as line items like "Cactus Plant," "Leo," "Bernie," "Have Trump," "Theme Castle," "Honey Badger," and "Tacit Rainbow" filled the pages of the public ledger.

From his job site on the huge scaffolds, Wally had a panoramic view of the secret air base where a new generation of "silver bullet" weapons was first flying.

If Wally obeyed his orders not to look up when a classified airplane flew overhead, then he would have spent an awful lot of time looking at the ground. All sorts of exotic birds tore through Groom Lake's skies during the 1980s. There was TACIT BLUE (the stealth prototype that looked like an upside-down bathtub outfitted with short, stubby wings I mentioned in chapter 5) and the YF-113G, an airplane whose purpose remains classified. A steady pace of acceptance tests for the top-secret F-117A stealth fighters took place at the base and the Red Hats flew Soviet MiGs from a collection of hangars in the north they called Red Square. Somewhere in an unmarked hangar, the National Reconnaissance Office was developing a giant aircraft code-named QUARTZ (also known as the Airborne Reconnaissance Support Program) as an unmanned follow-on to the SR-71. It would never fly, and to this date, it remains classified, although the Air Force Flight Test Center's Web site cryptically refers to a "classified, high-flying, large-payload, stealthy, autonomous, modest-cost UAV to eventually substitute for the U-2 and the SR-71," and says that "the program proved too great a challenge." There were undoubtedly many other projects.

But there was something else in the air around Walter Kasza each day as he helped build the ever-expanding site. A cloud of smoke billowing from a collection of trenches at the southern end of the base enveloped Wally as he worked. Smoke from burn pits created a haze so thick that workers took to calling it the London Fog.

With so many top-secret projects under way at the base and across the Southwest, the Air Force and its contractors developed a problem: what to do with all the top-secret trash? How should it dispose of the exotic refuse from crashed experimental aircraft, the toxic by-products from stealth aircrafts' radar-absorbent coatings, and the leftover composites and polymers developed for next-generation weapons systems? The Air Force settled on a crude answer: burn it.

Air Force officers at Groom Lake ordered workers to dig trenches the size of football fields, throw the secret trash into the pits, douse the concoction with jet fuel, and light it on fire. Waste from other secret projects started arriving. On Mondays and Wednesdays, trucks hauling classified detritus from projects based in Southern California made their way to Groom Lake, driving past the dormitories and down a road toward the base of Papoose Mountain. In lieu of shipping manifests, when they had paperwork at all, the drivers submitted documents covered with an indecipherable haze of code names. With each arriving convoy, the workers reignited the toxic fires. The London Fog enveloped the base. Walter Kasza, his friend Robert Frost, and many others worked in the thick of it.

It didn't take long for Wally to develop bizarre skin problems. "He'd come home from work on Friday covered with a red rash," said Nancy, "but it would be gone by Monday." After seven years working at the secret base, Wally's rashes worsened. A chronic cough joined the bleeding cracks in his skin. His doctors prescribed everything they could think of, but nothing helped. Toward the end, Wally was crippled. He died in April 1995. He wasn't the only one. Five years earlier, Wally's good friend Robert Frost, "Frosty," as the others called him, had passed away at age fifty-seven. Wally and Frosty shared the same symptoms: Their bodies were covered with fishlike scales that seeped blood when they moved. They hacked, coughed, and bore the red welts and scars from an unknown sickness. When Frost had a biopsy, doctors found his flesh interlaced with an assortment of dioxins, dibenzo-furans, and other industrial chemicals known to be highly dangerous to human beings.

When Frost died from a kidney illness his doctors said was related to the industrial toxins found in his body, his wife, Helen, wanted to file a wrongful death suit against his employer, the Reynolds Electrical and Engineering Company (REECO). She eventually found a Washington-based watchdog group called the Project on Government Oversight to investigate. The case found its way into the hands of Georgetown law professor Jonathan Turley. Other workers at the site who'd developed similarly bizarre illnesses joined the class-action suit.

"We never knew who the other people in the suit were," Stella told me. "Turley set it up so that we didn't have contact with each other." Their lawyer borrowed a trick from the black world he was taking on, compartmentalizing information so that if one person's identity became compromised, it wouldn't lead to the others. In Turley's estimation, going after an Air Force black site was not only unprecedented but dangerous. Frost, Kasza, and everyone else at the base had signed secrecy oaths condemning them to years in prison if they had the temerity to talk about their jobs to any outsiders. To hide their identities, the workers became a class of John Does. In a certain sense, they had become like the black site where they worked. Their very physiology, changed by their exposure to the base's unpronounceable toxins, had become just as secret. Their identities became like the unacknowledged name of the base itself. Turley told the Kaszas to assume their phones were tapped; the Air Force's Office of Special Investigations was most certainly keeping tabs on them. "We started to notice cars parked outside our home," said Nancy, still unsure if they were just being paranoid or if the old saying "Just because you're paranoid doesn't mean they're not after you" might apply to her family.

The lawsuit had several goals: The John Does wanted the Air Force to acknowledge the burning; they wanted the Air Force to disclose what kinds of chemicals they'd been exposed to so that they could receive proper medical treatment; and they wanted an apology. Turley hoped they might receive care from military doctors with the proper security clearances to know what chemicals the workers had been exposed to. Time was short; the men's health was rapidly deteriorating.

Responding to the lawsuit, the Air Force took a startling position: The base "did not exist." Turley proceeded to produce hundreds of documents with the name "Area 51" on them. There were old radiation-monitoring reports from the Department of Energy, pay stubs, and Air Force documents. Turley even produced a security manual for the base. Nonetheless, when the judge asked Justice Department lawyer Richard Sarver point-blank about the existence of the base, the lawyer replied, "That is a subject probably better taken up at another time." Eventually, the Air Force would begrudgingly admit to the existence of an "operating location near Groom Lake," but nothing more.

Next, the Air Force moved to invoke the state secrets privilege, claiming that the federal court had no jurisdiction over the matter. The following March, Las Vegas judge Philip Pro dismissed the lawsuit against the Air Force, invoking the circular logic of state secrecy:

> The court holds that federal defendants were not required to admit or deny allegations as to whether hazardous waste had been stored, treated, or disposed of at the site, because such information was classified and encompassed within the priv-

ilege . . . the court next holds that plaintiffs could not provide the essential evidence to establish a prima facie case for any of their RCRA [Resource Conservation and Recovery Act] claims. The defendants' assertion of the military and state secrets privilege prevented the plaintiffs from providing detailed photographic evidence, sealed affidavits, and information in other exhibits.

Because all references to operations or activities at the unnamed operating location were state secrets, wrote Judge Philip Pro, Turley and the John Does were not allowed to submit any of their evidence of wrongdoing because the evidence in a public court would compromise the secret. Because it was impossible to have a lawsuit without any evidence, the lawsuit, like the base and the mysterious aircraft tested there, could not exist.

In the middle of the court process, Wally passed away. With his death, the need to protect his identity became moot. The lawsuit then took on his name as its own, becoming *Kasza v. Browner.* In November 1998, the Supreme Court refused to hear a final appeal. Stella would never have her day in court.

10

The Precedent
Robins Air Force Base, Near Macon, Georgia

It began outside Waycross, Georgia. The crumpled hull of a crashed B-29 Superfortress smoldered in a swampy field on the Zachry family farm. Charred and shredded debris from the hulking plane was strewn about. An unfurled parachute lay near the fuselage. Attached was a man's body laying facedown in the water. Other bodies lay strewn among the wreckage. The scene on the Zachry farm looked like a battlefield. Before long, crowds of people arrived. Then the military. The soldiers took over, holding everyone, even local police and firemen, back from the site. Four men had survived; nine had not. Robert Palya was among the dead.

There's nothing natural about how state secrecy carved a blank spot into the law, creating legal no-man's-lands wherever government attorneys cried secret. In a field near the Okefenokee Swamp on October 6, 1947, a B-29 crashed and created a collection of facts on the ground. In the name of protecting a secret project aboard the crashed plane, the White House would appeal a lawsuit brought by the families of the deceased men, *United States v. Reynolds*, up to the Supreme Court. The executive branch would find a favorable decision, and the state secrets privilege would become a juridical precedent. More than a half century after Robert Palya's death, his daughter Judith would come to learn that the whole thing was based on a lie.

The Manhattan Project was by no means the only secret weapons technology program to come out of the Second World War. There was Secret Project MX-397, the first U.S. jet fighter, the XP-59A. The Norden Bombsight was so secret that its operators swore to defend it with their lives. One of the more bizarre was Project X-Ray, a "bat-bomb" containing hundreds of live bats strapped with incendiary devices designed to create firestorms. After the war, top-secret weapons research continued. The XP-59A program developed into the first operational jet fighter, Lockheed's P-80 Shooting Star. In 1946, the military contracted RCA to develop project MX-767, an avionics package that would convert B-29 bombers into unmanned drones. It was the precursor to guided missiles, cruise missiles, and modern-day unmanned aerial vehicles (UAVs). Its code name was PROJECT BANSHEE.

Robert Palya was an engineer assigned to the project. After two years on the job, he and his team from RCA were starting to make real progress, although the work remained highly experimental. "The plane [flies] in the right direction," Palya had written to a colleague the previous summer, "but the run is by no means a straight line. We have not progressed far enough to determine what exactly the trouble is." The following year, PROJECT BANSHEE approached its conclusion; the last mission was scheduled to fly a B-29 out of Robins Air Force Base near Macon, Georgia, on October 6, 1948.

Just after 1 P.M., Palya and his team of technicians and engineers, including a man named Bob Reynolds, boarded the hulking bomber and prepared for the day's experiment: a five-hour test flight between Georgia and Florida.

The World War II–era bomber lumbered down the Air Force runway and into the autumn sky. As the bomber lifted through the clouds at four thousand feet, the flight engineer reported the engines running hot, not unusual for the notoriously troublesome B-29s. The pilot adjusted the bomber's pitch to increase the airflow over the engines and cool them down. At eight thousand feet, engine number one blew out. In and of itself, that wasn't a crippling problem, but the pilot advised the crew to strap their parachutes on. At twenty thousand feet, the engine burst into flames. A few moments later, the whole wing was ablaze. "Stand by to abandon ship," barked the pilot. When the pilot opened the bomb-bay doors to allow his crew to escape, the aircraft careened into a spin. Centrifugal forces pinned the crew and engineering team against the walls as the hulking bomber spiraled toward the ground.

At 2:08 P.M., the sound of an explosion tore through the town of Waycross, Georgia. Only four men had managed to parachute out. The other nine were lost. The bodies, including those of Robert Palya and Bob Reynolds, lay strewn around the plane's wreckage in a farmer's field outside of town.

Newspaper accounts of the crash made elliptical references to the project's purpose. The plane "was on a secret mission testing secret electronic equipment," said one account. A separate account held that "full details of the plane's mission were not disclosed, but it was believed that it may have been engaged in cosmic ray research."

The dead men's widows hired Charles Biddle, of the law firm Drinker Biddle & Reath, to represent them. Under the Federal

Tort Claims Act, the families alleged that Air Force neglience caused their husbands' deaths. During the discovery phase of the lawsuit, Biddle sought a document that would most likely confirm or dispel the widows' suspicions of Air Force malfeasance: the official crash report. Biddle asked the Air Force for the file. Instead, he got a stone wall. The documents, said the Air Force, were "a privileged part of the executive files." There was no invocation of state secrets, no mention of national security. The Air Force was arguing that the crash report, like other executive files, shouldn't be made public because their publicity could impede internal Air Force deliberations and self-criticism.

U.S. District Court judge William Kirkpatrick didn't buy it. "The Government does not here contend that this is a case involving the well recognized common law privilege protecting state secrets," he ruled. In this case, wrote Kirkpatrick, "the Government claims a new kind of privilege. . . . I can find no recognition in the law of the existence of such a privilege." Hand over the documents, the judge told the Air Force. The Air Force replied, "No."

In April 1950, government lawyers showed up in court with affidavits from Secretary of the Air Force Thomas Finletter and the Air Force's judge advocate general supporting the nondisclosure. The tune had changed. Now it was invoking a "state secrets privilege." In his affidavit, the Air Force secretary insisted that the aircraft and its crew "were engaged in a highly secret mission of the Air Force. The airplane likewise carried confidential equipment and any disclosure of its missions or information concerning its operation . . . would not be in the public interest." "Such information and findings of the accident investigation board which have been demanded by the plaintiffs cannot be furnished without seriously hampering national security," added the judge advocate general.

Kirkpatrick took note of the Air Force switch, the argument changing from one of executive privilege to state secrets. Fine,

said Kirkpatrick. In cases where the government alleges state secrets, the custom is to produce the documents in question for the
judge to review, for any compromising information to be excised,
and for the case to proceed. Once again, the Air Force refused.

"We do not believe that is good law," stated government lawyer
Thomas Curtin, seeking to justify the Air Force's decision to withhold the documents from the judge. "We contend that the findings of the head of the department are binding, and the judiciary
cannot waive it." It was a bold assertion, a claim of executive
power far beyond what the government had made in previous
cases involving potentially sensitive materials. Kirkpatrick responded with a hypothetical question: "Suppose you had a colli-
sion between a mail truck and a taxicab, and the attorney general
came in and said that in his opinion discovery in the case would
imperil the whole military position of the United States, and so
forth. Would the court have to accept that? Is that where this argument leads?" Curtin let the judge know that that was exactly
his meaning. Again, Judge Kirkpatrick didn't buy it. Once again,
he ordered the Air Force to produce the documents. When it refused, Judge Kirkpatrick ruled in favor of the widows.

On appeal the following year, the Third Circuit Court concurred with Kirkpatrick's decision. The government was claiming
vast new powers, the appeals court warned, attempting to create a
space in the law where the executive branch—and only the executive branch—had the power to review and quash lawsuits that al-
legedly involved matters of national security. "The Government
contends that it is within the sole province of the Secretary of the
Air Force to determine whether any privileged material is contained in the documents and that his determination must be accepted by the district court without any independent
consideration," wrote Judge Albert Maris in the appeals court's
decision in favor of the widows. "We cannot accede to this propo-
sition." Again, the Air Force appealed.

When the widows' case reached the Supreme Court, it found a cast of presiding justices with a robust view of executive power. The Vinson court was composed of Roosevelt appointees who'd been specifically selected to authorize the sweeping powers the late president sought to implement the New Deal and the Second World War. The *Reynolds* case was the latest in a series that had culminated with the *Youngstown Sheet & Tube Co. v. Sawyer* decision that same year. In *Sawyer*, the question before the Court was whether the president had the power to nationalize private industries in times of war, as Truman had done with the steel industry at the end of World War II.

Before the district court in the Sawyer case, Truman's attorneys argued that there were essentially only two limitations on executive power: "One is the ballot box and the other is impeachment." Was the administration arguing that when a "sovereign people" elected a government, it was limiting the Congress and the judiciary but not the executive, asked District Judge David Pine? "That's our conception, Your Honor," Assistant Attorney General Holmes Baldridge answered. Pine flat-out rejected the Truman administration's sweeping claims, writing that Truman's theory "spells a form of government alien to our Constitution of limited powers." The consequences of the steel strike, he opined, were far less dangerous to democracy than Truman's expansive interpretation of his authority. The Supreme Court concurred with Pine's decision, with Chief Justice Vinson, Justice Reed, and Justice Minton dissenting. In his dissent to the Sawyer decision, Vinson wrote that while Truman may have been seeking extraordinary powers, "these are extraordinary times."

Though the Supreme Court shot down the Truman administration's vast conception of executive power in the Sawyer decision, the *Reynolds* case proved different. Vinson's logic, that "extraordinary times" justify extraordinary powers, led the majority reasoning in the Reynolds case.

When *Reynolds* reached the Supreme Court, Chief Justice Vinson discarded the lower courts' rulings and sided with the executive, finding that the government does indeed possess a state secrets privilege and that "it is not to be lightly invoked." But the crucial question was whether the courts should have the power to review claims of state secrets by seeing the materials the government sought to keep confidential. Did a judge get to see the files? The case was less about secrets than it was about the court's ability to place checks on those secrets. In the passages where Vinson took that question on, the Court's decision begins to defy logic.

"The court itself must determine whether the circumstances are appropriate for the claim of privilege, and yet do so without forcing a disclosure of the very thing the privilege was designed to protect," wrote Vinson. He went on to state that "too much judicial inquiry into the claim of privilege would force disclosure of the thing the privilege was meant to protect, while a complete abandonment of judicial control would lead to intolerable abuses." Vinson argued it was the court's job to oversee claims of privilege but did not explain how the courts should exert "judicial control" if they abdicated the tradition of reviewing, in camera, the materials the government sought to protect. Moreover, why would in-camera review "force a disclosure" of the alleged secrets? Surely an in-camera view was something altogether different than the front page of *The New York Times*. While Vinson appeared to be arguing for a modicum of judicial review over state secrets claims, the effect of his opinion was quite the opposite. The Supreme Court decision in *United States v. Reynolds* handed the executive branch vast new powers.

The executive would henceforth be able to quash lawsuits involving alleged state secrets without any interference from the judicial branch. As constitutional scholar Louis Fisher points out, Chief Justice Vinson allowed "the government to withhold documents from a federal judge, even in chambers, simply by having a government official sit down with the judge and explain why certain documents could not be seen." In his analysis of the case, Fisher concludes that the *Reynolds* decision had "little to do with the briefs, merits, the law, or the facts," and that "it reads more like a decision designed to meet institutional and political needs."

In the majority opinion, Vinson recognized that "abandonment of judicial control" over the state secrets privilege "would lead to intolerable abuses," even as his own opinion effectively abandoned the very principle of judicial oversight. Vinson never saw the evidence in the *Reynolds* case, nor did any other judge. Half a century later, it would turn out that the accident reports related to PROJECT BANSHEE, the documents that the government had tried so hard to protect, contained absolutely no classified information whatsoever. They did, however, contain ample evidence of government negligence, evidence that if revealed would have proved the widows right. The state secrets privilege, it would turn out, was based on a lie.

Judy Palya Loether grew up curious about the father who died when she was only seven months old. She knew her mother was one of the first people to sue the government under the tort laws and that her mother received some money. She assumed her mother had won the case. As an adult, she spent time in her mother's attic rummaging through boxes filled with her father's photographs and notebooks. His papers bore the bold stamps of a classified life story. The "Secret" and "Top Secret" markings intrigued her, but she could make little sense out of the mathematical formulas and geometric drawings they contained. News clippings about the crash made cryptic references to the secret project housed in the B-29. It drove home the sense of mystery surrounding her father and made her imagine that her father was someone important. Her uncle only added to the intrigue by suggesting that the Russians had blown up the airplane her father had died on. Later in her life, the birth of her own children made her far more interested in her own father. By this time, she found a new tool of research: the Internet.

One day in February 2000, she put the words "B-29" and "accident" into the AltaVista search engine. The results brought back the domain name Accident-report.com, which advertised "Complete Accident Reports from 1918 through 1955." She sent a check for $63. About a week later, she received a stack of documents and photographs in return. Sitting on the sofa with the two-inch-thick envelope, she debated actually looking at them. The initial perusal of the file was a letdown. "I was disappointed," she said. There were no secrets. No description of the BANSHEE project, no mention of another secret project called Shoran that he worked on. It was technical, barely comprehensible, and boring. The secret project that cost her father his life was barely mentioned. Her fascination with the secrecy surrounding his death wouldn't be ameliorated by the report in her hands. But something else emerged from the crash report.

As Loether spent night after night reading through the documents, she realized that they read like a detailed description of exactly what not to do when flying B-29s. There was overwhelming evidence of negligence. The civilian crew hadn't been briefed on the aircraft's emergency procedures; the crew had never flown together (causing numerous mistakes during the emergency). The Air Force, well aware of the B-29 engines' propensity for overheating, had ordered heat shields installed on its B-29s, but none were installed on her father's plane. Indeed, the report found that Air Force regulation "T.O. 01-20EJ-177 was not completely complied with," and that "the aircraft is not considered to have been safe for flight."

Loether went from being disappointed that the crash report contained no secrets to being upset about the Air Force's recklessness, "not angry but upset." She wrote to other surviving family members of the crash victims, asking them whether they'd like a copy of the report she had. It had answered questions for her; maybe it would do the same for them. When Loether started talking to the other families, she learned about the Supreme Court case and about the state secrets privilege. Her mother had never mentioned that the case had gone before the nation's highest court. Back at home, she researched the case. Within four minutes of another AltaVista search, her demeanor changed from upset to angry. "The government claimed that the secrets in the crash report were so important that a justice of the Supreme Court couldn't see them. . . . The negligence made me upset, but the lie made me angry . . . how could the government stand before the Supreme Court and lie!?"

After more time on the Internet, Loether started realizing the case's significance. She found other court decisions citing *United States v. Reynolds.* She found a course syllabus on national security law from George Washington University organized around only a few cases. There was *US v. Nixon* ("I knew what *that* was"), *US v. Burr* ("Aaron Burr!"). "I got goose bumps realizing what a big deal it was . . . they were teaching this in college! Someone ought to know they lied!"

Loether's investigation eventually brought her back to the law firm of Drinker Biddle and Reath, the same firm who'd litigated the *Reynolds* case. She found the Web page of a lawyer charged with handling government cases and sent a short but passionate e-mail to the person listed on the "contact" link. She got a response from Wilson Brown III, one of the firm's lawyers. "I am interested in following up with you about the *Reynolds* case," he wrote in an e-mail. "This was well before the time of most of us, but the past of this firm means a great deal to all of us who carry on in its name, and we are intrigued with the cause you have outlined." After talking to Judith, Brown decided to accept the case.

Asking the United States Supreme Court to reconsider an al-most five-decade-old decision, a decision that gave the executive branch extraordinary powers that the Bush administration (like other administrations before it) had come to rely on as part of its business-as-usual, was not something to take lightly. In fact, at first it was unclear how to actually go about doing it.

"We thought that the only, the best, approach was to go direct to the top," Brown told me. To undo the *Reynolds* decision, he said, "you'd have to undo the assumption that the accident report was secret. The only people who could do that was the Supreme Court." The problem was: how to get to the Supreme Court? "That usually requires certiorari," said Brown: an appeal from a lower court. "There's an act called the All Writs Act that was part of the original judiciary act of 1789, and among those writs is a *coram nobis* writ."

Coram nobis is one of the most obscure legal motions out there. The Latin reads "in our presence" but is usually translated as "the error before us." It is a petition to retroactively correct an error before the court. *Coram nobis* cannot be used to challenge the law or previous rulings but is instead a motion to bring new facts to an old case, facts whose revelation could retroactively bear on a settled decision. Use of the writ is extraordinarily rare; there are only a few contemporary examples. In the early 1980s, Alger Hiss filed a *coram nobis* petition in district court after substantial new information about his case became available through the Free-dom of Information Act (his motion was denied); in 1984, Fred Korematsu, convicted of disobeying orders to report to a Japanese internment camp during World War II, successfully overturned his conviction using a *coram nobis* writ in district court. Recalling the Korematsu case, district court judge Marilyn Patel said, "A petition for a writ of *coram nobis*? What is that? I'd never seen one before, and I've never seen one since."

Neither, apparently, had the Supreme Court clerk who took

Brown's petition: At first, the clerk rejected the request, claiming that no such thing could be filed. When Brown protested that it was, in fact, possible to file such a claim, a more senior clerk at the Supreme Court made a "compromise" with the firm, asking them to file a "motion to file."

"*United States v. Reynolds* stands exposed as a classic 'fraud on the court,'" wrote Wilson Brown in his *coram nobis* petition to the Supreme Court, "one that is most remarkable because it succeeded in tainting a decision of our nation's highest tribunal. The fraud is clearly established by the Air Force's recently declassified materials." The entire case was premised on a lie, wrote Brown. When the Air Force found that it could not keep the self-incriminating documents secret, "it determined to resort to the lie that they contained, and might compromise, 'military secrets.'" As the case moved up through the district and appellate courts, the lie grew and grew. Covering it up required bolder and bolder claims of executive power. In the end, the Truman administration rolled the dice, hoping that the courts would grant them that power, and they won.

After receiving Brown's petition, the Supreme Court asked Solicitor General Theodore B. Olson if his office wished to reply. Olson, charged with arguing cases on behalf of the Bush administration, was a political appointee, a stalwart conservative lawyer who'd participated in Richard Mellon Scaife's "Arkansas Project" to find dirt on the Clinton family and successfully represented the Bush campaign at the Supreme Court over the disputed 2000 election. In 2001, his wife was killed aboard the hijacked airplane that crashed into the Pentagon.

In Olson's reply to the *coram nobis* petition he argued that "the law favors finality." He went even further, contending that the government had committed no fraud at all. Back in 1950, Olson wrote, the government never stated that "the particular accident reports or witness statements in this case in fact contained military secrets." Instead, the Air Force worried that secrets might be contained in internal memos or in letters to RCA. Finally, argued Olson, the decision had to be seen in light of the times. "The claim of privilege in this case was made in 1950, at a time in the nation's history—during the twilight of World War II and the dawn of the Cold War—when the country, and especially the military, was uniquely sensitive to need for 'vigorous preparation for national defense.' . . . The allegations of fraud . . . must be viewed in that light." In other words, Olson's argument for dismissing the petition relied on Justice Vinson's words that while the state secrets privilege might represent newfound extraordinary powers, "these are extraordinary times." A few months later, Olson went on to argue before the Supreme Court that men held at Guantánamo Bay were "constitutionally committed to the executive branch" and their voices had no place in the federal court system.

On June 16, 2003, the Supreme Court issued its decision on Brown and Loether's *coram nobis* petition. Without fanfare or explanation, the Court wrote that "the motion for leave to file a petition for a writ of error *coram nobis* is denied."

From a plane crash in 1947, to the London Fog at Groom Lake, to more contemporary controversies surrounding everything from extraordinary rendition to NSA wiretapping, the state secrets privilege proliferated in tandem with the black world itself. Blank spots on maps begat dark spaces in the law.

On March 3, 2007, Khaled El-Masri wrote the words "I Am Not a State Secret" on the op-ed page of the *Los Angeles Times*. El-Masri, a Lebanese-born German citizen, had been kidnapped by the CIA in Skopje, Macedonia, and taken to the agency's Salt Pit prison on Kabul's outskirts, where he was subjected to months of incommunicado detention. Arriving back home outside Munich after his long ordeal, no one would believe his story, but when human rights researchers, lawyers, and journalists started following up the details he provided, his story started to look true. Working with the ACLU, the former "ghost detainee" filed a lawsuit entitled *El-Masri v. Tenet* and looked forward to his day in court.

It never came.

"The claims and defenses pertinent to this lawsuit would require the CIA to admit or deny the existence of a clandestine CIA activity," wrote the lawyers at Alberto Gonzales's Justice Department, citing the *Reynolds* and *Kasza* precedents:

> To avoid the consequences that flow from either admitting or denying the existence of CIA clandestine activities, the United States has intervened in the case and the Director of the Central Intelligence Agency has formally interposed the privilege for secrets of state. As is made clear in the classified *in camera ex parte* declaration of CIA Director Porter J. Goss, proceeding any further in this matter would create an unacceptable degree of risk that information the revelation of which would damage the national security and international relations of the United States will be disclosed.

In every case where the black operations and machinations of Dick Cheney's "dark side" of the war on terror might be subject to juridical review, the state secrets privilege popped up. El-Masri's case was dismissed; ditto for Maher Arar, another victim of the rendition program. The state secrets privilege was "absolute," wrote Justice Department lawyers over and over, "including in cases alleging constitutional violations . . ." Government whistleblower lawsuits like Sibel Edmonds's met the same fate, as did a sixth-grade boy who was investigated by the FBI for corresponding with foreigners for a school project.

Back in Berkeley, Lee Tien and I continued our conversation about the state secrets privilege and the NSA wiretapping case at a sidewalk café. He seemed far more optimistic about the Electronic

Frontier Foundation's chances than I would have expected. "In *Reynolds*," he explained between bites of his sandwich, "the Supreme Court ruled that it was the court's responsibility to review claims of a state secrets privilege." That interpretation startled me: It was the opposite conclusion from the one I'd drawn from my own reading of the case. What about Justice Department claims that the privilege is "absolute," I asked, referring to the language in motions to dismiss so many cases on secrecy grounds.

Tien stared down at his ham sandwich and shook his head.

"Am I totally confused?" I asked.

"No, you're just making the same mistake that district court judges and DoJ attorneys make all the time," he said. "Go back and look at the decision; it's clear that the courts are supposed to review the privilege claims." Tien was referring to those twisted phrases back in Vinson's majority opinion:

> The court itself must determine whether the circumstances are appropriate for the claim of privilege, and yet do so without forcing a disclosure of the very thing the privilege was designed to protect . . . too much judicial inquiry into the claim of privilege would force disclosure of the thing the privilege was meant to protect, while a complete abandonment of judicial control would lead to intolerable abuses.

The passage contradicted itself. In light of the rest of the ruling and the subsequent case history, I assumed that the state secrets privilege was absolute. Focusing on this muddled-sounding passage, Tien saw something different in executive claims to privilege: Vinson had ruled that it was up to the judiciary to decide the merits of state secrets claims. For Tien, Vinson was not arguing for a "complete abandonment of judicial control." The question for Tien was how often there were cases in which the judges weren't allowed to see the secrets. "There's one way of interpreting *Reyn-*

olds which says that in ninety-nine point nine percent of the cases, the judge doesn't get to see the secret sauce," he said. "I think that in ninety-nine point nine percent of the cases, the judges can." The only real precedent that mattered was the Supreme Court ruling, and *Reynolds* remained the only high court ruling on the state secrets privilege. In other words, Tien was saying, it was still an open question.

"Suppose this goes all the way up to the Supreme Court, they decide to hear it, and you win?" I asked.

"I would die of a heart attack," laughed Tien. "In all honesty, if the Ninth Circuit affirms the district decision," he explained, "they can still appeal to the Supreme Court. If we win there, then all that means is that we can go to step two in the process." It could be years before the case even began in any substantive way. Between now and then, Tien hoped, Congress or a new president could step in, open the files, and tell the truth, making the lawsuit moot.

"Let's say this question goes to the Supreme Court and you lose," I asked. "What would that say?"

"It would be saying that even when there are constitutional or statutory violations, violations of laws specifically put in place to restrict the executive, even when there's evidence *in the record* of unlawful and unconstitutional behavior, they could keep challenges to their actions out of court. . . . That would be a devastating decision. It would send the worst possible message to the executive branch: that they can do what they want as long as they cloak it with the state secrets privilege. . . . They are acting that way already, but they're still rolling the dice in each of these lower courts. If they were to get a Supreme Court ruling, there isn't going to be any way around it."

11

Money Behind Mirrored Walls
Farm Credit Drive, Washington, D.C., Suburbs

When in D.C., a visit to the Mall is practically obligatory. I was staying near Dulles Airport in Northern Virginia and had taken the train into town from Chantilly for some interviews on K Street. Not knowing exactly how long the ride would take, I arrived early and strolled past the White House, through scurrying swarms of smartly dressed young wannabe politicos, and over to the Mall. It was late spring, a time of year when the first waves of wet heat arrive in town, a prelude to the long, hot, humid summer that the capital is notorious for. If it weren't for the National Archives and the critical mass of people to talk to, I'd avoid this time and place as much as possible.

Standing next to the towering stone of the Washington Monument at the heart of the nation's capital, the iconic white dome of the Capitol building looms to the east, topped with Thomas Crawford's bronze statue of a robed woman holding a sheathed sword in her right hand and a laurel wreath and shield in her left. To the north, the White House's Aquia sandstone facade is visible just past the nation's Christmas tree's unadorned green column; to the south, the Jefferson Memorial's rounded architecture recalls the Roman Pantheon. On the shores of the Potomac to the west, on the far side of a long reflecting pool, is the Lincoln Memorial. The steps of its Doric architecture mark the place where Martin Luther King Jr. delivered his "I have a dream" speech in 1963. The Capitol's layout isn't an accident. The monuments serve as a form of myth-making, creating a set of historical reference points to sculpt a national story about what it means to be an American, to help forge a national identity in a country largely founded by immigrants. If you want a green card, you have to know who George Washington and Abraham Lincoln were. But the urban layout also serves as a spatial metaphor for the structure of government and the separation of powers the Founding Fathers, determined to leave monarchy back in the old world, sought to build into the new state. The architecture and urban design is in this sense a story about who we are and who we want to be.

Ask six literature professors how to interpret *Hamlet* and you're likely to get six different answers. Some students of the nation's capital read different meanings out of the city layout; they see secret conspiring and hidden hands behind the nation's workings. Author David Ovason writes of a veiled cosmological order behind Washington's urban planning. At sunset on August 10 of each year, he points out, a view from the Capitol down Pennsylvania shows a setting sun briefly eclipsed by a pyramid atop the Old Post Office in the Federal Triangle before reaching the horizon and setting behind the White House. For him, the Masonic symbolism of the sun and pyramid is no coincidence, nor is the statue of Benjamin Franklin below the Post Office holding up his hands in wonder. Moreover, explains Ovason, the first stars to set in the sky after sunset, Spica, Arcturus, and Regulus, outline the constellation Virgo and appear in the night sky where the sun had just been. The triangle they form mirrors the Federal Triangle's layout in the city below. For Ovason, Washington, D.C.'s urban layout is meant to "celebrate the mystery of Virgo—of the Egyptian Isis, the Grecian Ceres, and the Christian Virgin," and "this truth— and this truth alone—explains the structure of the city."

Perhaps there's something to this hidden architectural text; perhaps not. The point is that there are many ways to read the landscape. When I look at the landscape of the nation's capital, I also see something far subtler than the towering monuments and Doric columns. The architecture I'm referring to lies among Washington's suburbs and outskirts, hidden in plain sight among Burger Kings and Starbucks, primarily in Northern Virginia. I explored this "other" capital in a rented Hyundai from a hotel south of Dulles Airport just off Brookfield Corporate Drive in Chantilly, a collection of suburban suites inhabited by construction crews drawn to town by the region's rapid growth. Just across the street were the nondescript buildings of the National Reconnaissance Office. On the hotel's other side was a CIA drop box.

The NRO's office complex just on the other side of Highway 28 looks like any other of the collections of blue-mirrored glass buildings that house corporate offices in the area. The NRO's headquarters is a collection of buildings laid out in a crescent shape, connected by glass-enclosed, elevated walkways. Maybe once its reflective glass was supposed to blend into the office park background like a stealth satellite blending into the blackness of space; in any case the building was supposed to be a secret. The complex's true function became public in 1994, two years after the space agency's existence was revealed. Ironically, the eventual reason the $310 million building's true identity became public was the very secrecy surrounding it.

Before the NRO's headquarters was "outed," the National Reconnaissance Office used one of its contractors, Rockwell International, as a cover story for the complex. When the land was first purchased in 1990, Rockwell described the complex as a corporate park for their own company, pitching the project to the local board of supervisors and asking for a zoning waiver to install sophisticated security measures at the site. The board, welcoming the economic influx from what they were led to believe was a new defense contractor, expedited the approval process. With the permits in place, the NRO hired Collins International Service Corp., a Rockwell subsidiary, to build the new headquarters. Throughout the early 1990s, a blue sign outside the complex read simply ROCKWELL.

The NRO built the complex in much the same way that it goes about building classified spacecraft: financing the building through their normal intelligence budget instead of presenting a new line item. This, combined with the NRO's circumvention of normal Pentagon contracting channels, roused the Senate Select Committee on Intelligence's ire. "We are shocked and dismayed to learn that the facility cost for the new NRO headquarters at Westfields may reach $350 million by completion, nearly double the amount most recently briefed to the committee," wrote senators Dennis DeConcini and John Warner in a series of secret letters to the agency. "In fact, the total anticipated cost was never effectively disclosed to our committee, either in the annual budget submissions or in related briefings."

Across the street from the National Reconnaissance Office, on the eastern side of Highway 28, Chantilly's local post office is an unremarkable white concrete building complete with glass facade, pale blue trim, and cookie-cutter suburban landscaping. The Stars and Stripes hang from a flagpole; the mailbox at the building's entrance is painted to look like R2-D2. Inside, a line of people wait for their turn at the teller. A young mother in pink sweatpants stands in line behind a stroller; a thirtysomething man wearing a blue baseball hat opens a P.O. box to retrieve his mail. There's something strange about the box next to the man with the blue cap, Box 221943. More than a hundred people claim to live there. Moreover, they don't live anywhere else. This P.O. box, along with countless others scattered throughout Northern Virginia, is part of the CIA's covert action infrastructure.

I located the P.O. box by running database searches on names I found on documents related to CIA front companies. Among the almost two hundred names registered to Box 221943 is "Eric Matthew Fain," whose name also appeared in documents that police in Palma de Mallorca assembled in an investigation into whether the CIA used the Mediterranean island as a stopover point for rendition flights. Eric M. Fain and eleven others flew a Boeing business jet with the tail number N313P on CIA missions through the island. On a January 2004 stopover en route to Afghanistan via Macedonia, Fain and his compatriots ran up an enormous tab at the Gran Meliá Victoria luxury hotel. That March, Fain returned to the hotel on a stopover between Tripoli, Libya, and Örebro, Sweden. He did it again the following month. The only known address of the plane's pilot, James R. Fairing, was the same cramped space that Eric lived in: the P.O. box in Chantilly. Both of these men now have international arrest warrants out for them; they're wanted for illegally kidnapping terror suspects. In actuality, however, neither Eric Fain nor James Fairing is wanted at all, because there are no such persons. Fain and Fairing, like most of the other 168 personas registered to P.O. Box 221943, are "sterile identities." The small mailbox is haunted by a legion of ghosts.

A sterile identity is a fake identity operatives use on covert actions, not unlike Niels Bohr using the name Nicolas Baker while attached to the Manhattan Project. James Fairing, for example, holds an American passport—supplied by the State Department— a pilot's license, and maybe even an international driver's license. With these official documents, Fairing passes through customs at foreign airports, checks into hotels, and establishes his identity overseas. But if a border guard or hotel desk clerk were to attempt to verify this sterile identity they would discover that Fairing has no credit history, no bank loans, has never owned a car, and lacks an employment history. In other words, Fairing has none of the qualities that, in the information age, establish one's existence in the ordinary geography of our country. Fairing is as close as it gets to being an invisible man. The P.O. box in Chantilly is part of the covert architecture that conceals him.

This other architecture of the nation's capital, from secret space industries to above-top-secret covert action forces, extends in all directions from its locus in Northern Virginia. All of the big-five intelligence agencies have their headquarters in the capital's suburban outskirts. North of D.C., out toward Baltimore, lies the National Security Agency, a looming glass and steel complex of buildings, antennas, barbed wire, and blast walls in the forest of the Maryland suburbs. On the Maryland bank of the Potomac a few miles northwest of D.C. proper sits the National Geospatial-Intelligence Agency, an agency of geographer-spooks tasked with producing and interpreting maps, digesting reconnaissance photos, and delivering condensed "product" to their military and intelligence "customers." Just across the river on the Virginia side lies the Central Intelligence Agency, whose name remains synonymous with the Langley suburb surrounding it. Further south is the Pentagon and its own intelligence agency, the Defense Intelligence Agency. Those agencies are the monuments of the intelligence community, behemoth organizations occupying so much space they have freeway exits named for them. Every single one of these agencies, moreover, has numerous and far less visible satellite offices and subagencies in its orbit.

Just a short drive from CIA headquarters is one of the region's newest "undisclosed locations": the National Counterterrorism Center, a one-stop hub of interagency counterterrorist work. Driving south on Dolley Madison Boulevard in my rented Hyundai, I imagined CIA officials barreling down this same street to an emergency meeting at the new center. I took a right on Lewinsville Road, expecting to see the operation on the left side of the street (I'd located the building by comparing AP photos of the president visiting the facility with aerial photos of the McLean area). I quickly found myself on an overpass with Highway 495 below me. I'd gone too far. Turning back to find a place to stop and check the map I'd marked, I turned right on Farm Credit Drive, hoping for a place to stop and get my bearings. But both sides of the tree-lined side street were marked with red paint—no stopping. And then, at the top of an incline was the building I recognized from the photos. No signs. No guards.

The National Counterterrorism Center's dry corporate architecture is a testament to the post-9/11 boom in secret intelligence spending, an off-the-map cornerstone of a new "war on terror intelligence complex." Established by Executive Order 13354 in August 2004, the NCTC descends from the CIA's old Counterterrorist Center, established in the 1980s. Inside the NCTC, analysts and operatives from various intelligence agencies work side by side in a work environment designed by a Walt Disney Imagineer for maximum interaction. The main working areas have no walls.

I stopped for a moment, nervous at having stumbled onto one of the intelligence community's more secure facilities. It was a familiar feeling. Here I was in a place that had no outward signs of being anything other than another run-of-the-mill office park, but it didn't feel that way to me. It was the same feeling I had outside the AT&T building in San Francisco (which houses the NSA surveillance room) months before: When you know what's behind the facade of everyday landscapes, the familiar architecture becomes unsettling, even frightening. A sunny corporate park in the suburbs wasn't the most obvious place to experience what Freud called "the uncanny."

The NCTC is designed to blend in with the corporate architecture of the surrounding area, but the relationship goes both ways: The corporate landscape also blends into the NCTC. Inside the complex, it's not clear where the corporate world ends and the civic world starts.

If I'd been able to enter the complex that day, more than half the people I'd have met inside would have been private contractors, or "green badgers," pulling paychecks from corporations like Lockheed Martin or Northrop Grumman and sending the bill (with a nice profit margin) to the taxpayer. Since the 1990s, and especially after 9/11, the spy business has become big business.

Nowadays, the intelligence community is cheerfully described as a "public-private partnership." Contractors perform everything from designing and implementing software systems, to analyzing raw intelligence, to producing classified reports for policy makers. Overseas, private contractors have taken over some of the government's most sensitive jobs. For-profit corporations "run" foreign agents out of American embassies in faraway places, staff secret CIA black sites, and conduct "enhanced" interrogations of terror suspects. At a February 2008 congressional hearing, Rep. Jan Schakowsky (D-IL) asked CIA director General Michael Hayden about the extent of intelligence outsourcing:

> REP. SCHAKOWSKY: Are contractors involved in CIA detention interrogation programs?
> GEN. HAYDEN: Absolutely.
> REP. SCHAKOWSKY: Were contractors involved in the waterboarding of al Qaeda detainees?
> GEN. HAYDEN: I'm not sure of the specifics. I'll give you a tentative answer: I believe so.

Three quarters of the people working at the CIA station in Islamabad, Pakistan, are said to be contractors. At the CIA headquarters in Baghdad, contractors outnumber agency employees. Back at Langley, green-badgers outnumber civil servants. They attend meetings about everything from how many office supplies to buy to managing the most questionable of covert operations. The scale of privatization extends far beyond the halls of the CIA. The National Reconnaissance Office is almost entirely staffed by corporate contractors, and approximately $7 billion of the agency's estimated $8 billion budget goes to private industry. At the Pentagon, 35 percent of the Defense Intelligence Agency's staff is contractors. In the contemporary intelligence community, there is no distinction between public and private.

Except pay. With the sizable disparity in wages between a civil servant and a private specialist, the old "revolving door" between government and business once open to only the highest officials now includes even career civil servants. During the height of the dot-com boom in Silicon Valley, recruiters randomly called engineers and other dot-commers' workstations to offer better jobs at competing companies. That practice has migrated to the halls of Langley. Private intelligence recruiters have become so aggressive that former director of central intelligence Porter Goss issued warnings to several companies to stop making pitches to CIA officers in the agency cafeteria.

This didn't start on September 12, 2001. Throughout the 1990s, privatizing government services was one thing that both parties could agree on. Al Gore spearheaded the process of "reinventing government," as he called it. The Republican Congress was only too happy to go along with the widespread diversion of public funds into private hands. Gore imagined government working like a corporation when he described what he meant by the privatization boom he helped inaugurate: "We need governments that are as flexible, as dynamic, as focused on serving their customers as the best private companies around the world. We need to adopt the very best management techniques from the private sector to create governments that are fully prepared for the Information Age." Gore wanted to "do more with less." So the Clinton administration and the Republican Congress "downsized" and privatized a host of government services, including the intelligence community. Then 9/11 happened.

Among the mirrored windows and manicured lawns of Northern Virginia, new and old intelligence companies are enjoying boom times. The spy business is big business. Booz Allen (the company behind the "Total Information Awareness" system), for example, boasts of "[employing] more than 10,000 TS/SCI cleared personnel"—people holding those "above top secret/sensitive compartmentalized information" security clearances with bizarre names such as "Gamma," "VRK," and "Credible Wolf." The taxpayers pay to train, vet, and clear these folks, then companies like Booz Allen recruit them and rent them back to their old jobs at much higher rates. It happens at every level: Booz Allen's executives include former CIA director James Woolsey, George Tenet's former chief of staff Joan Dempsey, and Keith Hall, a former director of the National Reconnaissance Office. Director of National Intelligence Mike McConnell's career is typical: After serving as director for the National Security Agency, McConnell became an executive at Booz Allen in charge of military and intelligence projects for the Department of Defense until the Bush administration tapped him to replace John Negroponte as director of national intelligence.

Booz Allen's offices on Greensboro Drive in McLean lie next to the Science Applications International Corporation. Sometimes called "the largest government contractor you've never heard of" (with $8 billion in revenue for fiscal year 2008), the majority of the company's forty thousand employees possess security clearances, and much of the company's work comes in the form of classified contracts. Former SAIC board members include NSA director and CIA deputy director Bobby Inman, who served on the board for more than twenty years. Other former SAIC board members include CIA directors John M. Deutch and Robert M. Gates.

If CIA front companies had Web sites promoting their classified work, they might look something like the advertisements for companies like Abraxas, the Baer Group, SpecTal, or Total Intel. The Abraxas Corporation, for example, "gives you the most qualified and respected professionals from every facet of private industry, national and homeland security, law enforcement, and diplomatic service to define and defeat risk." SpecTal advertises "All-source regional, functional, and technical analysts; field operations officers; trainers; software engineers; program managers; specialized government consultants; and operational support professionals." Their team of "veterans of the CIA, DIA, NGA (NIMA), NRO, FBI . . ." and other intelligence agencies include "speakers of more than 20 languages, including Arabic, Farsi, Chinese, [and] Korean . . ." The Center for Intelligence Research and Analysis, another private intelligence company, advertises that it "supports a variety of national security operations such as interpersonal deception detection, undercover/clandestine operations, psychological operations and mass persuasion, cross-cultural applications of intelligence tradecraft, understanding and mitigating terrorist recruitment, threat assessment, interview and interrogation techniques, and risk communication, among others." Its promotional copy explains that the company "[harnesses] a broad range of social sciences, including social, cognitive, forensic and cultural psychology, sociology, social and cultural anthropology, and political science" in its intelligence work.

The scale of private intelligence contracting is, as you might have guessed, secret. Even *unclassified* intelligence-related contracts don't appear in the USAspending.gov database, an application designed to increase government transparency. Perversely, the creation of the database has had the opposite effect with regard to intelligence contracts: Previously accessible information has disappeared.

Trying to track intelligence spending by "following the money," as the old Watergate cliché goes, leads immediately and unavoidably to blank spots in the federal ledger, the black budget. Most of the intelligence budget is hidden somewhere in the sections dealing with the Department of Defense.

You can download a copy of the Department of Defense budget (available as an Excel or PDF file) by doing a simple Internet search for the comptroller's office at the DoD. Print it out and the defense budget is about the size of a phone book, an enormous document composed of thousands of pages detailing the DoD's projected expenditures for each year. Here are some random line items for fiscal year 2008:

- Amount the Army's Base Operations Support forces intended to pay the U.S. Postal Service: $7.054 million
- Amount the Air Force receives from leasing a communications site at Vandenberg Air Force Base out to AT&T: $10,500
- Amount the Air Force's Air Operations Training program expects to spend on commercial transportation services: $1.965 million
- Amount the Army wants to "enhance soldier efficiency, effectiveness, and sustainability" by providing "laundries, latrines, and showers which directly affect combat readiness and sustain combat power by promoting wellness and preventing disease" in the global war on terror: $12.3 million

But there's much more to the military budget than cell phone towers and toilet seats. Nestled among the budget's countless line items, the funding for secret parts of the military and intelligence agencies is masked by code names and blank spaces. Much of the black budget resides in the section of the Air Force budget dealing with research, development, testing, and evaluation (RDT&E) programs.

At first glance, the RDT&E section looks unremarkable. It details how much the Air Force wants to spend flight-testing MQ-9 Reaper drones, researching secure communications for its space operations, and developing safety procedures for armaments through the SEEK EAGLE program office. On closer inspection, however, an entirely different kind of spending appears.

Program Element

Number	Item	FY 2007	FY 2008	FY 2009
0603576N	CHALK EAGLE	131,863	207,230	352,858
0603734N	CHALK CORAL	28,097	30,384	117,543
0603746N	RETRACT MAPLE	342,183	340,318	138,091
0603801F	Special Programs—MDA	347,337	196,892	288,315

(Note: each digit represents one thousand dollars, so CHALK EAGLE, for example, is allocated $352.86 million)

The difference between SEEK EAGLE and CHALK EAGLE (0603576N) is that CHALK EAGLE has no corresponding program description. It is a classified project. Nonetheless, the Air Force does provide a budget number for the classified program ($352.86 million for FY 2009). The same isn't true for other names and code names of these projects:

Program Element

Number	Item	FY 2007	FY 2008	FY 2009
0301314F	COBRA BALL			
0301324F	FOREST GREEN			
0304345BQ	Cryptologic Activities			

At the most secret end of the budgetary spectrum is a collection of programs that have no associated code names or budget numbers:

Program Element

Number	Item	FY 2007	FY 2008	FY 2009
0304111F	Special Activities			
0305124F	Special Applications Program			
0305172F	Combined Advanced Applications			
0301555BB	Classified Programs			
0301556BB	Special Program			

There is, however, a small and telling quirk in all of this. By adding up all of the individual items in the various parts of the defense budget and comparing that number to the published total, one can derive a very basic sketch of the black budget's scale. For the fiscal year 2009 RDT&E budget, for example, the sum of all the line items is about $64,091,301,000. The published total is $79,615,941,000. The difference between the two numbers is the total cost of unacknowledged programs: about $15,524,640,000. This number is the black budget's cornerstone, but is only part of the overall black budget.

By taking the numbers of all three categories—classified programs with code names and budget numbers, programs with code names without budget numbers, and programs with no names and no numbers—one can derive a more accurate "best guess" estimate of the Pentagon's black budget.

Steven Kosiak, an analyst at the Center for Strategic and Budgetary Assessments in Washington, D.C., conducted an analysis of classified defense spending for FY 2009 for both the procurement and research sections of the defense budget. His calculations show a black budget of $34 billion for the year, the highest since the Reagan-era peak in 1987. The Pentagon's black budget, however, doesn't represent the entirety of secret spending. Intelligence funding comes from another black budget, although the two can significantly overlap.

"The black budget is like a Venn diagram between intelligence and military dollars," Kosiak told me. "There are parts of the intelligence budget that are classified, but other parts are unclassified." Black military dollars for classified aircraft don't necessarily come out of the same accounts as the CIA payroll, but they aren't easy to separate from one another, either.

Back in the heart of the nation's capital, amid monuments to Abraham Lincoln, Thomas Jefferson, and George Washington, the National Gallery of Art's sculpture garden sits among the national museums lining the Mall. I have a special fondness for art, so when I had a moment of downtime, I visited the sculpture garden, which houses work by some of the United States' most celebrated artists. There was Ellsworth Kelly's *Stele II*, a large, rounded sheet of inch-thick weathering steel, and conceptual artist Sol LeWitt's *Four-Sided Pyramid*, fashioned from concrete blocks and mortar. One of the garden's prized possessions is a piece by Claes Oldenburg and Coosje van Bruggen, who made their mark by taking everyday objects and turning them into monumental sculptures: clothespins, pickaxes, shuttlecocks, pieces of pie. Their contribution to the national sculpture garden is a large steel and cement sculpture in the shape of an old typewriter eraser.

Across the street from the sculpture garden is the National Archives, whose Rotunda for the Charters of Freedom houses original copies of the Declaration of Independence, the Bill of Rights, and the Constitution. From the Bible, to Shakespeare, to Sun Tzu's *Art of War,* historical documents are constantly reworked and reinterpreted in ways that make them relevant to the present. This is also true of the U.S. Constitution in the National Archives. But as the black budget became a permanent feature of the state, something particularly brutal happened. It was as if Claes Oldenburg's oversized eraser crossed the street and did a job on Section I, Article 9, Clause 7 of the U.S. government's founding document.

Section I, Article 9, Clause 7, the Constitution's "receipts and expenditures" clause, is straightforward:

> *No money shall be drawn from the treasury, but in consequence of appropriations made by law; and a regular statement and account of receipts and expenditures of all public money shall be published from time to time.*

The language is deliberately unambiguous. Congress has to authorize every dime that the government spends with attendant legislation, and every dime the government spends has to be reported to the public.

The Founding Fathers understood the golden rule: "He who has the gold makes the rules." They understood that, in the halls of government as it is in so many other affairs, money is both information and power. As such, Section I, Article 9 is a rebuke to the old monarchism the Founding Fathers wanted to free themselves from. "The people," argued George Mason, "had a right to know the expenditures of their money." Open books, argued James Madison, imparted both knowledge and responsibility upon a democratic citizenry: "A popular Government without popular information, or the means of acquiring it is but a prologue to a Farce or a Tragedy; or perhaps both," he wrote. "Knowledge will forever govern ignorance. And a people who mean to be their own Governors, must arm themselves with the power which knowledge gives." Open books were a fundamental check on presidential power and a prerequisite to democracy. Congress's power of the purse combined with the mandate to publish all government expenditures, the idea went, would help guarantee democracy. Open books would enfranchise the citizenry, prevent corruption, and put significant checks on future presidents' monarchical whimsies. "The purse and the sword ought never to get into the same hands, whether legislative or executive," said George Mason at the Constitutional Convention.

Nonetheless, there are precedents for the contemporary black budget in the earliest days of the Republic. The first Congress, for example, gave George Washington a "contingency fund" of $40,000 that the first president could use for special diplomatic missions and in foreign affairs. But this was a far cry from creating a permanent, statutory, institutionalized basis for classified spending; a "contingency fund" is not quite the same thing as a permanent multibillion-dollar black budget and a global black world.

Niels Bohr's "huge factory" of secrecy and weapons development became permanent in a few short years after the Second World War. The Atomic Energy Act of 1946 essentially continued the Manhattan Project in perpetuity and established a norm that information relating to nuclear weapons was "born classified." Although the Atomic Energy Commission would be a civilian agency, it would be charged with developing a classification system to preserve nuclear secrets and directed that scientific research related to nuclear weapons remain secret. Research data would not appear in scientific journals. Patents related to nuclear weapons would be kept under commission control, outside the normal patent system. The plants at Oak Ridge and Hanford and the secret laboratory at Los Alamos would continue the top-secret work they'd begun during the war.

The black budget, one of the Manhattan Project's foundations, was also formalized in the Second World War's aftermath. Like the top-secret project to build the bomb, it began as a temporary wartime measure and became permanent in the war's aftermath. Congress wrote the black budget into law when it created the CIA. Apart from a few lonesome protests in Congress, there was little debate. For most of the U.S.'s postwar history, the black budget has gone unnoticed in the halls of the legislature. On the few occasions where the subject has been taken up, most notably during the Nixon meltdown and in the 9/11 Commission, its legitimacy has been called into question.

As I sat in my rented car back on Farm Credit Drive, illegally stopped along the red-lined sidewalk surrounding the National Counterterrorism Center, there was really nothing to see beyond the manicured lawns and corporate landscaping. I knew that the facility was a sinkhole for black dollars, but its mirrored windows simply reflected the landscape around it. To understand how this place, the black budget, and the secret state in general came into existence, I needed to turn my attention away from its architecture and toward its archaeological record, preserved in the yellowed pages of the *Congressional Record*.

12

Nonfunding the Black World
United States Capitol, Washington, D.C., 20515

It was 1947 and the House chambers were in bad shape. Congressmen complained about the wooden row seats creaking, about the dilapidated interior, and about the bad acoustics, which made it difficult to hear congressional proceedings. Above the chamber's blue-green carpet and white marble rostrum backed by a hanging American flag and portraits of George Washington and the Marquis de Lafayette, a bare steel frame was all that kept the chamber's aging and corroded roof from collapsing. For years, renovations promising new "theatrical splendor" and "Technicolor" halls had been planned, but the Second World War and the ensuing postwar recession had put the remodeling project on the back burner. The chamber wouldn't be renovated until the summer of 1949. The smaller Senate chamber, in the other wing of the Capitol, wasn't in much better shape. It was here, in the crumbling and cavernous legislative chambers where congressmen could barely hear the day's proceedings, that the secret world went from being an ad hoc (and possibly illegal) infrastructure to being enshrined as a legitimate part of the state.

It began with the National Security Act. Signed on July 26, 1947, it laid the contemporary foundations of the military and intelligence communities. It created the Department of the Air Force as an independent branch of the military (it had previously been under the Army) and combined it with the Department of War and the Department of the Navy to form the Department of Defense. The law created the National Security Council to act as an arm of the executive branch. And it created the Central Intelligence Agency.

The idea of having a secret, peacetime intelligence agency wasn't without its critics: The recently defeated Nazi regime in Europe had shown what atrocities became possible when agencies like the S.S. and Gestapo were given dual powers of secrecy and coercion. Truman's secretary of state Dean Acheson told the president that he had the "gravest forebodings about this organization" and that the agency was being set up in such a way that "neither [the president], the National Security Council, nor anyone else would be in a position to know what it was doing or to control it." During the congressional debate over the 1947 bill, Congressman Clarence J. Brown stood firmly against the proposed agency, declaring that the president should not have "a Gestapo of his own." But the CIA's advocates quelled Congress's fears enough to pass the bill. Future CIA director Allen Dulles assured Congress that the agency would consist of no more than "a couple dozen people throughout the United States" and a "certain number" of people abroad. Future secretary of defense James Forrestal promised the CIA would never conduct secret operations. The CIA's advocates won out, and the agency came to life when President Truman signed the National Security Act into law.

Section 102 of the National Security Act outlines the CIA's duties, all of which seem relatively harmless, even boring. The National Security Act charges the CIA with correlating, analyzing,
and evaluating intelligence, and "[performing] such other functions and duties relating to intelligence affecting the national security as the National Security Council may from time to time
direct." In these "other functions" was a loophole, a subtle yet
open-ended set of powers that would come to define much of the
agency's activities. These exceptions would come to define the
rule: The CIA would be much more than the graduate-school
study group Dulles had helped sell to the legislature. Immediately
after the bill's passage, the NSC began expanding the CIA's powers, and by the end of 1947, Forrestal, who had assured Congress
only a few months before that the CIA would never conduct secret
operations, was ordering the CIA to begin a secret war against the
Soviets. Its first task was a covert operation to prevent a Communist victory in the upcoming Italian election.

In May of 1948, the NSC issued directive NSC-10/2, creating
the Office of Policy Coordination. Like the Manhattan Project's
Engineering District, this was another instance of a nondescript
line item concealing something far more interesting. The OPC
was, in short, the CIA's covert action arm: NSC-10/2 authorized
the CIA to practice "economic warfare; preventative direct actions, including sabotage, anti-sabotage, demolition, and evacua-
tion measures," and "subversion against hostile states." The CIA
was now authorized, in secret, to wage equally secret wars against
anyone the president deemed hostile. The authority for the CIA's
entry into the covert action business came from that single, am-
biguous line in the National Security Act of 1947: the "other functions and duties relating to intelligence affecting the national
security as the National Security Council may from time to time
direct."

But NSC-10/2 contained another provision that would have an

equally important legacy. Even as it authorized the CIA to act as the president's secret paramilitary force, it directed these covert operations to be "so planned and executed that any U.S. Government responsibility for them is not evident . . . and that if uncovered the U.S. Government can plausibly disclaim any responsibility for them." When the CIA fought the president's secret wars, it was to conduct them in such a way that the president could lie about them and get away with it. Policies and de facto laws associated with the CIA were established so that the agency and its activities were, paradoxically, legally immune from legal oversight.

Curiously, the agency did not yet have any funding, at least on paper. During the 1947 deliberations, Walter L. Pforzheimer introduced a clause into the CIA section of the National Security Act that would have authorized "covert and unvouchered funds" for the agency but withdrew it because it would have "opened up a can of worms." He decided that "we could come up with the house-keeping provisions later on." In the meantime, the CIA's budget was surreptitiously gleaned from disguised Pentagon appropriations. In 1949, the director of intelligence, Admiral Roscoe Hillenkoetter, brought Pforzheimer's "house-keeping provisions" to Carl Vinson, Democratic chairman of the House Armed Services Committee. The result was the Central Intelligence Agency Act of 1949—a law that allowed the agency to have a seal of office, authorized training for officers, and laid out employment conditions for CIA employees. Furthermore, the act would permit the CIA to circumvent normal government employment practices: the CIA could "borrow" officers from other agencies (for example, the Air Force) and hire political defectors. Finally, and most importantly, the bill would formally create a black budget to fund the agency.

Congressman Vito Marcantonio of New York was among the few dissenters to the CIA Act of 1949. Addressing his colleagues, Marcantonio warned that they were on the verge of creating a precedent of profound significance: "I call the attention of the Members of the House who are present to the language on page 6 of the report," he began. "I think that it can be said without any fear of contradiction that this is the first time in the history of the United States that this language is found in any report accompanying a bill coming before the Congress. It reads as follows." Marcantonio continued, quoting from the text in front of him:

> The report does not contain a full and detailed explanation of all of the provision of the proposed legislation in view of the fact that much of such information is of a highly confidential nature. However, the Committee on Armed Services received a complete explanation of all features of the proposed measure. The committee is satisfied that all sections of the proposed legislation are fully justified.

"Let us look at this a moment," Marcantonio exclaimed. "We are being asked to vote for legislation without having full explanation of all of the provisions of the bill." He was pointing out one of the most startling aspects of the Central Intelligence Agency Act of 1949: *The bill itself was secret.* Only members of the Armed Forces Committee had seen the bill's entire contents.

As Marcantonio continued his address, the congressman lamented that "as a result of the hysteria under which this bill is being passed I suppose a majority of the House will vote for the bill, even though in doing so you are suspending your legislative prerogatives and evading your duty to the people of this Nation. . . . I refuse to believe that our Nation is so unsafe from a security standpoint that we have to suspend not only the civil liberties of the people but the legislative prerogatives of the Representatives of the people in the Congress."

That same day, the bill passed 348 to 4 in the House. The Senate went on to pass it in a voice count.

The Central Intelligence Agency Act of 1949 was, and remains, the only statutory basis for the black budget; one of its key provisions was that the CIA's funding would be exempt from congressional oversight. The CIA's budget would be hidden within the line items of other governmental bodies, agencies, or programs in a collection of secret earmarks—pieces of the CIA's finances could be hidden in the Air Force budget, or in the Department of Agriculture, or anywhere else, for that matter. With the Central Intelligence Agency Act, the doctrine of "plausible deniability" extended from the specific operations of the fledgling agency to the lifeblood of the agency itself. The act would ensure that not a single congressperson or senator would know what was actually in the budgets they were called to vote upon.

When Congress passed the secret CIA Act that year, they may have imagined themselves in the same situation Leo Szilard, Niels Bohr, and the other progenitors of the Manhattan Project had felt a decade earlier as the Nazi war machine rolled across Europe. In 1949, the Cold War's intensity was increasing day by day, and the fear of communism—whether imagined or real—was bringing the nation's temperature to a feverish state. The Hollywood blacklist was now two years old. Howard Hughes shopped scripts like *I Married a Communist* to test his directors' patriotism. That spring, eleven leaders of the Communist Party USA were found guilty under the Smith Act of promoting communism in the USA, and party leader Eugene Dennis landed on the cover of *Time* magazine. Defense lawyers for the party members were imprisoned on contempt of court charges. Less than a year later, Joe McCarthy would famously claim at a speech to the Republican Women's Club in Wheeling, West Virginia, to have information on fifty-seven Communists working in Truman's State Department. It would be twenty-five years before Congress revisited the question of the black budget. Meanwhile, the money flowed.

Revelations that the CIA had raised an army in Laos (a continent and ocean away from the Capitol) and was spending more than $300 million a year on a secret war in Southeast Asia put the first chink in the agency's armor. The proprietary airline it ran for clandestine logistics, Air America, had grown into one of the largest air carriers in the world, and agency pilots were moonlighting couriering Golden Triangle Hmong heroin from the Laotian hinterlands to Long Tieng and Vientiane.

Some of the main players in Laos were men whose names would come up over and over again in connection with off-the-books covert actions. Richard Secord was part of the spooky teams of Special Forces operatives, CIA officers, and local paramilitaries who ran the secret war. So was Jim Rhyne, who'd go on to found Aero Contractors, a CIA airline, in the late 1970s. In Vietnam, Felix Rodriguez flew helicopters for the CIA and trained "provisional reconnaissance units" for the CIA's PHOENIX program.

Congress balked at the news stories. On the Senate floor, Senator J. William Fulbright of the Foreign Relations Committee asked Senator Allen Ellender of the Appropriations Committee about Laos. "It has been stated that the CIA has 36,000 there. It is no secret. Would the Senator say before the creation of the army in Laos [the CIA] came before the committee and the committee knew of it and approved it? . . . Did the Senator approve it?" Ellender responded, "It was not—I did not know anything about it. . . . I never asked, to begin with, whether or not there were any funds to carry on the war in this sum the CIA asked for."

Laos was the first crack in the wide levee holding back the CIA's secrets: Leaks turned into streams, then a torrent and flood. In December 1971, Congress cut off funding for the war in Laos, the first time that the American legislature had attempted to exert some control over the agency. More attempts followed.

On June 17, 1972, police arrested a group of men caught breaking into the Democratic National Committee headquarters at the Watergate complex, on the Potomac's banks just a couple of short miles from the nation's Capitol. They were no ordinary burglars: James McCord was a former chief of security at the CIA; Bernard Barker was attached to the Bay of Pigs; Eugenio Martinez was a former CIA boat captain; Frank Fiorini, aka Frank Sturgis, was a longtime CIA agent. The team's leader was E. Howard Hunt, who'd cut his teeth as a CIA operative back in the 1954 coup in Guatemala and the Bay of Pigs. During the 1960s, Hunt rose to become chief of covert action in the Domestic Operations Division. The CIA wasn't supposed to have a domestic operations division—the agency was legally barred from operating against Americans. At the time of the break-in, Hunt had officially retired from the CIA but held on to his connections to the agency. Hunt was using a CIA-supplied fake identity to conduct much of the job's logistics work.

The extent of CIA involvement in Watergate may be debated by historians for years to come, but revelations about former CIA personnel working for Nixon to discredit Nixon's enemies set off a campaign by journalists and, later, congressmen to find out just what the agency had been up to since its murky inception.

That didn't stop Nixon from trying to hold back the gathering waters—a few days after the break-in, Nixon conspired with H. R. Haldeman to use executive secrecy and "national security" to thwart the looming FBI investigation. Their conversation, recorded on a White House taping system, would eventually become the "smoking gun" leading to Nixon's resignation.

When special prosecutor Archibald Cox subpoenaed Nixon's White House tapes, Nixon responded with the "Saturday Night Massacre." The president forced Attorney General Richardson to resign and ordered Solicitor General Robert Bork to fire the special prosecutor. It was a desperate and transparent move. Protesters outside the White House held up signs saying HONK TO IMPEACH, turning Pennsylvania Avenue into a circus of protest and blaring horns. The new special prosecutor, Leon Jaworski, picked up where Cox had left off. Nixon continued resisting the subpoena, citing national security. In July of 1974, the House Judiciary Committee voted to recommend articles of impeachment against Nixon. That same month, the Supreme Court ruled that Nixon had to release the tapes. Ten days later, Nixon resigned.

In the meantime, Nixon replaced Director of Central Intelligence Richard Helms with James Schlesinger, an intelligence outsider with instructions from Nixon to turn the agency upside down. Helms suspected that Schlesinger's appointment as DCI was part of a White House plan to deflect Watergate in the agency's direction. Before leaving office, Helms destroyed records of the CIA's drug experiments from the fifties and sixties. Helms, like the White House, also had a taping system in his office that allowed him to record his conversations and held the transcripts on thousands of pages of paper in his files. On his way out of office, Helms destroyed every last page.

Schlesinger's tenure at the CIA was short and bitter. The new DCI set about cleaning house by firing more than a thousand CIA employees. He expected his deputy directors to give him a list each morning of people to cut. Schlesinger was so hated in the agency that the Office of Security provided him with extra bodyguards. When his portrait went up in the CIA's main corridor, a hidden surveillance camera was aimed at the painting to catch anyone trying to deface it.

A few months into his tenure, the new director got hit with devastating news. On April 15, 1973, John Dean reported to federal prosecutors about the burglary of Daniel Ellsberg's psychiatrist's office in Los Angeles, a scheme engineered by E. Howard Hunt. The point of the burglary was to find information that could go into a CIA psychological profile of Ellsberg, who'd leaked the Pentagon Papers to *The New York Times*. The CIA had previously created profiles on Ellsberg twice at Hunt's request, developed the film Hunt used in the "black bag" jobs, and provided Hunt with the sterile identity he was working under.

When Schlesinger found out about the agency's ties to Watergate, he was enraged and threatened to "fire everyone if necessary." Schlesinger didn't want any more unseen land mines detonating under his feet. William Colby, Schlesinger's deputy director for operations, proposed that the DCI issue an agency-wide order directing anyone who had information about anything the CIA may have done outside its charter to come forth with the information. The order was distributed on May 9; in it Colby instructed all agency employees with damning information to "call my secretary (extension 6363)." That same day, Nixon appointed Schlesinger secretary of defense. Colby became DCI. Extension 6363 started ringing off the hook.

Colby proceeded to do what spies are never, ever supposed to do. He made a list of secrets, taking the most sordid details of the agency's improprieties—facts that had been compartmented, made "need to know," "eyes only," and operations so black that there wasn't a paper trail at all—and put them all in one place. In the charged political atmosphere of the Watergate era, listing the secrets was like stockpiling dynamite in a match factory.

As the calls rolled in, Colby's list grew to 693 single-spaced pages. CIA officers gave the sensitive file a nickname: the "Family Jewels." The dossier teemed with everything from the merely immoral to the downright inhuman, from petty improprieties to out-and-out felonies. The CIA had bugged and burgled Americans in their homes, put dissidents under illegal surveillance, and experimented on unwitting people with dangerous drugs. The NSA tapped countless Americans' phones. And then there were the assassination attempts: Lumumba in the Congo, Castro in Cuba, Trujillo in the Dominican Republic—incidents that the CIA was either directly involved with or far too close to. The stockpile of combustible secrets grew. On December 22, 1974, someone lit a match.

HUGE CIA OPERATION REPORTED IN U.S. AGAINST ANTIWAR FORCES, OTHER DISSIDENTS IN NIXON YEARS, read the headline of *The New York Times*. Investigative journalist Seymour Hersh had spent more than a year picking up bits of the Family Jewels. In his front-page exposé, Hersh detailed Operation CHAOS, the CIA program to report on antiwar activists. The CIA had infiltrated antiwar groups, photographed protestors at antiwar marches, and was keeping files on more than ten thousand antiwar activists. The agency even put members of Congress under surveillance.

Hersh's article was one of countless revelations that brought a newfound activism to Congress. After revelations of the secret wars in Laos and the bombings of Cambodia came to light, Congress overruled a Nixon veto to pass the 1973 War Powers Resolution, requiring presidents to consult with the legislature before engaging U.S. military forces around the world. On December 30, 1974, Congress passed the Hughes-Ryan Amendment, requiring the president to issue written "findings" for each CIA covert operation and to report all CIA covert operations to relevant congressional committees.

On January 27, the Senate voted 82 to 4 to form the Select Committee to Study Governmental Operations with Respect to Intelligence Activities, chaired by Idaho Democrat Frank Church, which became known as the Church Committee. The House moved to establish the Select Committee on Intelligence, chaired by New York Democrat Otis Pike. The star witness would be CIA director William Colby.

William Colby is one of the more peculiar figures in the black world's history. He was one of the last CIA directors whose legacy went back to the agency's prehistory as the World War II–era Office of Strategic Services (OSS), the wartime spy outfit whose ranks swelled with Ivy League playboys, businessmen, and Eastern aristocrats. Himself a Princeton man, Colby twice parachuted behind enemy lines, and he led a sabotage mission into Norway. After the war, Colby briefly worked at OSS director William "Wild Bill" Donovan's New York law firm. One of the firm's projects involved helping establish Civil Air Transport (CAT), the aviation firm that would evolve into Air America and later Aero Contractors. Donovan's law firm played a central role in establishing the CIA's front companies or proprietaries. But Colby isn't usually remembered for his clandestine operations during the Second World War.

On one hand, there was William Colby the loyal soldier: He had overseen the Vietnam War's notorious Phoenix program and its architecture of secret prisons, death squads, torture, assassination, and massacre. During Colby's confirmation hearings, "wanted" posters for him appeared all over town. On their face was an ace of spades—a symbol used in Vietnam to signify death or killing—with a drawing of Colby's face. The posters echoed tactics employed in the Phoenix program. During his confirmation, Colby put the Phoenix body count at more than twenty thousand.

On the other hand, water-cooler gossip at the agency held that the new director himself might be a Soviet agent planted into the intelligence community's heart at its very inception. To some people in the agency, Colby's performances before Congress were at best designed to cripple the intelligence community. At worst, as hallway murmurings attested, Colby's testimony was tantamount to treason. According to his memoirs, Colby was convinced "that [the Rockefeller Commission, convened by President Ford, which preceded the Church Committee] would not be the end of the matter, and that the President's carefully circumscribed investigation of CIA's domestic affairs would not stop Congress from conducting its own probe . . . the atmosphere in the nation had far too radically changed—in the aftermath of Vietnam and

Watergate—for the Executive Branch to get away, as it always had in the past, with keeping the cloak-and-dagger world of intelligence strictly its own prerogative and affair. . . . Intelligence," he mused, "was entering a new era, and the country was in the process of redefining its correct position under the Constitution." And so, in his testimonies before the investigative committees, Colby was far more forthright than any of his predecessors.

Before the Rockefeller Commission, Colby revealed so much that the commission's chairman, Vice President Nelson Rockefeller, pulled him aside and said, "Bill, do you really have to present all this material to us? We realize that there are secrets that you fellows need to keep and so nobody here is going to take it amiss if you feel that there are some questions you can't answer quite as fully as you seem to feel you have to." In his memoirs, wrote Colby, "I got the message quite unmistakably and I didn't like it. The Vice-President of the United States was letting me know that he didn't approve of my approach to the CIA's troubles, that he would much prefer me to take a traditional stance of fending off investigators by drawing a cloak of secrecy around the agency in the name of national security."

Colby believed that if the CIA was going to survive, he had to cooperate with Congress. Stonewalling Congress, he thought, would challenge them to dismantle the agency altogether. By employing a policy of moderate openness with the committees, Colby reasoned, he could get Congress to "buy into" the intelligence community. Colby would recruit Congress like a spy recruiting a foreign agent. If the CIA could weather the congressional investigations, the intelligence community might come out even stronger. Thus, Colby started talking, and he instructed his officers to do the same.

Drawing from his experience at William Donovan's law firm, the CIA director would later explain that his strategy was based on how he beat antitrust investigations: "In those cases, an enormous number of documents are demanded by the prosecution, meticulously examined and then three or four specific papers are extracted to prove the case. The only real defense in such actions," Colby wrote, "was not to fight over the investigators' right to obtain the documents, as the courts would almost invariably rule against you, but to come forward with the documents and information so as to place in proper context the documents selected by the investigators and to explain that they had another significance than guilt." But, Colby realized, "Since this strategy often required the revelation of even more material than the investigators sought, it was greeted with very little enthusiasm within both the administration and the intelligence community." That was an understatement.

Richard Helms, Colby's old boss at the CIA, was livid: "It was Colby's sworn responsibility to protect 'CIA sources and methods,'" he wrote, a responsibility Colby abdicated as he went about "dumping files on the Rockefeller Commission, and subsequently the Senate and House committees." Helms compared Colby's testimony before Congress to the Bolsheviks opening up the czar's intelligence files after the revolution, or the Allied intelligence services pillaging secret Nazi files after World War II. "The DCI's unilateral actions effectively smashed the existing system of checks and balances protecting the national intelligence service," Helms concluded, without explaining what those "checks and balances" actually consisted of.

Colby was fired.

On November 2, 1975, President Ford instigated a staff shakeup the press called the "Halloween Massacre." In the span of a few days, Ford fired Henry Kissinger as national security advisor (he retained his position as secretary of state), William Colby as CIA director, and James Schlesinger as secretary of defense. Moving up the ranks to become secretary of defense was Donald Rumsfeld, and Dick Cheney became chief of staff. In Colby's place, Ford put a man named George Herbert Walker Bush.

In June of 1975, the Rockefeller Commission issued its report. Appointed by the president and designed to draw attention away from exposing the intelligence community, the Rockefeller Commission strongly suggested that the black budget was unconstitutional: "Congress should give careful consideration to whether the budget of the CIA should not, at least to some extent, be made public, particularly in view of the provisions of Article I, Section 9, Clause 7 of the Constitution."

During the hearings, DCI Colby explained that the black budget was legal in his opinion. The crux of Colby's argument was that since House members could view congressional subcommittee hearings on the CIA budget, the constitutional requirement had been fulfilled. The Church Committee disagreed: "Not only does [Colby's] position ignore the plain text of the Clause, but is not supported by the debates, either at the Constitutional Convention or in the ratifying conventions in the various States . . . the Constitution requires that the *public* know how its funds are being spent" (emphasis in original).

"It is clear," concluded the committee, "that the present secrecy surrounding the appropriations and expenditures for intelligence—particularly the inflation of unspecified appropriations in which funds for intelligence are concealed—vitiates the constitutional guarantee. Under the present system neither the public nor the Congress as a whole knows how much is being spent on national intelligence or by each intelligence agency. In addition, both Congress as a whole and the public are 'deceived,' as one Senator put it, about the 'true' size of other agency budgets. . . . It is impossible for most Members of Congress or the public to know the exact amount of money which actually is destined for any government agency."

Despite the bad blood between himself and his predecessor Richard Helms, Colby joined Helms to testify at a 1978 hearing on "whether disclosure of funds authorized for intelligence activities is in the public interest."

Colby and Helms advanced the standard argument against the budget's disclosure: "The single figure I don't have any great problem with one way or the other. I just think it is a mistake to take that first step." For Colby, "any effort to release an official figure for the intelligence budget would have to be accompanied by considerable description of exactly what kinds of programs were covered and what kinds of programs were excluded . . . this kind of clarification would have to go on until a very clear line appeared between the kinds of operations covered under the budget and those left out." This, in his estimation, would lead the country down a dangerously slippery slope: "The result would be only to outline in public more and more details of our overall intelligence program."

George Bush concurred. "I have concluded that one figure, standing alone, is all but meaningless," he wrote, but "this 'meaningless' figure will inevitably lead to a demand on the part of some for more detail. . . . I worry about the whittling away process that might take place." Like Helms and Colby, Bush's conclusion was clear: "I hope this Committee will resist the urge to move towards accommodation by revealing the budget figures. The demand will not cease."

No one from the intelligence community—not a single person—argued that publicly disclosing the intelligence budget would put anyone's safety in jeopardy. The Church Committee had refuted the "slippery slope" argument in its 1976 report, pointing out that "for many years, Congress has refused to reveal the figures for the national intelligence budget and the aggregate budgets of the intelligence agencies. It seems unlikely that given this past history, Congress will suddenly reverse itself and fail to protect information whose disclosure would endanger the national security." Congressman Ed Koch summed up the committee's argument, saying:

> The real fear on both sides of the aisle that some have expressed is, "Gee, if we do that, that is the first step."
>
> Maybe it is, but, whatever the second step is, it is what this House wants it to be, and if this House decides that this is the last step, so be it. If the House decides that it wants to have more information it will have to have a vote on it.
>
> What's wrong with that? That is what is called the democratic system. We are sent here to be a part of that system.

In conclusion, the Church Committee argued that the "slippery slope" rationale could legitimize anything. "It could be used to justify much greater secrecy. It could be used to justify the withholding of all information on the Defense Department because information which the Congress wishes to protect would be threatened by pressures caused by the publication of any information on that Department."

The intelligence budget stayed an official secret. And then one day it wasn't. Sort of.

In 1998, the Federation of American Scientists prevailed in a Freedom of Information Act lawsuit aimed at forcing the CIA to disclose the intelligence budget. On March 20, 1998, CIA director George Tenet wrote, "After careful review, I am announcing the release of the aggregate amount appropriated for intelligence and intelligence-related activities for fiscal year 1998 because it has been determined that this release will not harm national security or otherwise harm intelligence sources and methods. The fiscal year 1998 figure was $26.7 billion." The following year, however, Tenet changed his mind, and the top line was reclassified. Still, the top line crept out from time to time, mostly when intelligence officials slipped up and inadvertently revealed the number. At a speech in 2005, Deputy Director of National Intelligence Mary Margaret Graham let it slip that the number was $44 billion.

When the 9/11 Commission took up the question of the black budget, they came to the same conclusion that the Church and Pike commissions had come to decades earlier. The intelligence community was "too complex and too secret." Keeping the intelligence budget's top line secret was symbolic of an intelligence community marked by fiefdoms and by a lack of coordination and cooperation, a community that hoarded secrets to hoard power at the expense of the country's greater good. The commission blamed the intelligence failures leading to the attacks, in part, on secrecy itself:

> Secrecy, while necessary, can also harm oversight. The overall budget of the intelligence community is classified, as are most of its activities. Thus, the Intelligence committees cannot take advantage of democracy's best oversight mechanism: public disclosure. This makes them significantly different from other congressional committees, which are often spurred into action by the work of investigative journalists and watchdog organizations. . . .
>
> To combat the secrecy and complexity we have described, the overall amounts of money being appropriated for national intelligence and to its component agencies should no longer be kept secret. . . . The top-line figure by itself provides little insight into U.S. intelligence sources and methods. . . . But when even aggregate categorical numbers remain hidden, it is hard to judge priorities and foster accountability.

The executive branch stuck to its traditional line. In 2003, George Tenet had told a federal court in response to a Freedom of Information Act suit, "Information about the intelligence budget is of great interest to nations and non-state groups (e.g., terrorists and drug traffickers) wishing to calculate the strengths and weaknesses of the United States and their own points of vulnerability to U.S. intelligence and law enforcement agencies." Disclosing the top line would cause "serious damage" to national security, he testified. The Bush administration opposed a bill to implement the 9/11 Commission's recommendation to disclose the top-line budget figure: "The Administration strongly opposes the requirement in the bill to publicly disclose sensitive information about the intelligence budget," said a Bush administration policy statement from early 2007.

Nonetheless, the bill passed. With little fanfare, the number $43.5 billion for fiscal year 2007 was declassified. The administration had lost. Sort of.

Although Congress compelled the director of national intelligence to disclose the top lines of the National Intelligence Program for 2007 and 2008 (after that, the president could reclassify the top line by issuing a memorandum to that effect each year), it didn't exactly reveal the true scope of the intelligence budget. The National Intelligence Program, whose budget disclosure Congress had compelled, was only one branch of the intelligence community at large. In addition to the NIP, there's TIARA (Tactical Intelligence and Related Activities), which involves tactical intelligence for the military, and the JMIP (Joint Military Intelligence Program), the Defense Department's own intelligence infrastructure, which supplied the DoD with information that isn't part of the National Intelligence Program. The budgets for those two programs, TIARA and JMIP, remain classified.

Reluctant disclosures from the director of national intelligence notwithstanding, the most accurate top-line number may have been located when R. J. Hillhouse of the *Spy Who Billed Me* blog downloaded an unclassified PowerPoint presentation from the Office of the Director of Intelligence. Hillhouse, a former history professor who blogs about intelligence privatization from her home in Hawaii, was interested in a pie chart contained in the PowerPoint showing the intelligence budget percentage going to outside contractors: The chart revealed that a staggering 70 percent went straight to private companies. Another PowerPoint slide illustrated the growth of intelligence outsourcing since 2001. The graph showed a clear rise, but the actual dollar numbers were hidden. Using the "edit" function in PowerPoint, Hillhouse accessed the spreadsheet used as a basis for the graph. And there it was: The graph showed $42 billion in contracts for the fiscal year. From there, it was just a matter of some simple math to calculate the total budget: 70 percent (the number of intelligence dollars going to contractors) of X (the total budget) is $42 billion. To solve for X, divide $42 billion by .7 and you get the total: $60 billion. It's hard to say what's more shocking—the $60 billion figure (a number roughly comparable to what the Chinese military—the second-largest military in the world—spends each year), or the fact that a whopping 70 percent—$42 billion—is outsourced to private industry.

Since day one, black budgets have lined the pockets of industry, whether it was Dow Chemical doing work on the Manhattan Project or Lockheed building secret bases and spy planes for the CIA. But privatizing covert actions and intelligence analysis is a problem for democracy. The corporations who provide services to the intelligence community, and by extension the people, exist to enhance their bottom line. Government service is of course a different kind of social contract.

In a different PowerPoint presentation Hillhouse unearthed, the Defense Intelligence Agency shows that it is fully aware of the potential conflicts of interest that arise in a privatized intelligence world. One slide of the unclassified briefing lays out the differences between a government employee and a contractor employee: A government employee had a "taxpayer funded salary; [a] fiduciary obligation to serve the public good; no profit motive; [and]

universal and strict conduct standards," while a contractor had a "private business salary; fiduciary duty to employer only; profit motive; employers have diverse and different [conduct] standards." In other words, the DIA was warning that outsourcing the intelligence business meant creating a class of intelligence professionals with corporate rather than public interests at heart. That, however, wasn't stopping the DIA from outsourcing over $1 billion in intelligence work to fulfill "operational and mission requirements," including "Gathering and Collection, Analysis, Utilization, and Strategy and Support."

Given the divergent interests between the intelligence community and its corporate kin, the opportunities for abuse are both predictable and legion. Intelligence community "product" is supposed to provide objective (insofar as that's possible) information to policy makers. If there's one thing that the CIA was supposed to do from its inception, that's it. Replace a civic institution such as the CIA with a for-profit institution, and the results quickly diverge.

Even executives at private intelligence firms recognize the potential problems. "This is a personal view, but I happen to believe analysis is the responsibility of the government, and the government is accountable for it and you can't delegate that and pass it off to contractors," said former CIA deputy director for intelligence John Gannon, who went on to head BAE Systems' Global Analysis Group. "A contractor is going to look at a government requirement and it's going to go and find people wherever it can and get the greatest number of people at the lowest price and maximize the profit to the business to do it," he says. "When I was in government hiring people, I was looking for the best possible people I could get against the priorities I fully understood and the mission that I had. That is not what the private sector does. I know that from personal experience because I've worked on both sides of the house here."

■ ■ ■

Throughout postwar American history, the creation of the secret state and the budget that funds it has been a distinctly bipartisan project. A Republican Congress and Democratic president created the CIA back in 1947, and a Democratic Congress wrote the black budget into the books in 1949. It became law with the signature of a Democratic president. Nixon broke the rules most spectacularly, but Kennedy and Johnson had overseen the rise of covert wars in Southeast Asia and the secret infrastructures that went along with them. In the 1980s, a Democratic Congress signed off on the largest black budgets seen up until that point. When Clinton came to office in the early 1990s, he collaborated with a Republican Congress to privatize much of the secret world. Under a Democratic Congress, the black budget reached historic highs for fiscal year 2009.

Back in 1949, Congressman Marcantonio was a lone voice in his outrage over Congress's willingness to cede its legislative prerogatives to the president and the secret state he controlled. Under subsequent administrations, that world had grown and thrived in the darkness. Congress had gone along with it. With an influx of antiwar legislators in the 1970s, Congress had held the first hearings on the secret state in decades. It passed legislation aimed at curbing its excesses and abuses. The incoming Reagan administration, however, would change the rules. It would lay the foundations of the secret state anew.

13

Plains of Death
Outside Tegucigalpa, Honduras

The pavement ended on the far side of Las Tapias, just past a collection of military ranges in the hills west of Tegucigalpa. Although Lepaterique was only another twelve miles or so to the west, it took more than an hour to get there on the winding dirt road. It was slow going: Packs of dogs ran alongside our Toyota pickup; shirtless men wearing cowboy hats led firewood-laden mules along a dirt road cutting through the thick pine forest extending from Nicaragua up to Chiapas, Mexico. A barefoot girl around seven carried a baby on her hip. On either side of the road, small peasant houses sat among makeshift cabbage fields and plantain trees cut out of the teeming deep-green forest. A truck full of Honduran Special Forces, all gripping M-16s, bounced past us from the opposite direction. The road began to climb. It was hot and humid, and the horseflies were starting to bite. The day before, two dead bodies—a man and his wife—had shown up somewhere on the side of this road. No one knew who they were or why they were killed.

Months earlier, at Berkeley, my friend and fellow geographer Joe Bryan had been mumbling something about old Contra camps and airfields he kept running into while doing fieldwork in Nicaragua and Honduras. Joe is a soft-spoken guy whose boyish looks and cheerful demeanor make him wholly disarming, but he's got an incredibly sharp mind and works under some very difficult circumstances. Joe has spent most of his career working with indigenous peoples throughout the Americas, trying to understand what happens when traditional attitudes and ways of using land come up against territorial claims made by nation-states. He'd spent time with the Western Shoshone in Nevada mapping out traditional native lands. In Central America, Joe was working primarily with the Miskito people to negotiate land claims with national governments. It was complicated work: The problem Joe constantly faced was that traditional lands just don't have the same kinds of borders that places on maps have, but to make a land claim, the native peoples had to draw maps. The process set off a kind of mapping arms race among the various indigenous peoples, each eager to claim as many "traditional" lands as possible. In these land struggles, drawing maps was like stockpiling strategic weapons: "Map or be mapped," Joe explains. Then there was the whole Contra thing. Joe ran into old Contras all the time in the course of his work in the Central American hinterlands, but something was changing. It took me a while to figure out what he was talking about from the short conversations next to the water fountain in the hallway outside our adjacent offices. I finally got the story.

One day in 2004, Joe was sitting on the steps of the YATAMA party headquarters in Puerto Cabezas, Nicaragua, when a Miskito man with a tattered T-shirt and dirty jeans came up to him and offered his hand.

"Do you have a project here?" the man asked, assuming that no gringo would be hanging out in Puerto Cabezas without some sort of angle.

With no visible association to the Peace Corps or an NGO, Joe's presence in the town was an anomaly. Local rumor held that Joe was DEA, or maybe from an "other government agency." He certainly didn't look like a cocaine runner.

"No, I'm just a student," replied Joe.

The man ignored the answer. In the cocaine-soaked Wild West atmosphere of the Miskito Coast, "grad student" was just as easily a discreet way of saying "CIA officer." The man started telling Joe about a trip he'd once made to the United States, about the nice Spanish-speaking cook who gave him slugs of whiskey from time to time at a military base in North Carolina. It struck a chord; Joe had heard that anti-Sandinista Miskito fighters had been brought for training to Fort Bragg—the North Carolina home of the Army's Special Forces community—after Congress repealed the Boland Amendment in the late 1980s. While the Iran-Contra scandal tore through Washington, the United States continued training Contras on U.S. soil. When Joe asked the man what he learned in North Carolina, the man rattled off a list of commando skills: blowing up bridges, small-party raids, training in communications, map reading. Again, the man asked for a job. Joe assured him that grad students don't have either the money or inclination to hire old Contras, even if they did have a project for them to work on. The man didn't give up.

"Look, I haven't had a job since the war. . . . I can do lots of things, anything you want. I'll find bin Laden. I'll fight Saddam Hussein. Give me a job."

Joe insisted he couldn't help.

"Look, I can give you the coordinates of a place in the *llano*. . . .

You tell me when you want to come, and I will have three hundred men waiting for you there. You can take us away in a helicopter, we'll go to Iraq, Afghanistan, it doesn't matter. We'll go there and no one will have to know. Think about it, boss."

Joe's encounter with the broke Contra on the streets of Puerto Cabezas turned out to be a vision of what was to come. In September 2005, an advertisement appeared in *El Heraldo*, one of Honduras's major daily papers. A company called Your Solutions was recruiting "security forces"; applicants had to be willing to work overseas. By Central American standards, the pay was great: between $990 a month for non-English-speakers and up to $1,500 for English-speaking contractors with military experience. The same thing was going on elsewhere in Central and South America—countries racked by years of civil war, death squads, insurrections, and disappearances. In Nicaragua, someone named David Godoy recruited for Your Solutions. The company was also hiring in Chile. Before deploying to Iraq, the men would receive training outside Tegucigalpa, at an old camp built in the 1980s at Lepaterique. I convinced Joe that we should go there together.

Our 4x4 bounced through the mountain town of Lepaterique toward the two-story cross overlooking the village, past the cemetery, and into the gate of the camp. Quonset huts and dormitories lay scattered around. A row of crashed trucks and cars lined the center divide. In black letters above the entrance to a teal shack were the words CLUB SOCIAL. On a board nailed to a tree, green letters spelled SECTOR I. Down the hill was a lake and small pier. It felt like an abandoned summer camp—the kind of place kids might spend their summers away from their parents. Cows milled around the abandoned wood shacks and buildings. As we sat in the truck looking around, a dark-skinned, shirtless, middle-aged man sauntered out from a building with a Pepsi machine outside. The caretaker. He welcomed us and asked what we were doing. When we replied that we were from U.C. Berkeley and interested in the Your Solutions story, he turned away. He either didn't know the story (unlikely) or was unwilling to talk about it. But he invited us to look around the camp as much as we wanted.

At the far end of the camp we found the shooting range. It was little more than a piece of wire strung from wooden posts in front of a dirt berm on the base's far end. Sheets of cardboard taped with photocopied targets of bull's-eyes and human torsos hung from a clothesline. TARGET PISTOL, 50-FOOT, TIMED AND RAPID FIRE, STANDARD AMERICAN read the words. Some of the bullet holes were taped over with masking tape so that the targets could be reused. In the middle of the range, a piece of poster paper had a drawing of a man's torso in blue marker, his body divvied up into regions worth different points. It was as if someone had left the camp abruptly, not even bothering to take the targets down. Littered on the ground was more evidence of what had taken place here: shotgun shells, casings from 38mm handguns, and the brass full metal jackets of spent Philippine-made M-16 ammunition. It was sloppy work—automatic weapons outside the military are illegal in Honduras, as they are most other places.

If Your Solutions's intent was to generate controversy by seeking out relatively low-paid Central American mercenaries to complement the American "coalition" in Iraq, they couldn't have picked a more inflammatory location to conduct their training. This place was home to a long history of covert collaborations between the darker elements in both countries. Honduras announced its withdrawal from the "coalition of the willing" on April 20, 2004. That same day, the Bush administration declared that Paul Bremer's replacement in Iraq would be John Negroponte. It's not clear if Negroponte's appointment directly prompted the Honduran withdrawal, but the symbolism was nonetheless telling. Negroponte remains widely reviled in Honduras for his role as ambassador to the country in the early 1980s. During Negroponte's ambassadorship, American aid to Honduras increased from $3.9 million in 1980 to $77.4 million in 1984. It came with serious strings attached: Honduras became a giant staging ground for the quasi-secret American war against the Nicaraguan Sandinistas to the south. And once Negroponte arrived, Honduran dissidents began disappearing. When their cast-off bodies showed up in the mountains around Tegucigalpa, the corpses showed signs of torture and execution-style killing. Nevertheless, at Negroponte's confirmation hearings to become ambassador to Iraq, he repeated his longstanding assertion that there were no "death squads" operating in Honduras on his watch. In fact, there were. The most notorious of them was Battalion 316. Beginning in 1981, more than twenty-five years before Your Solutions showed up in the hills outside Tegucigalpa, Battalion 316 trained at this very same camp in Lepaterique.

Battalion 316 was the brainchild of Gustavo Alvarez. The son of a high school principal, Alvarez was obsessed with military history. He admired Nazi general Erwin Rommel so much that he named his sons Erwin and Manfred, after the German general and his son. By the early 1980s, Alvarez had graduated with honors from the Argentine Military Academy, risen to the rank of colonel, and become head of Honduras's national police force, the Fuerza de Seguridad Pública (FUSEP). On the side, Alvarez created a secret intelligence unit that would be the basis for Battallion 316.

As Alvarez rose to power in Honduras, revolution broke out in Nicaragua. On July 17, 1979, dictator Anastasio Somoza, whose family had ruled Nicaragua since 1937, ceded power. Two days later, the Sandinistas took Managua and, with assistance from Cuba, instituted a series of literacy programs, agrarian reforms, and other leftist social and economic projects. In the United States, the Carter administration took a lukewarm attitude toward the Sandinistas. Carter felt that U.S. hostility toward the Cuban revolution two decades prior had done much to radicalize the Cuban government. Carter believed that American assistance to the newly formed government would help the new state steer a more moderate course and give the United States a degree of leverage over Sandinista policies. Moreover, there was little doubt about the brutality of the deposed Somoza regime. Over strong resistance from right-wingers in Congress, Carter passed a series of moderate aid packages to the fledgling government. All of this would change with the incoming Reagan administration, with its vision of a Soviet beachhead in Nicaragua.

On Honduras's northern border, Alvarez saw a peasant revolution in El Salvador growing into a brutal civil war. Fearful that the insurgencies in the north and south might inspire a revolution at home, Alvarez reckoned he could solve any potential political problem by emulating the Argentinean police state. On February 6, 1981, Col. Alvarez told U.S. ambassador Jack Binns (a Carter appointee whom Negroponte would replace later that year) that he admired the way that the Argentines dealt with suspected leftists and planned to emulate them.

Beginning in the early 1970s in Argentina, the Argentine Anticommunist Alliance (the "Triple A" death squad) undertook a campaign of assassinations against suspected leftists, killing 458 people and "disappearing" another 600. When a military junta took power in 1976, it institutionalized state terror, assassinations, torture, and disappearances against leftist "subversives"—students, trade unionists, and other critics of Argentina's military rule. Tens of thousands of people were "disappeared" or murdered between the junta's 1976 coup and the regime's 1983 end.

When Binns heard about Alvarez's plans for Honduras, the alarmed American ambassador sent a cable to Washington:

> Alvarez stressed theme that democracies and West are soft, perhaps too soft to resist Communist subversion. The Argentines, he said, had met the threat effectively, identifying—and

taking care of—the subversives. Their method, he opined, is the only effective way of meeting the challenge.

Binns feared the Argentines "might be helping the Hondurans set up an extralegal countersubversion operation that would resemble and emulate that of Argentina." His fears were well founded. A team of ten to twelve Argentine military "advisers" was already in the country training Honduran military intelligence. This was part of the Argentine government's Operation Charly, a covert action designed to export the "Argentine method" of counterinsurgency to other countries. In an interview with the *Baltimore Sun*, Alvarez's son Oscar would explain that "the Argentines came . . . and they taught how to disappear people."

"This place is called the S-Turns," said Maria, a staffer at the Comité de Familiares de Detenidos Desaparecidos en Honduras (COFADEH), an NGO formed by the families of Honduras's disappeared to investigate the past and to advocate for human rights. We'd driven several miles into the mountains outside Tegucigalpa, past the last shantytowns and suburbs, onto a steep dirt road that makes sharp 180 degree turns as it winds up to a radio antenna overlooking the city. The mountain, once a pine forest before the logging industry stripped its trees, teemed with shoulder-high overgrowth. Maria pointed to a clump of thick bushes and said, "That's where they found the first body." One morning in November of 1981, as peasants from a hamlet atop the mountain made their long daily walk to the market at the mountain's base, they found a human body half-buried on the roadside. A dog was making off with a piece of its flesh. The peasants buried the corpse to keep the dogs away. The body was never identified.

Further up the hill, Maria stopped the truck next to a gate leading down a road to a small school. "They found the next bodies here," she said, "one month after the first." Again, it was the villagers who found the half-buried corpses, and once again, the dogs had found them first. This time there were five. These bodies were also never identified.

The trip continued like this, winding through the mountains on dirt roads, Maria stopping at landmark after landmark where the bodies showed up once the Argentines came to Honduras. Two pine trees standing next to one another far up in the mountains mark where the body of an unidentified woman wearing white pants was found. More bodies were found in a ravine where two trees cross to form an X shape. More in a dark gully off the side of the red dirt road. So many unidentified bodies had shown up here that locals took to calling it the "plains of death," Maria explained.

After the sun had fallen and the foliage had turned black, we arrived at a locked gate in the Amarateca Valley where a long dirt driveway leads up toward a walled hacienda, its thick concrete walls beginning to crumble. Lightning bugs glided through the dark underbrush. As we walked up the driveway hill, we saw the silhouettes of three children sitting in each other's arms on the wall above us. They said little. Their mother had yet to come home from town. Maria knew the children. Their family had moved into the smaller of two houses on the property a few years ago. The children had watched as a team of forensic anthropologists excavated the white plaster house adjacent to their own, the former home of General Amilcar Zelaya.

We walked through the open doorway into the cavelike concrete house. It was too dark to make out anything more than the scuffed white walls and empty window spaces. Maria pointed out how the architecture is set up so that there are independent entrances and exits to nearly every part of the concrete house, allowing rooms to be effectively cordoned off from one another. I started to take pictures. The white burst of my camera flash lit up the walls for an instant, revealing black outlines drawn with magic markers. Numbers next to each shape identified the uneven circles, oblongs, and amoebalike figures. Some covered entire walls; others were the size of silver dollars. One outline took the shape of a deformed handprint. The forensic team had drawn the marks around places where Luminol sprayed on the walls glowed bright blue as it reacted with the trace iron in human hemoglobin. Residue from bloodstains someone had tried to wash away. Zelaya's house was a torture chamber where an unknown number of disappeared people had spent their last days. Outside the house, Maria led us into a small, square brick building with a water tank on top. Inside, the back wall was riddled with bullet holes. When the forensic team applied Luminol to the brick room, the whole interior lit up. This was where Battalion 316 carried out the final executions.

Learning of the disappearances, Ambassador Jack Binns continued sending alarmed cables to Washington: "I am deeply concerned at increasing evidence of officially sponsored/sanctioned assassinations . . . of political and criminal targets, which clearly indicate GOH [Government of Honduras] repression has built up a head of steam much faster than we had anticipated." The ambassador urged the United States to "try to nip this situation in the bud," recommending that the United States should threaten to block military aid to Honduras if the repression continued. "There was no official response to this cable or to the strategy I proposed. In fact, State and the Reagan administration continued to ignore Honduran human rights abuses . . . ," he said.

Washington had already warned Binns to "back off all that liberal stuff." A few months later, Reagan replaced Binns with John Negroponte. Instead of canceling military aid to Honduras, the Reagan administration increased it dramatically. Disappearances, death squads, and torture aside, Honduras would be the staging ground for not-so-secret wars against Nicaragua.

In the white world, military aid to Honduras rocketed from $8.9 million in fiscal year 1981 to $31.3 million in FY 1982. In FY 1983, it shot to $48.3 million, and it reached a plateau at $77.3 million in FY 1984. Other forms of aid, often indirectly intended for the Contras, came in other forms. From August 1983 until January 1984, the U.S. military staged the BIG PINE II military exercise involving four to five thousand troops, mock bombing runs by fighters based on offshore aircraft carriers, amphibious Marine landings, and large-scale "counterinsurgency operations" along the Nicaraguan and El Salvadorian borders. Nineteen warships, over two hundred jet fighters, and twenty thousand personnel were marshaled to the region.

The BIG PINE exercises created a substantial new military infrastructure in Honduras. U.S. engineers built new roads, improved old ones, and constructed barracks, training camps, hospitals, and storage depots. Construction began on air bases at San Lorenzo, Trujillo, and Tiger Island. At Palmerola Air Base (later known as Soto Cano), north of Tegucigalpa, the military built a state-of-the-art command center to support the exercises. By 1985, the country was home to so much U.S. military basing that it earned the nickname the USS *Honduras*, as if the country had become a giant American aircraft carrier.

But the USS *Honduras* was only the visible part of an undeclared war.

From secret air bases and safe houses scattered throughout Central America, black Army units and CIA operatives waged very hot and very secret wars in El Salvador, Guatemala, Panama, Honduras, and, above all, against Nicaragua. The black war in Central America, moreover, would become more than just a blueprint for the post-9/11 war on terror. In a very real sense, the war on terror was already in full swing twenty years before September 12, 2001.

■ ■ ■

On November 4, 1979, Iranian students stormed the U.S. embassy in Tehran, initiating a 444-day hostage crisis and a geopolitical domino effect across the world. That event would transform geographies from Iraq to Honduras, Beirut to Washington. Facts on the ground in Iran would change the makeup of American politics and serve as a backdrop to a dramatic expansion of the secret state.

Responding to the hostage situation, President Carter authorized Operation RICE BOWL, an ad hoc rescue attempt drawing on disparate units from all of the armed services. It failed spectacularly. When an RH-53D helicopter crashed into a fuel-filled C-130 at the Desert One staging site, the ensuing explosion killed eight servicemen, ended the mission, and left a scene of smoldering wreckage in the Iranian desert. Members of the newly formed Delta Force unit and other soldiers working with Joint Task Force 179 flew dejectedly home from Egypt on a C-141 transport.

Within hours of the failed rescue attempt, President Carter authorized planning for a follow-on operation that would become known as SNOWBIRD. Its various components would fall under code names like CREDIBLE SPORT and HONEY BADGER. An investigation led by Admiral James Holloway found that the first operation had failed, in a nutshell, because Joint Task Force 179 was ill-prepared. The units hadn't properly trained together; the military had no long-range, quick insertion helicopters and no aircraft designed to covertly insert Special Forces troops into a country undetected. Moreover, the CIA had been either unwilling or unable to provide tactical intelligence to the task force over the course of the mission. To remedy the situation and to prevent a repeat of the fiasco, Holloway recommended the creation of "a Counterterrorist Joint Task Force . . . as a field agency of the Joint Chiefs of Staff with permanently assigned staff personnel and certain assigned forces."

The Pentagon set to work creating a series of new units specifically designed to conduct black operations like the operation in Iran.

To fill the need for highly trained special operations helicopter pilots, the Army created a Special Operations helicopter unit called Task Force 160, which eventually became the 160th Special Operations Aviation Regiment (SOAR). Based at Fort Campbell, Kentucky, the mottoes of these "Night Stalkers" were "NSDQ" (Night Stalkers Don't Quit) and "Death Waits in the Dark" spoke to the unit's expertise: flying low-altitude, long-range night missions in support of Special Forces operations.

The Night Stalkers had a black counterpart in a second aviation unit called SEASPRAY. SEASPRAY was a joint Army-CIA unit flying Cessnas, King Airs, and Hughes MD500 helicopters. Although the unit took its funding from the Army, SEASPRAY took the CIA as its model: Its equipment was kept "off the books," its aircraft were kept out of the official Army inventory (the "Gold Book"), and the operation was hidden from the "uncleared" Defense Department brass and congressional reviewers. Modeled on a classic CIA proprietary, SEASPRAY used a civilian cover called Aviation Tech Services to hide the aircrafts' true ownership and purpose. The unit had its headquarters at Fort Eustis, Virginia, under the name First Rotary Wing Test, a bland name that served as an internal Army cover. SEASPRAY also operated out of a secret site in Tampa to support activities in Central America.

The Army created other black units to fill gaps that the failed mission in the Iranian desert made so dramatically visible. One of the problems, in the Army's estimation, was that it had no independent tactical intelligence capabilities: It had to rely on the CIA for up-to-the-minute information about the hostage situation in Iran, but the CIA hadn't delivered. To prepare for SNOWBIRD, the Army wanted to know as much as possible about the situation at the embassy. The Army wanted to know where guards were positioned, how many rounds their weapons carried, and what kinds of locks were on the gates. The Army, in short, wanted its own clandestine boots on the ground, its own mini-CIA. In order to meet this need, the Army created an outfit called the Field Operations Group, or FOG: a collection of fifty temporary-duty personnel who would serve as an "ad hoc organization composed of selected personnel who were trained to fill critical intelligence and operational [needs]." FOG would later become one of the most secret units in the Army, the Intelligence Support Activity (ISA).

The "go" command for operation SNOWBIRD never came. On January 19, 1981, the United States and Iran signed the Algiers Accords. Iran released the hostages the next day, just minutes after Ronald Reagan's inauguration to the White House.

Although the black army units such as Task Force 160, SEASPRAY, the ISA, and Delta Force had been created in response to events unfolding in the Middle East, they quickly found themselves conducting massive operations in Central America.

In February 1982, SEASPRAY set up shop at San Pedro Sula in northwest Honduras. Using a modified Beechcraft 100, the unit flew surveillance missions over El Salvador, monitoring the positions of guerillas and relaying the information to the Salvadorian army. Operation QUEENS HUNTER was so successful that the Special Operations Division had to fight off the Army Southern Command, who wanted to take control of the mission. When U.S. ambassador to Honduras John Negroponte sided with the Special Operations contingent in the ensuing intra-Army turf war, the Special Operations Division program not only stayed in place but started to dramatically expand. Operation QUEENS HUNTER quickly outgrew its base at San Pedro Sula as more planes and personnel arrived: SEASPRAY units, Delta Force "shooters," and ISA signals intelligence operators. The covert operations expanded to Honduras itself and Nicaragua.

As the black operations spread throughout Central America, so did the scale and scope of their civilian cover. Congress had prohibited the military from using proprietary companies during the 1970s as part of the post-Watergate reforms, so the Special Operations Division's civilian fronts were slightly different than their CIA counterparts in that they weren't financially independent, as some of the CIA proprietaries were. It was, at best, a technical distinction. One of the SEASPRAY "cutouts" was a paper company called Airamco, based in La Jolla, California, which could issue checks for services to SEASPRAY aircraft, keeping the Army's name off the paper trail. Airamco had a subdivision called Shenandoah Aerolease, which owned and leased SEASPRAY aircraft. In the QUEENS HUNTER program, for example, Shenandoah owned the planes, while Airamco contracted with the Honduran government to fly "electromagnetic surveys." Other front companies hid related parts of the operation. The Army was creating its own version of the CIA.

Bill Casey, who assumed the CIA helm with the incoming Reagan administration, was determined to win back ground the agency had ceded during the Church and Pike investigations. An old OSS veteran, the new director referred to congressional intelligence committees (instituted in the aftermath of Watergate) as "those assholes on the hill." He mumbled incomprehensibly through his briefings, when he bothered to brief the intelligence committees at all. Moreover, when he accepted the job as DCI, Casey had insisted that the post be elevated to a cabinet-level position in the Reagan administration. This would make him one of the most powerful CIA directors in history.

Casey chose former Rome station chief Duane "Dewey" Clarridge as his new Latin America Division chief and asked for a proposal. Clarridge turned around with a simple two-point plan:

1. Take the war to Nicaragua.
2. Start killing Cubans.

"It was exactly what Casey wanted to hear," Clarridge recounts in his memoirs. "A smile broke across his rumpled countenance as he asked me to produce a Presidential Finding to cover and fund the operation." Shortly thereafter, swarms of unmarked planes began filling the skies over Honduras, often intruding into Nicaraguan airspace. The CIA replaced the Argentine trainers at Lepaterique with its own people.

The long-held fiction behind the massive covert action effort was that its purpose was nothing more than "interdicting arms" that were supposedly flowing from Nicaragua to El Salvadorian rebels. In the aisles of gun shows and in hushed tones among soldiers of fortune, word was out that there was good money to be made in Central America doing work behind Nicaragua's borders.

Casey first heard of the black army units in a secure room at Langley at a secret briefing on the Army's Special Operations Division in October 1982. Casey learned about the special operations, the counterterrorism forces, and the SOD's access to the incredible resources of the U.S. Army. He liked what he saw. The DCI understood immediately the possibilities that a close collaboration with the Army might open up. Casey requested a formal liaison between the CIA and SOD. Casey may have realized something else at the briefing: that the military wasn't subject to the same executive and congressional oversight over its covert activities. The SOD didn't require presidential "findings," nor was it explicitly required to inform congressional intelligence committees of its work. For the most part, the post-Watergate rules applied to the CIA, not the military. In the words of author Steven Emerson, the secrecy afforded the Special Operations Division a huge amount of autonomy: "[The division] was building to something much greater than its present form, but at the same time, the chain of command that mattered most—the Army leadership—had little idea of what was going on . . . the Division was emerging as a parallel military organization within the Army."

The new black military units started becoming intertwined with the CIA as the division's liaison to the CIA, James E. Longhofer, worked closely with Rudy Enders, head of the CIA's Special Activities Group. Their close collaboration meant that the CIA gained access to the division's secret army.

The covert war against Nicaragua escalated. On March 14, 1982, a squad of CIA-trained and -equipped saboteurs bombed two bridges in northern Nicaragua: one near Somotillo and the other near Ocotal. "Who lives? Somoza!" was the battle cry before the destruction of a bridge at Rico Coco.

September 8, 1983, saw two lightweight planes appear over Managua, Nicaragua's capital. One dropped bombs on a residential neighborhood near the home of the foreign minister Miguel D'Escoto. That plane escaped. The second, a Cessna 404, wasn't so lucky. After attacking the Managua airport with two 150-pound bombs, it was shot down by antiaircraft fire and crashed into a control tower. Although Eden Pastora's faction of southern Contras claimed responsibility for the bombings, the CIA's fingerprints were all over the wreckage. The pilot, Agustin M. Roman, was a former Sandinista who'd defected to Pastora's ARDE group the previous year. The plane itself had been recently owned by a McLean, Virginia, outfit called the Investair Leasing Corporation, whose manager was a man named Edgar L. Mitchell. It turned out that Mitchell had been an executive at Intermontain Aviation, which had been one of the CIA's largest proprietary companies before it was liquidated in 1975. Investair's marketing director, Mark L. Peterson, had a similar past with agency proprietaries: He'd been an executive at Air America. Officials in the Reagan administration acknowledged providing support to Pastora's group.

The same day as the Managua bombings, a Nicaraguan pipe-line at Puerto Sandino exploded. Although FDN Contras took responsibility for the bombing, Contra spokesperson Edgar Chamorro would later explain that "the FDN had nothing what-soever to do with this operation . . . we were instructed by the CIA to publicly claim responsibility in order to cover the CIA's involvement. We did." In reality, American covert operatives from the CIA and the Army's Special Operations Division were working with mercenaries recruited from throughout Central America to conduct covert operations against Nicaragua and, according to one former mercenary, "make it appear that the Contras had done it."

One of the problems of having so many new undercover Army units had to do with operational security (OPSEC): how to keep their activities and existence secret. Although the Army's assis-tant chief of staff for intelligence (ACSI) was nominally in charge of providing OPSEC to military units, when the SOD went to ask for help, ACSI told them to take a number. The Special Opera-tions Division took matters into their own hands. Their solution to the OPSEC problem? Create a new black unit in charge of oper-ational security. In June of 1982, the Army leadership approved the creation of an "operational security/counterintelligence de-tachment" within the Special Operations community. Run by a young officer named Lieutenant Colonel Dale E. Duncan, the new outfit took the name YELLOW FRUIT.

With YELLOW FRUIT, Special Operations division chief James Longhofer (who also acted at the division's CIA liaison) wanted "an organization that was a hidden circle within a circle within a circle. So as people pulled those onion skins away, it would take them a long time to get to the core of the onion to find out that it was really an Army unit." As part of YELLOW FRUIT's cover, Lieutenant Colonel Duncan "retired" from the Army to set up a "private" consulting company called Business Security International, or BSI. Working out of an office suite at 4306 Evergreen Lane, Suite 204, in Annandale, Virginia, the company claimed to help commercial firms with security and overseas operations, and to provide services such as "threat analysis, plant security, asset and executive protection . . . private communication systems and providing technical countermeasures." On the record, BSI's "customers" included local law enforcement and federal agencies, but in reality, BSI only had one "customer."

At YELLOW FRUIT's Annandale office, black dollars gushed like a broken fire hydrant. More than $300 million disappeared into the Special Operations Divisions' black world. Unit operators controlled $64,292,335.50 in secret checking accounts. YELLOW FRUIT personnel had expensive tastes: $600 hotel rooms, $1,200 monthly liquor bills. Its accounting files bulged with bogus receipts for tens of thousands of dollars. There were rumors of prostitutes and drugs.

But there was something else besides the vast network of cutout companies and secret bank accounts, the lavish hotel rooms, and the covert operations. In a YELLOW FRUIT safe was a three-ring binder that Longhofer and Enders dropped off only a few weeks after the secret unit's offices first opened. On plain white paper without a CIA letterhead was a draft for a remarkable undertaking: to fund the Contras when, as it was becoming clearer was going to happen, Congress unambiguously cut off money for the undeclared war.

The document called for a three-point plan. First, generate money by selling weapons to other countries at inflated prices (the plan mentioned Honduras, Guatemala, Brazil, and Argentina). Second, set up offshore bank accounts for the Contras. Third, send YELLOW FRUIT operatives to Costa Rica tasked with building clandestine airstrips, opening up a "southern front" against the Sandinista regime in Nicaragua.

■ ■ ■

Congress tried to definitively end the secret war in Central America in 1984. That March, a Soviet oil tanker bound for Nicaragua hit an American-laid mine. The explosion injured five crew members and caused heavy damage to the ship. Mining Nicaraguan ports had been Duane Clarridge's idea, inspired by the efficacy of mines in the Russo-Japanese war. Using Piranha speedboats, UCLAs and Special Forces had laid the mines, although, once again, the Contras took credit. And once again, in reality, the Contras had nothing to do with it.

Barry Goldwater, chair of the Senate Intelligence Committee, was furious. "You get hold of Bill Casey, and find out what the fuck's going on." Mining another nation's harbors was an act of war. Daniel Patrick Moynihan threatened to resign from the Intelligence Committee over the mining, while Senator David Durenberger complained that "There is no use in our meeting with Bill Casey. None of us believe him. The cavalier, almost arrogant fashion in which he has treated us as individuals has turned the whole committee against him."

In 1982, Congress had passed the first Boland Amendment, prohibiting the CIA from spending money "for the purposes of overthrowing the government of Nicaragua." The second Boland Amendment, a bill outlawing "military or paramilitary activities in Nicaragua" came in July 1983. In the mining incident's aftermath, Congress tried once again to shut the secret war down. On October 12, 1984, the last in a series of Boland amendments became law:

> During fiscal year 1985, no funds available to the Central Intelligence Agency, the Department of Defense, or any other agency or entity of the United States involved in intelligence activities may be obligated or expended for the purpose or which would have the effect of supporting, directly or indi-

rectly, military or paramilitary operations in Nicaragua by any nation, group, organization, movement or individual.

Fortunately for the group of people who'd become known as "the Enterprise," a backup plan lay in the YELLOW FRUIT vaults. And the Enterprise took over where YELLOW FRUIT left off.

14

Anything You Need Anywhere
Aguacate

The road to Aguacate runs east from Tegucigalpa on a two-lane highway that narrows and crumbles as it leaves the nation's capital and meanders toward Honduras's historic frontier. We've driven about five hours toward the mouth of the Black River, the point demarcating Honduras's west from territory nominally controlled by the Miskito Indians in the east. "About as far from Hondurans' imagination as northern Alaska is in the U.S.," says fellow geographer Joe Bryan as our pickup truck lumbers on eastward.

The highway winds over lush hills and valleys, past thick green ferns, past ubiquitous banana, jacaranda, and acacia trees, past mothers and daughters washing family clothes by hand on the sides of rivers, and past the downed palm trees where peasants brew up powerful *coyol* liquor (nicknamed "mule kick"). It didn't used to be as easy to travel through the Olancho province as it is now. A checkpoint controlled all traffic between the cities in the west and the eastern hinterlands. No cameras were permitted into the area. No maps were allowed either. Even homemade sketches of the area were strictly prohibited. The Hondurans, working closely with the Reagan White House, declared that the whole region would be a blank spot on the map as a matter of national security. The reason? There were no Contras in Honduras. That was the official line of the Honduran government, anyway. One stray photograph, one wide-angle camera lens whose angle was a little bit too large, could have easily dispelled that myth.

It was Ninoska's idea to visit some of the farmers working in the overgrown fields around the old secret base at Aguacate. A staffer at COFADEH back in Tegucigalpa, she'd been involved in a 2000 excavation where human rights investigators unearthed a mass grave. Ninoska hadn't been back to Aguacate for nearly a decade. We turned down a dirt road; in the distance a lone woman walked along the roadside carrying a plastic tub on her head. "Can you tell me where the home of Marcos Rivera is?" asked Ninoska. The woman pointed to a small ranch further down the road. We drove up to the makeshift gate, held together with a piece of wire from a coat hanger. A small boy played in the overgrown weeds consuming much of Marcos's property. His father wasn't there, said the boy. After a few minutes, a bright red truck turned down the road toward us.

"It's a miracle!" Marcos exclaimed when he saw Ninoska. He was wearing shorts, a black T-shirt with an American flag and the words NEW YORK on it, and a yellow baseball hat. A short, stocky man with a warm face and fingers the size of bananas, he was strong but didn't look old or jaded. Marcos and Ninoska had met when the local man helped out with the mass grave excavation years before. After a round of Cokes on his porch, Marcos agreed to show us the base. Along the way, we picked up his friend Vicente, whose property includes a hill overlooking Aguacate.

Now little more than a blurred-out patch of jungle on Google Earth, Aguacate had once been a logistics hub and training center in the covert war that "wasn't happening" in Central America. Helicopters and propeller-driven aircraft had once been the soundtrack to this forgotten piece of the forest, as unmarked aircraft took off to fly clandestine reconnaissance missions over Nicaragua and swooped down to deliver pallets of small arms, cash, and supplies for Contra units based here.

On the far side of the strip, a collection of Honduran soldiers milled around a UH-1 "Huey" helicopter. We drove up and introduced ourselves to the local colonel, who shook our hands and politely asked us to stay away from the area until his crew got the helicopter off the ground. How different a scene it was from only a few years ago, when the Contras tried to kill a journalist who slipped into the area and photographed the base. The Honduran military detachment here at Aguacate was about to conduct a surveillance flight over the adjacent national park.

The truck ambled further into the base and Marcos's friend Vicente pointed to different holes in the foliage, explaining what structures used to be there. There had been a big generator, storage facilities. "Over there," he said, pointing to an enclave off to the dirt road's left side, "was the CIA." They had big radio antennae, and absolutely no one was allowed in there, he explained. Aguacate had once been his land, said Vicente. The military, he explained, had forced him to sell it for pennies in the early 1980s but allowed him to continue farming parts of it. He was now trying to get the land back.

When the helicopter took off for its reconnaissance mission over the forest, Ninoska steered our pickup down the dilapidated dirt runway, stopping near a small overgrown path that led into a thick morass of green overgrowth. Joe and I followed Ninoska,

Marcos, and Vicente through ferns and bushes to a brick room the size of a big chimney. It was only a few yards away from where Vicente said the old CIA transmitter had been. The forest was slowly taking the brick room back: Its roof had fallen in; the floor was stones and rubble. This was the torture chamber, Vicente explained. They'd put people in here barefoot, he said. The floor used to be a metal slab that they'd heat up with embers. A bar across the ceiling was used to hang people up by their wrists. Prisoners had scratched their names into the brick interior: Seto Lopez, Leche, Mario . . . Vicente himself had spent some time there too, he said obliquely.

We asked about the bodies investigators uncovered in 2000 behind the old base hospital. "Those were all Contras," said Vicente, fighters who'd died at the base hospital and had been laid to rest outside. The other bodies, those of the rural leftists and their supporters who'd been tortured and executed at the base, lay elsewhere. "They loaded *those* corpses onto helicopters at night," and took them somewhere nearby, said Vicente. "The flights took only fifteen minutes." Those bodies are still missing.

As we walked back to the truck, Marcos pointed out where the old hangars had been. There were always planes there, he said, coming in at all hours, "Caribous, Hercules, helicopters, push-pulls." They were all unmarked, he said, except there was a sky-blue C-130 that would come around. If you looked really closely, Marcos explained, you could see Air Force insignia on it.

The image of a sky-blue C-130 made me think of Tepper Aviation. A Tepper plane had crashed in the late 1980s while resupplying CIA-supported guerrillas in Angola. Another one of their C-130s had landed at the Desert Rock Airstrip in 2002 as part of the ANABASIS project. They were the only C-130s I knew of with blue paint jobs, but that's not to say that there weren't others. Besides, Tepper planes didn't have Air Force markings.

"I got to fly on it once," Marcos offered, "to Swan Island." I knew that Swan Island was a longstanding CIA outpost in the Caribbean north of Honduras. The agency had used it since the late 1950s, when it set up a radio station on the island to transmit propaganda into Cuba before the Bay of Pigs invasion.

"What!?"

"How'd you end up on a U.S. plane going to Swan Island?"

"I was a mercenary!" he laughed.

"This Aguacate has a tremendous history," Vicente said as we walked around the remains of the once-covert airstrip. He pointed to a cul-de-sac at the far end of the runway. A collection of unmarked airplanes lay buried under the red clay dirt over there, he said. Base officials had buried the aircraft once stationed here, lest curious investigators start tracking their registration histories. Digging up aircraft parts and tracing their serial numbers back to the planes they belonged to might be the way things would turn out in a movie, but in this hot, remote land, no one cared enough. Even with the serial numbers, determining their identities would mean spending months trying to piece together a labyrinthine paper trail of front companies and false identities that were both the CIA and the Special Operations Division's modus operandi. All this would only confirm something everyone already knew.

There was, however, another possibility. According to the final version of the Iran-Contra report, the fleet of aircraft used by Ollie North and Richard Secord's Enterprise was last seen at Aguacate.

The Enterprise started unraveling October 5, 1986, when Sandinista ground forces shot down a DC-123 over Nicaraguan airspace. Inside were a hundred thousand rounds of ammunition, seven grenade launchers, and seventy automatic weapons. Eugene Hasenfus was the only survivor from the four-person crew. Hasenfus, who once worked as a loadmaster for the agency in Laos, claimed he was working for the CIA. The CIA denied everything. But littered throughout the downed DC-123's wreckage were clues to the aircraft's true purpose.

At the crash site, the Nicaraguans recovered flight records showing that the plane's base was at Ilopango, El Salvador, and that it made frequent flights to Aguacate and Morocon, Honduras. Hasenfus told his captors that two Cuban-Americans based in El Salvador—"Max Gomez" and "Ramon Medina"—coordinated the operation for the CIA. In reality, "Gomez" and "Medina" were aliases for Felix Rodriguez and Luis Posada Carriles. Both men had long-standing relationships with the CIA but weren't, strictly speaking, working for the agency on this mission.

Felix Rodriguez was a longtime CIA operative whose paramilitary work for the agency went back to the Bay of Pigs, where he'd joined David Atlee Phillips, David Morales, Ted Shackley, E. Howard Hunt, Frank Sturgis, and others in the failed 1961 attempt to overthrow Castro. Rodriguez formally joined the CIA in the late 1960s, where he posed as a Bolivian military officer named Felix Ramos, assisting in the hunt for Che Guevara. After capturing Guevara in the Bolivian forest, Rodriguez instructed a soldier to execute their prisoner in a way that made it look like Guevara had been shot while fighting. Rodriguez took the slain guerrilla's Rolex and strapped it on his own wrist as a trophy.

Rodriguez's partner at Ilopango was Luis Posada Carilles. Nicknamed "Bamby," Posada was a former CIA agent trained at Fort Benning in demolitions and guerrilla warfare in the 1960s. In 1976, Posada was responsible for bombing Cubana Airlines flight 455, a Cuban passenger plane, and killing all seventy-three people on board. Imprisoned in Venezuela after the bombing, Posada escaped to Aruba in 1985 by bribing a prison supervisor. Rodriguez supplied Posada with a false passport and a fake identity as "Ramon Medina," and gave him a $3,000-a-month job on the Iran-Contra staff. Upon his arrival in El Salvador Posada took charge of finances, housing, transportation, and refueling Iran-Contra flights.

In 1998, Posada claimed responsibility for a series of bombings in Cuban nightclubs the previous year. In 2000, he was arrested in Panama with two hundred pounds of explosives, plotting the assassination of Fidel Castro. After a sudden pardon from the Panamanian government, Posada surfaced in Miami in May 2005, where he was arrested for illegally entering the country. When Venezuela and Cuba demanded his extradition, the United States refused, saying that Posada faced the threat of torture in both countries.

Headquartered at a restricted section of the Ilopango air base, Rodriguez and Posada ran Iran-Contra's covert airlift operations with a fleet of five aircraft and a team of about fourteen pilots and crew members. On the books, an unimaginatively named shell company called Corporate Air Service Inc. owned the aircraft. After Hasenfus's capture, the Salvadorians immediately ordered the operation out of Ilopango. Rodriguez and Posada sent the aircraft to Aguacate.

When Nicaraguan authorities questioned Hasenfus about Ilopango, the former CIA loadmaster gave up addresses for three San Salvador safe houses. When local investigators checked the phone records from the addresses, they found numerous calls to Lieutenant Colonel Oliver North.

After a seven-year investigation, Independent Counsel Lawrence Walsh issued a 1994 report on the Iran-Contra Affair. The Enterprise's off-the-books activities were as labyrinthine as they were impetuous. They had solicited private funding for the Contras from a diverse network of wealthy allies, including H. Ross Perot, beer magnate Joseph Coors, the Saudi royal family, and the sultan of Brunei. Iran-Contra managers colluded with arms merchants such Manucher Ghorbinafar, sold arms to Iran, and pocketed much of the proceeds. Continuing the CIA's off-the-books war in Central America, the Enterprise hired British mercenary

David Walker to conduct "special operations" inside Nicaragua, including blowing up an arms dump and providing helicopter pilots.

According to Senate Iran-Contra Committee chairman Senator Daniel Inouye (D-HI), the Enterprise was "a secret government—a shadowy government with its own Air Force, its own Navy, its own fund-raising mechanism, and the ability to pursue its own ideas of the national interest, free from all the checks and balances and free from the law itself."

At Marcos's dairy farm near Aguacate, we sat on the porch drinking cold water, hiding from the summer sun under the canopy of potted plants surrounding his house and talking about what happened to Honduras after the American military (and American money) left the country. Joe had heard rumors that Aguacate became a major hub of cocaine smuggling after the CIA, the SOD, and the Enterprise left. "That was nothing compared to the eighties," said Marcos. He started rattling off the names of people he said were from the Medellín cartel who frequented the air base during the eighties. A man named Michelangelo, a pair of brothers. "Every night, there was plane after plane ... they had some kind of arrangement with the military and with the Americans."

In Marcos's estimation, things had gone to hell with the end of the Cold War. The USS *Honduras* was dismantled; American military dollars dried up. It was like, "Take all these guns! Go sell cocaine! Go join private security firms!" laughed Marcos about the prevailing spirit after the wars.

The statistics confirm Marcos's analysis: At the end of the secret wars, El Salvador, Nicaragua, and Honduras had higher unemployment, lower literacy rates, and lower standards of living than they had before the billions of U.S. dollars had come. Nicaragua and Honduras became second and third only to Haiti as the Americas' most impoverished countries.

Back in Tegucigalpa, the legacy is everywhere. Private security has become one of Honduras's biggest industries. On every street corner and outside almost every shop, for-hire guards cradle shotguns. Restaurants and nightclubs search patrons with handheld metal-detecting wands; there are lockers in front where people check their firearms along with their coats. The private security industry feeds on itself, creating the conditions for its own growth. As unemployment rises, there's more work to be done protecting the increasingly conglomerated wealth. As guns in private hands proliferate, things happen. Blame it on the gangs, and there's an argument for even more private security.

At COFADEH's headquarters on Avenue Cervantes, I sat across from Dina Meza, the Honduran recipient of the Amnesty International Special Award for Human Rights Journalism Under Threat for her work investigating the rise of privatized violence in Honduras. In a car outside, a bodyguard waited for her in the car. While reporting for the online magazine *Revistazo*, Meza has had her phone tapped and received multiple death threats. On the online comments section under one of her stories, someone wrote that her daughter was "very good looking." In December 2006, her lawyer, Dionisio Díaz García, was assassinated. Meza's assessment of the situation in Honduras echoed Marcos's: After the Cold War, she said, the military and wealthy landowners were looking for ways to maintain influence (the influx of American military aid to Honduras had greatly expanded their power). Combine that with a flood of small arms from demobilized fighters along with the economic instability of reduced American aid and neoliberal "free trade" ideologies, and you have a situation where the old Army establishment can step in to fill a "security gap," this time under the guise of for-profit "security" companies. It was getting to the point where Honduras's ruling class commanded their own armies, she said.

In a 2007 report, the United Nations concurred, saying, "Some

PMSCs [private military and security companies] are committing human rights violations which go unpunished," and that "it is worth asking how far a State can cede control of public security to foreign private security companies before losing part of its sovereignty and before the situation becomes one of interference in the internal affairs of that State."

Among the ubiquitous armed shopkeepers and handheld metal detectors of Tegucigalpa's narrow streets, it's easy to see how local private security industries are both the legacy of American black operations in the region and part of the war on terror's contemporary geography. Under the Central American Free Trade Agreement, Honduras competes with El Salvador and Nicaragua for outsourced American jobs. A plentiful supply of cheap labor has lured American T-shirt and clothing manufacturers to the country. Cheap labor and outsourcing, however, come in many forms. Your Solutions, the American company that trained cheap fighters at Lepaterique to join the mercenary "coalition" in Iraq, was helping outsource the war. It was doing the same thing as the T-shirt companies.

In a less visible way, Iran-Contra's legacy also shaped the United States' future. The secret wars, off-the-books units, and privatized violence of the 1980s drew a blueprint for the U.S.'s post-9/11 war on terror.

Aboard an Air Force Two flight between Pakistan and Muscat, Oman, a reporter asked Vice President Dick Cheney about presidential power. Cheney recalled Iran-Contra:

"Yes, I do have the view that over the years there had been an erosion of presidential power and authority . . . ," began the vice president, "a lot of the things around Watergate and Vietnam, both, in the '70s served to erode the authority," he continued. "If you want reference to an obscure text," Cheney continued, "go look at the minority views that were filed with the Iran-Contra

Committee; the Iran-Contra Report in about 1987." The minority views, said Cheney, "are very good in laying out a robust view of the President's prerogatives with respect to the conduct of especially foreign policy and national security matters. It will give you a much broader perspective."

Cheney's mention of the Iran-Contra report, especially the minority opinion, was indeed a reference to an obscure text. I remember reading the bulk of the report one lazy summer in the early 1990s while waiting for college classes to begin. I, like most people who read it, spent far more time trying to understand the intricate machinations of government and wondered why Ronald Reagan hadn't been impeached and George H. W. Bush indicted. Above all, I wondered what additional crimes remained uncovered when George H. W. Bush pardoned a slew of conspirators in the early 1990s. I hadn't bothered to read the wonkish "recommendations," and definitely not the minority opinions.

In the majority opinion to the Iran-Contra Affair, Congress described the scandal as "characterized by pervasive dishonesty and inordinate secrecy." The majority concluded that the Reagan administration violated the Hughes-Ryan Act by failing to inform congressional intelligence committees about its covert actions in the Middle East and Central America, violated the Boland Amendment by supporting the Contras, then lied about it and covered it up. The majority opined that a "cabal of zealots" had been in charge and concluded its executive summary by saying, "The idea of monarchy was rejected here 200 years ago and since then, the law—not any official or ideology—has been paramount. For not instilling this precept in his staff, for failing to take care that the law reigned supreme, the President bears the responsibility."

Dick Cheney's office authored the minority opinion.

Out of the five recommendations, four were recommendations to *increase* secrecy. The dissenting opinion advocated secrecy oaths for members of Congress, coupled with "stiff penalties" for its violation. It recommended strengthening "sanctions against disclosing security secrets or classified information" and enacting legislation that would allow the president to inform even fewer members of Congress about covert actions. For the minority, the lesson of Iran-Contra was the exact opposite of what common sense dictated. Less oversight, more secrecy. That was the recipe. How to prevent presidents from abusing their power? Give them more power so that whatever they decide to do isn't an overreach.

With a few exceptions, the Iran-Contra conspirators came out relatively unscathed. Oliver North went on to make a serious bid for the Senate and enjoyed a healthy career as a public speaker, talk show commentator, and host of his own TV show on Fox News. Elliott Abrams became an official in the George W. Bush administration. John Poindexter went on to become a well-paid defense industry consultant and executive.

In early 2005, according to Seymour Hersh, the principle players in the Iran-Contra scandal held an informal "lessons learned" meeting about what they'd done nearly twenty years prior and how those lessons could be applied during Bush the younger's administration. Their conclusions included some familiar cornerstones of the war on terror.

> Even though the program was eventually exposed, it had been possible to execute it without telling Congress. As to what the experience taught them, in terms of future covert operations, the participants found: "One, you can't trust our friends. Two, the C.I.A. has got to be totally out of it. Three, you can't trust the uniformed military, and four, it's got to be run out of the Vice-President's office.

All the various aspects of Iran-Contra, from the black Army units that the Enterprise borrowed its structure from, to the mercenaries it employed to conduct its operations, to the informal, quasiprivatized organization, to the "robust" view of executive power its participants adhered to, would create new blank spots on maps in the war on terror. The transformation would begin as CIA operatives fought alongside secret Army units and Afghan warlords on their way toward Kabul, Afghanistan. In Central America, the executive branch had learned that if you did it right—and kept it black—you could get away with it. "We can do whatever we want. . . ." That's where the logic led. In 2004, a man named Khaled El-Masri would hear those very words at a CIA black site outside Kabul.

15

Bobs
Kabul

I got an unmediated glimpse of the war on terror's geography long
before arriving at Kabul's Khwaja Rawash International Airport,
whose international code, OAKB, I knew by heart from flight
plans of numerous CIA planes. My friend A. C. Thompson was
sitting next to me in the coach cabin on a six-hour flight from
Amsterdam to Dubai. Thompson is an old friend from the East
Bay punk rock scene who went on to become an award-winning
journalist. He speaks in thick street slang he picked up covering
the criminal justice beat for a handful of local papers. He doesn't
look a whole lot different from some of the folks he writes about:
He's covered with tattoos and his arms and shoulders are bruised
and battered from his other passion, training to be an ultimate
fighter. Our KLM flight was filled with American defense con-

tractors eventually bound for Baghdad and Afghanistan, along with workers bound for Middle Eastern oil fields.

As we crossed over into the Middle East, the airplane icon on the in-flight screen veered east over Turkey and curved far out of its direct path, steering clear of Iraq. The route arced over Iran before touching down well past midnight in the Gulf kingdom. From there, it was a cab ride through sauna-like heat and humidity to a spartan terminal on the airport's far side. On the way to the Ariana Afghan Airlines building, my Pakistani driver worriedly asked whether the United States plans to attack Iran.

Two distinct types of people filled the waiting area for the flight to Kabul: full-bearded Afghan men wearing traditional clothes and hats, and an equally large contingent of mostly overweight Americans wearing the shorts, T-shirts, and fanny packs that seem de rigueur for Americans overseas.

Smartly dressed "team leaders" in khakis and polo shirts rounded up the motley crew of American contractors like counselors at a summer camp, the men and women who serve the food, pump the gas, manage the books, indeed do just about everything at Bagram, the main military air base north of Kabul. They had their own charter plane.

Identification cards dangling from their necks said who they were: These men and women worked for Kellogg Brown and Root, the giant engineering and construction firm that was a subsidiary of Halliburton until April 2007. KBR's name has long been synonymous with private military contracting. In the early 1990s, then–defense secretary Dick Cheney commissioned the company to undertake a classified $3.9 million study on how to privatize military logistics and support services. When the Clinton administration assumed office in 1993, Cheney became CEO of KBR's parent company. During the Clinton years, KBR built Camp Bondsteel in Kosovo under the Army Corps of Engineers' direction and took responsibility for the base's operation. Government contracts to KBR peaked in FY 2004, when the company received $7.5 billion, the vast majority coming from military logistics contracts. In FY 2007, the company received $4.2 billion in military contracts. KBR ran much of the logistics at Bagram Air Base in Afghanistan just north of Kabul.

KBR's charter plane from Dubai departed for Bagram an hour before our flight to Kabul. The group of men and women were bound for an oasis of American suburbanism on the Afghan plains: Bagram is an American superbase complete with movie screenings, a Burger King, and a post exchange (PX) offering soldiers and contractors everything from Doritos to iPods. At the base cafeterias, where KBR serves the food, calorie numbers are posted next to each dish. It's a not-too-subtle hint: American soldiers could actually gain weight eating too much cheesecake while serving in one of the war on terror's hearts of darkness. Across the street from Bagram's PX, a razor-wire fence marks the perimeter of one of the war on terror's most controversial sites, the Bagram prison, known on base as "the other Gitmo." But Thompson and I weren't on our way to Bagram.

Kabul International Airport is an entirely different affair: a boneyard of aluminum aircraft corpses left over from the American bombing and, before that, attacks by Gulbuddin Hekmatyar's faction in the post-Soviet, pre-Taliban civil wars that reduced much of the city to rubble. In the early days of the American-led invasion, frustrated American commanders complained that they couldn't bomb Afghanistan back to the Stone Age after 9/11 because it had already been done. Fluorescent lights flicker inside the airport, held together with duct tape; the X-ray machines are broken; the stepladder going up to the airplane is a gift from Japan; the bathroom is worth avoiding, to put it mildly. An overweight American sporting Oakley sunglasses, a shaved head, a bulletproof vest, and a black submachine gun keeps watch over the baggage claim.

Kabul's streets are a paradigm of informality. Everything is up for negotiation, from cab fares to traffic rules, or from the amount you pay little kids to show you how to avoid the lingering land mines on a hike through the hills to the *baksheesh* the customs man asks for to expedite your way through the airport. It's debatable whether one could call the ousted Taliban regime a state, but what followed certainly wasn't.

Violence, like the traffic rules, is another informal affair. Hotels, NGOs, and nouveau-riche opium barons in the hills near the InterContinental Hotel all claim their own private security forces. The for-hire gunslingers protecting Afghan president Hamid Karzai, known locally as the "mayor of Kabul," are employees of DynCorp, an American military contractor. At the Mustafa Hotel, the price of a room includes a man whose job it is to sit outside my room with an AK-47. Could he do anything for me, he asks in broken English.

"Can I have a towel?"

Outside in the streets, informality characterizes the built environment itself. Much of the city is an architecture of shipping containers. Around the corner from the Mustafa Hotel, across from the bus station, shipping containers act as storefronts. One sawdust-filled container acts as a furniture-making workshop. Another is a kebab restaurant. An Internet café is built into another. This is an architecture of flexibility and impermanence. A shipping container might host a business, a storage space, even a prison as the situation on the ground changes. In any case, the containers can be quickly and easily abandoned.

The contrasts between Kabul and the Northern Virginia home of much of the intelligence community couldn't be starker. In Tysons Corner, flush with classified dollars from a booming espionage industry, fashionable thirtysomething men and women cruise suburban Virginia in hybrid SUVs and Lexuses, spending weekends at boutiques and cafés, shopping malls, and multiplex

theaters. By contrast, Kabul's streets teem with thick-bearded tra-
ditionally garbed men passing time with their friends while
burka-clad women and children accost white-skinned foreigners
to beg for a few pennies. In the outskirts of suburban Virginia,
imperial estates of Saudi billionaires and old-world princes and
kings sit by the mansions of impossibly rich new-world CEOs and
aristocrats along the Potomac's banks. In the hills overlooking
Kabul, families live in mud-brick squalor with open latrines and
filthy children whose eyes and noses drool with easily cured but
untreated infections. Red-painted rocks warn of unexploded land
mines. And yet, the American and Afghan capitals' geographies
are profoundly interwoven. The war on terror justifies the escalat-
ing black budgets, the legions of contractors, the wiretappings
and waterboardings. Afghanistan and the United States are both
part of a "relational" geography. What happens in one place af-
fects the other. From Sunday morning news shows to the pages of
The New York Times, a cottage industry of pundits, academics,
and analysts dedicates itself to divining the future of Afghanistan.
I have a different question: How do facts on the ground in Afghanistan sculpt the future of the United States?

The Mustafa Hotel is the closest thing I've ever seen to the arche-
typal saloon in an old western movie. Home to one of the only
places serving alcohol in this deeply religious and conservative
culture, the hotel caters to the motley collection of mercenaries,
bounty hunters, undercover paramilitaries, and even shadier
characters who tend to congregate in war zones. Bullet holes riddle the second-floor dining room's marble walls and crusty ceiling: leftovers from more than one gunfight that's broken out
among the hard-drinking armed men who've called the Mustafa
home since the 2001 invasion. A twentysomething Afghan named
Abdullah managed the place. He wore a gold chain, slicked-back
hair, and kept a girlfriend in the back of the hotel (an astounding

transgression of Afghan culture). Asked whether the police were called after any of the gunfights, Abdullah looked at me as if I were insane.

Wais Faizi, dubbed "the Fonz of Kabul" by his American friends, ran the place. An Afghan-American from New Jersey who'd set up the hotel in late 2001, Wais struck me less like Fonzie than some kind of Afghan Samuel L. Jackson. He had a Glock permanently strapped under his arm and kept loads of vitamins on his desk (he was convinced that the Northern Alliance wanted to poison him). Wais spent the evenings watching *Scarface* over and over when he wasn't drinking with the hotel guests. One story held that he'd beaten up a man in Dubai when, after a drunken boast that Faizi was a "Pashtun Warrior," the man asked if that was a rock band.

The Mustafa hopped with action in the months after the war began. Packed to the gills with foreign correspondents, aid workers, daring backpackers, and an assorted collection of CIA officers, private security guards, and hacks, the hotel was the place to be for Thursday-night barbecues on the hotel roof. Visitors could kick back in pilot seats looted from old Soviet MiGs sipping the only "green grenades" (Heineken in a bottle) in town.

Those days were now over. In the West, the lingering war was all but forgotten, and the Thursday-night barbecues had migrated down from the roof and into the Mustafa's courtyard. The adventure of the initial invasion was gone. The mood was dogged and resigned. The Thursday-night parties were reduced to a handful of Americans sitting in metal chairs guzzling three-dollar Coronas without limes and listening to country music on a laptop.

All the Americans at the Mustafa Hotel were named Bob. At least, that's what they said their names were. A collection of mostly mustachioed white men in jeans and rumpled polo shirts, the Bobs were mostly friendly but had an edge that could come out in the blink of an eye. "You're not a journalist, are you?" barked one of the Bobs after we'd been drinking and chatting together for a while. I'd made the mistake of asking what he did for a living, who he worked for. I thought the question had come up naturally, but that question, maybe more than any other one, was a red flag. He'd paused for a moment before regaining his composure and broadly smiled. "The U.S. government."

I knew the Bobs from a previous life. As we sipped beers one Thursday night (Friday is the traditional Muslim holiday; whatever they did, the Bobs also had it off), the Bobs mentioned some of the other places they'd worked. These men spent their lives in the vicinity of major military installations, but not necessarily on them, places like Bad Aibling near Munich, Germany, or Misawa, Japan.

Growing up in the Air Force, I'd lived in Germany during the height of the Reagan administration. A lot of the other kids who went to the base high school had parents who were "civilians" working in things like "communication." I never thought this was unusual until my brother told me he'd gone with a civilian friend to drop his father off at work. The family car pulled up to a cornfield, the father disappeared into the field, and the family car drove away. We both agreed that was weird. My high school girlfriend's father was a civilian, not assigned to any specific base, who would answer all of our questions about his career in cryptic mumblings about "radar" and "communications." Another friend's father piloted C-130s and eventually confessed that his "supply plane" was actually stuffed with surveillance equipment. My teenage life was filled with Bobs. Coming to Kabul was, in this small way, like coming home.

The relational geography between Afghanistan and the United States began taking its contemporary form on September 17, 2001. That day, George Bush signed the new war on terror's birth certificate. Its contents are still secret.

In the hours after 9/11, it became clear to everyone in the Bush administration that there would be a war. "Any barriers in your way, they are gone," he told Defense Secretary Donald Rumsfeld. "I don't care what the international lawyers say, we are going to kick some ass." Someone—one agency or another—would be given extraordinary powers in the coming days. It was less clear who would be out front.

CIA director George Tenet envisioned his own agency acting as the sharp tip of the war's spear. Immediately after the attacks, he began frantically assembling a top-secret dossier: the CIA's proposal for what this war on terror might entail. Working together with CIA director of operations James Pavitt, Tenet sent cables to the CIA's regional stations around the world asking for "wish lists." What new powers would his operatives like to have? Tenet encouraged his agents to imagine "novel, untested ways" that the CIA might conduct overseas operations. The global covert action Tenet anticipated would "include paramilitary, logistical, and psychological warfare elements as well as classical espionage."

The weekend following the attacks the Bush administration's principal cabinet members met at Camp David. George Tenet, the director of central intelligence, handed out a packet entitled "Going to War"—the result of the agency's fast brainstorming and wish-listing. It called for a wide-ranging campaign of financial espionage, paramilitary operations, and surveillance. But "Going to War" contained much more.

Tenet's proposal was a vision of the future, a future in which the CIA would have "exceptional authorities," as he called them. New secret wars would begin across the world. Old ones would expand. Strict rules about congressional and executive oversight of covert operations would be a thing of the past. The agency would no longer have to get individual covert actions approved by the president. Age-old complaints about covert actions getting "lawyered to death" would now be gone. The CIA would be able to snatch people from around the world at will, and would now be able to kill.

The CIA director's vision saw new relationships and deeper collaborations with foreign intelligence services in Egypt, Jordan, and Algeria, whose cooperation the CIA would encourage with generous subsidies. There would be new covert relationships with regimes like Libya and Syria. Foreign intelligence services would serve as CIA proxies and force multipliers. At the same time, cooperation with states like Egypt and Morocco would help keep American fingerprints off the nastiest incidents that were bound to occur.

On Monday, September 17, the president announced that he intended to support every one of Tenet's requests for expanded power. Bush scrawled his name on Tenet's memorandum of notification.

The CIA, an agency designed to operate outside the law, was now free to pursue its vision of a new world, to create new geographies, and to keep that world's details far from the public record. The black world was supercharged with newfound life and purpose.

The CIA spearheaded the American invasion of Afghanistan. On September 26, veteran officer Gary Schroen led a team of operatives in an old Russian helicopter from Tashkent, Uzbekistan, over the Hindu Kush and into the Northern Alliance stronghold in the Panjshir Valley. Schroen's connections to the Northern Alliance went back to the days when he served as the CIA's Kabul station chief (posted in Pakistan) in the 1980s. As CIA station chief in Islamabad in the late 1990s, Schroen reestablished his connections to the mujahideen commanders to prepare for the upcoming campaign. Recalling the old British saying "You can't buy Afghan loyalty, but you can rent it," Schroen started handing out millions of dollars in fresh hundred-dollar bills to the U.S.'s prospective allies.

Within a few weeks, Schroen's team of CIA officers in northern Afghanistan was joined by Special Forces "A-Teams" from Task Force Dagger, based at Karshi-Khanabad ("K2") Air Base in Uzbekistan. One of the Special Forces soldiers' primary missions was to "paint" Taliban positions with SOFLAM (Special Operations Forces laser marker) target designators, which Air Force bombers used to guide their "smart bombs." The vast majority of the boots on the ground, however, did not come from American infantry divisions or joint Special Forces units, but from mujahideen commanders holed up in the northern regions of Afghanistan that the Taliban had failed to take.

The Northern Alliance was a loose federation of northern warlords and former mujahideen who had fought the Soviets in the 1980s and banded together out of necessity when the Taliban came to power in the mid-1990s. Their leader had been Ahmad Shah Masood, the "Lion of Panjshir," who led the dominant Tajik faction of the alliance from his base in the Panjshir Valley. After Masood's September 9, 2001, assassination by al-Qaeda operatives posing as journalists, a trio of Masood's deputies, including Mohammad Qasim Fahim Khan, Yunus Qanooni, and Abdullah Abdullah (Dr. Abdullah), took over the alliance leadership.

Other major Northern Alliance commanders included Ismail Khan, the Iranian-supported leader of Heart province, and General Abdul Rashid Dostum, an Uzbek warlord with a reputation for brutality. One story holds that when Dostum caught one of his soldiers stealing, he had the man bound to a tank tread, then drove the tank around, grinding the soldier into a bloody mass of meat. Another Northern Alliance commander was Abdul Rasul Sayyaf, a friend of Osama bin Laden from the anti-Soviet war in the 1980s. In 1985, Sayyaf started Dawa'a al-Jihad, a university in an Afghan refugee camp near Peshawar with a reputation for training terrorists. Its alumni include Ramzi Yousef, who led the first World Trade Center bombing in 1993. Sayyaf was also a mentor to Khalid Sheikh Mohammed, the alleged mastermind behind the 9/11 "planes operation." The two "journalists" who'd assassinated Masood had been able to gain the commander's audience with a recommendation from Sayyaf. When Schroen met with Sayyaf in preparation for the war, he handed the commander a $100,000 brick of cash.

As American teams of Special Forces, CIA officers, and Northern Alliance commanders and foot soldiers marched south with American B-52s, B-2s, fighters, and cruise missiles overhead, the ad hoc federation of fighters began taking prisoners. The immediate question was what to do with them. The answer was shipping containers: "low-value" prisoners went into shipping containers controlled by Northern Alliance warlords for transport to a prison in the northern city of Sheberghan; "high-value" prisoners went to the CIA, who put them in a collection of shipping containers surrounded with barbed wire at the recently captured Bagram Air Base for interrogation. Back in Washington, decisions about the fate of those battlefield prisoners would begin a radical transformation of American political institutions and culture.

At the Justice Department's Office of Legal Counsel, lawyers working with Dick Cheney's counselor David Addington discussed several interrelated questions about how to conduct this new secret war: What legal status (if any) would prisoners in the war on terror occupy? Where would they be held? How would they be held and interrogated? Whose jurisdiction would they fall under?

Alberto Gonzales, John Yoo, and Jay Bybee, accompanied by Addington, began outlining what they would call a "new kind of war" and a "new paradigm." They concocted new legal definitions carefully crafted to circumvent existing laws, institutions, and international norms. Chief among these new legal entities was the "unlawful enemy combatant." Gonzales opined that the Geneva Conventions would be little more than a "quaint" relic from a by-gone era. In effect, the White House was institutionalizing the Afghan battlefield's informality. The ad hoc extralegal structure they outlined closely resembled the CIA's newly found "extraordinary powers."

For the Bush administration lawyers working on these issues, the questions were not only about policy but about geography. *Where* would this "new paradigm" be exercised? Creating new spaces in (or outside, as it were) of the law, was also a spatial question: If you want to create a space beyond the purview of national and international legal institutions, and if a nation's soil imparts certain rights upon anyone standing on it, then this question of geography becomes paramount. It was a new version of the black world's original contradiction: how to create a "nowhere" when even nowhere must exist somewhere?

The White House devised three solutions.

The first was Guantánamo Bay, a space that fit the paradoxical requirement of being beyond the purview of the U.S. federal court system (it was, strictly speaking, not a part of the United States) but nevertheless under the control of the United States. In a no-man's-land like Guantánamo, the White House insisted it could suspend some laws while enforcing others, all without the oversight of the other branches of government. Justice Department memos note that the island prison would be a place where the Bush administration could "detain and try suspects 'for violation of the laws of war and other applicable laws' " while simultaneously suspending " 'the principles of law and rules of evidence generally recognized in the trial of criminal cases in the United States district courts.' " But Guantánamo Bay was only one solution to this problematic intersection of legality and geography. Bizarre as it may sound, Guantánamo was the closest thing to a white version of the war on terror's prison geography.

A second solution to the White House's geography problem came in the form of the rendition program—terror suspects kidnapped by teams of CIA officers and contractors who would bring them and other prisoners to third-party countries like Egypt, Syria, and Morocco, where local intelligence services (which were substantially funded by the CIA) could hold them in relative secrecy.

The third solution was the black sites.

From the beginning, Guantánamo Bay made the CIA nervous. The facility would be run by the Department of Defense, a potential political rival. Furthermore, there were too many competing agencies, too many different agendas at Guantánamo. Finally, Guantánamo was out in the open—no doubt journalists and human rights advocates would soon be demanding access. Federal courts might try to exert influence over the prisons. For the CIA, Guantánamo Bay was a "goat fuck," the last place the CIA wanted to keep its high-value prisoners.

A CIA black site program could meet the same extralegal requirements that the Justice Department laid out when they picked Guantánamo Bay, but they'd have an added element: Their very existence would be secret. In late 2001, the CIA built the first black site outside Kabul, the Salt Pit. With brick laid, the black world was constructing more than an unacknowledged outpost for ghost prisoners and "disappeared" people. It was building a new economic, social, and legal infrastructure within the American state. Facts on the ground a short drive from the Kabul airport would sculpt the United States' future.

16

Screaming Their Heads Off
In the Dark, Around the World

As A. C. Thompson; Maiwand, our aged Afghan taxi driver; and I drove past the Salt Pit, we could see that this once-isolated and nondescript outpost had grown dramatically. A brick fence topped with barbed wire surrounded a sprawling compound the size of a gated community in the American suburbs. Black SUVs with tinted windows patrolled the complex's perimeter, and a Humvee kept watch near an entrance gate. The old brick factory that had housed the first black site looked worn and crumbled, but newer buildings had been erected all around it. If the Salt Pit began as an informal and ad hoc solution to a battlefield prisoner problem, it was now an institution, as permanent-seeming as the National Counterterrorism Center's manicured campus near Tysons Corner.

By the time we arrived, this had become an international destination. Rendition victims from all over the world had been brought there. Majid Khan, captured by a CIA rendition team in Pakistan in March 2003, was held at the prison. Laid Saidi, an Algerian man kidnapped from Tanzania, spent time there. American interrogators told Saidi that he was in a place that was "out of the world," and said, "No one knows where you are, no one is going to defend you." After sixteen months of brutal interrogations, the CIA decided Saidi was a nobody. They delivered him to Algerian intelligence officials, who promptly concurred. The Algerians then gave Saidi some money and left him at a bus stop in Algiers. When the CIA kidnapped Khaled El-Masri from Skopje, Macedonia, in early 2004, he spent months at the Salt Pit before the CIA realized that he too was a nobody. They dumped him off on a rural roadside in Albania.

The former prisoners give similar accounts of what it was like inside the black site. El-Masri described a cell where filthy, worn clothes topped with a thin military blanket served as a bed. The drinking water was a plastic bottle filled with greenish-brown liquid. The walls were scratched with verses from the Koran, aphorisms, and dates in Arabic, Farsi, and Urdu. Masked men in black uniforms served as interrogators. One of the interrogators, who spoke Arabic with a south Lebanese accent, summed up El-Masri's fate with a telling sentence, whose verisimilitude extended far beyond the walls of the secret prison: El-Masri, said the man, "was in Afghanistan, where there are no laws . . . 'We can do with you whatever we want.' "

By the time El-Masri and Saidi arrived in Afghanistan, the world's attention had turned to Iraq. Afghanistan had become the forgotten war. The only people left in-country were a shady collection of Bobs. Afghanistan had, in other words, become a perfect place for blank spots on maps. With the world's attention diverted, the black sites proliferated in Afghanistan.

First was the Salt Pit, and then came the "Dark Prison," the "Prison of Darkness," the "Disco Prison." Saidi had spent time there before being transferred to the Salt Pit. Binyam Mohammed al Habashi also spent time there. Binyam Mohammed was first captured in Karachi, Pakistan, trying to travel on a false passport, then brought to Morocco, where he was tortured for eighteen months before the CIA arrived to bring him to Afghanistan. On January 21, 2004, a Boeing Business Jet arrived in Rabat, Morocco (the same 737 from the Desert Rock Airstrip that we encountered in chapter 1). He arrived in the country within days of El-Masri.

As he recounted in his diary, which his British lawyer Clive Stafford Smith provided to me,

There was a hall with rooms apart from each other. I am guessing there were about 20 rooms. I was told special people were housed in it, and I was "special" which is why I was being taken there. I later found out that these special people were people like Abdulsalam Hiera, the Yemeni businessman from Sana'a, and Dr. Gairat Bahir, the former Ambassador of Afghanistan.

They knocked my head against a wall a few times until I could feel blood, then I was thrown into a cell. It was cell number 16 or 17, the second or third last room from the shower room. The room was about 2m by 2.5m. The cell had a heavy metal door, all solid, then a second door with bars. There were speakers near the ceilings at both ends of the room. There was a watching hole low down on one wall. There was a hanging pole for people left there in a kneeling position. There was a bucket in the corner for a toilet. . . .

It was pitch black, and no lights on in the rooms for most of the time. They used to turn the light on for a few hours, but that only made it worse when they turned it back off. . . .

They hung me up. I was allowed a few hours of sleep on the second day, then hung up again, this time for two days.

My legs had swollen. My wrists and hands had gone numb. I got food only once all this time. After a while I felt pretty much dead. I didn't feel I existed at all. . . .

Then I was taken off the wall and left in the dark. There was loud music, Slim Shady and Dr. Dre for 20 days. I heard this non-stop over and over, I memorized the music, all of it, when they changed the sounds to horrible ghost laughter and Halloween sounds. It got really spooky in this black hole. . . .

Accounts from other prisoners, like Jamil el-Banna and Hassan bin Attash, provided consistent descriptions of the Dark Prison: They spoke of a darkness so thick they couldn't see their hands in front of their faces; Eminem's *Slim Shady* album and other kinds of abrasive music and sounds blasted twenty-four hours a day; interrogations were held under strobe lights; prisoners were hung for extended periods of time from bars across their cell's ceiling. Bisher Al Rawi, held in the Dark Prison beginning in December of 2002, described "some sort of satanic worship music" on constant rotation, impenetrable darkness, and the unsettling sight of masked guards periodically moving through the corridors with dim flashlights. "Plenty lost their minds," recounted Binyam Mohammed. "I could hear people knocking their heads against the walls and the doors, screaming their heads off. . . ."

"We can't comment on the subject of unacknowledged detentions," said Reto Stocker, the Swiss head of the Afghan Delegation of the International Committee of the Red Cross at their compound in the Shar-i-Naw section of Kabul. Our visit was unannounced, but after a few phone calls, the guards outside the Red Cross compound ushered us to an office in the back. Stocker said that he'd been expecting us. Strange . . . I imagined that in a small town like Kabul, word gets around pretty quickly when someone shows up asking about secret prisons.

Stocker wouldn't budge on the question of black sites. Asked about the work NGOs like Human Rights Watch had done on the subject, Stocker replied, "They're much more outspoken on the subject." I knew that the Red Cross isn't supposed to talk about the work they do. The reports they issue aren't meant for public consumption—the Red Cross is supposed to discreetly visit prisoners and submit reports only to host governments. In the case of prisoners held by the United States in the war on terror, that would be the executive branch. The point of the Red Cross's discreet approach is to ensure that the organization remains neutral in a given conflict and doesn't jeopardize its access to prisoners by publicly embarrassing governments. The Red Cross's system rarely breaks down, but a notable exception was Abu Ghraib. A Red Cross report on the prison leaked to *The Wall Street Journal* showed that the abuses at the prison had been documented by the aid agency (and promptly ignored by the Pentagon) long before the internal Army investigations into the prison began. Nonetheless, the Red Cross relies on secrecy as much as the CIA does. It might be called a Faustian bargain, but it's easy to understand the logic.

As our conversation spindled around the subject of black sites, Stocker talked about the work the Red Cross was doing in Afghanistan, visiting prisoners at Bagram's "other Gitmo" and at makeshift prisons on American FOBs (forward operating bases) in places like Gardez. Stocker had just come back from a visit with Jack Idema at the Pul-e-Charki prison outside Kabul. Asked about Idema, Stocker said that talking to Idema was like "talking to someone from Mars." Our conversation continued dancing around the subject of black sites. I finally got frustrated and threw my hands up: "I feel like you're implying the Red Cross knows a lot about this, and at the same time you won't talk about it! You're really confusing me!" Stocker's response was calm yet firm: "It's not my intention to make any of this clear to you."

As we got up to leave, Stocker's tone changed ever so slightly. "You know," he said, "we are interested in the same things. If you find out anything about this, we would like to know about it." I pointed down the street. Two blocks away, some kind of American outfit had walled off a city block with concrete blast walls, sandbags, and Nepalese Gurkha guards perched in a makeshift plywood tower pointing M-16s down the alley. Several journalists Thompson and I talked to had mentioned the site, recounting rumors that it might be one of the places where rendition victims wound up. Nobody seemed to know who ran the place. When Thompson and I approached the compound's blast walls, four layers of security—Afghans, Gurkhas, Bosnians, and finally an American—all declined to say who they were or what the installation was. "I heard that foreign prisoners had been held at that place," I said. Stocker nodded, acknowledging only what I'd said. He still wasn't giving anything up.

Back at the Mustafa Hotel, the Bobs and I had gotten off to an awkward start, but I started making friends with them after consciously steering conversations clear of anything remotely sensitive, like their names. I joined the Bobs each morning for a breakfast of flat bread, butter, and jam. We took to chatting.

One of the Bobs was different than the others. A fortyish African-American man who wore smart casual clothes, he stayed away from the nightly drinking that the other men in his crew took part in. He looked less jaded than the others, more resigned, less boisterous. One morning as we sat eating breakfast together, he confessed that he hated being in Afghanistan. He missed his wife and daughter back in the States but was now on his third rotation because it was the only way he saw to get ahead financially. With the earnings from his first and second stints in-country, he'd been able to save enough for a down payment on a house for his wife and himself. Another eight months and he'd be able to help put his daughter through college.

After a few days, some of the spookier Bobs started inviting me to drink with them in the hotel's back rooms when they had some downtime. At some point, I realized that my being a writer didn't upset them for the reasons I'd suspected. The Bobs weren't worried about me spilling whatever inconsequential secrets they might let slip. Journalist Peter Bergen had been through the Mustafa the previous year, working on a story for *Rolling Stone*. Setting the scene for his piece, Bergen casually mentioned that the Mustafa had an in-house massage parlor stocked with giggling young Thai women. There'd been hell to pay when the Bobs' wives back home had learned about it. As far as I could tell, the massage parlor was no more.

Over beers with one of the Bobs at the Mustafa one night, I mentioned what Stocker had said about Jack Idema. The Bob paused. "He wasn't such a bad guy," he finally said, in the kind of tone you might have if your brother had been sent to prison for armed robbery, but you thought he was a decent guy who got a bum deal. Before he was locked up in the Pul-e-Charki prison outside Kabul, Idema had been the king of the Mustafa scene. He even had a cocktail named after him in the hotel bar: the Tora Bora. The Bobs all knew him: They'd been part of the same gang.

Idema might have been a Bob once, but he went beyond that role. His story is filled with conflicting loyalties, secrecy, and violence. If Afghanistan and the United States affect one another through relational geographies of informality, secrecy, and violence, then Idema's story is an account of its logical outcome.

Jack Idema's military career began when he was a Special Forces operative in the late 1970s and early 1980s. The rest of the story gets obscure. Idema claims that, after being discharged from the Army in 1984, he signed on as a military adviser in El Salvador and Honduras as part of a black Special Mission unit. This claim is hard to verify: as Idema told Peter Bergen, the only record of this service is in files that the Army "[doesn't] want to give anyone." Idema also spent time in Haiti and Thailand training local forces. Back in his home of New York State, Idema was a partner in a counterterrorism training school called the Counter Group.

During this same time, Idema's police record started growing: There was a 1982 charge of possessing stolen property, a 1986 charge for resisting arrest and assault, a 1988 arrest for disorderly conduct, and a 1990 arrest for assault involving a firearm. Idema spent 1994 through 1997 in federal prison on more than fifty counts of wire fraud. According to Idema's version of the story, the charges stemmed from a Clinton administration conspiracy against him. Idema claims that in the early 1990s, he traveled to Lithuania to follow the trail of the illegal arms trade coming out of the former Soviet Union. According to Idema, he discovered in Lithuania a black market in tactical nuclear weapons, so-called "suitcase nukes." Idema says that he brought this information to the FBI, who asked for his sources. Believing the FBI to be penetrated by Russian moles, Idema refused, setting off a "shit storm of biblical proportions" that eventually led to the FBI investigation. But the record contradicts Idema: The FBI began their investigation a full year before Idema went to Lithuania.

Idema made up his mind to go to Afghanistan after 9/11, encouraged by the multimillion-dollar bounties on al-Qaeda and Taliban heads. With a documentary team from *National Geographic* in tow, Idema slipped into Afghanistan via Uzbekistan and Tajikistan in October 2001 and quickly joined up with Northern Alliance forces on the invasion's front lines.

When the initial battles for Afghanistan finished in early 2002, Idema settled into the Wild West life of post-invasion Afghanistan. Spooks were everywhere: undercover CIA officers, black Special Forces units, and hosts of "advisers" and "communications" people, many of whom camped out at the Mustafa Hotel.

Idema fit the profile to a T: by day, strapped with pistols and machine guns, he cruised the capital in an SUV wearing wraparound shades and a desert camo uniform that looked almost, but not exactly, like American military garb. By night, Idema held court at the Mustafa, where, unlike the other shady types living in the war on terror's dark corners, he was more than happy to regale his drinking buddies with outlandish tales of his past and present exploits.

Idema set up his own one-man war-on-terror operation, an ad hoc group composed of a few American bounty hunters and Afghan fighters. Edward Caraballo, an award-winning documentary cameraman, followed the group, recording their exploits. Echoing the code names of American Special Forces teams operating in Afghanistan, Idema called his crew Task Force Saber 7.

From time to time, Idema would disappear from the Mustafa with truckloads of machine guns, RPGs, radios, body armor, knee pads, and everything else one would need for scattershot paramilitary operations. "Top-secret mission," he'd tell the Mustafa crowd if they asked where he'd been. "We're closing in on the last terrorists," he'd whisper cryptically. Idema told the crowd that he was reporting directly to Donald Rumsfeld's office at the Pentagon for these "top-secret" missions, and in the post-invasion climate of Kabul, it seemed plausible. The only thing that didn't make sense was Idema's willingness to talk about himself. Soldiers assigned to black units outside normal chains of command aren't known to brag about their exploits to outsiders.

On July 5, 2004, Idema's world imploded. Days before, Idema had made an egregious political mistake when his Task Force Saber 7 raided the house of Afghan Supreme Court justice Maulawi Siddiqullah, who Idema believed was plotting an assassination attempt on Yunus Qanooni, the Northern Alliance commander serving as Afghanistan's education minister. In a dawn raid, Idema grabbed the Supreme Court justice and one of his brothers.

A group of German soldiers in an overhead helicopter provided backup. A few days later, Afghan police arrested Idema and the other members of his outfit. Afghan authorities found a private prison built into Idema's home. On the wall were two clocks, one showing local time in Afghanistan, the other showing the time in Fort Bragg, home of the Army's Special Forces community. A piece of paper tacked to Idema's wall was labeled "missions to complete." Number two was "Karzai"; number four, "pick up laundry."

Idema's trial took place only months after the publication of photos from Abu Ghraib. Idema's former prisoners described being scalded with hot water, dunked in ice water, kicked and beaten, chained upside down by their ankles, and hooded for days at a time. Idema admitted to running a private prison in Kabul but insisted that the men he'd captured were terrorists and that he'd used only standard interrogation techniques on them. Idema faced five charges before the Afghan court: taking hostages, having a private jail, torture, robbery of vehicles, and entering the country without a visa. He was looking at twenty years in an Afghan prison.

The story of Jack Idema gets as muddled and twisted as the American occupation of Afghanistan itself. When reporters showed up for the trial, Idema confidently claimed that "we were working for the U.S. anti-terrorism group. We were working with the Pentagon and some other federal agencies. We were in direct contact with Rumsfeld's office five times a day, every day." A spokesperson for the Defense Department said it wasn't true: "This group of American citizens does not represent the American government and we do not employ or sponsor them."

But as the trial proceeded, Idema and his lawyers started producing a stream of documents strongly suggesting that, while he may have not been in the direct employ of the Pentagon, they certainly knew what he was up to. At best, the Pentagon had indirectly authorized his activities. At worst, they let Idema's task force go about their "missions" with a wink and a nod. First, the Pentagon admitted that it accepted a prisoner at Bagram whom Idema handed over, saying that the man was a high-level Taliban intelligence official. Moreover, Idema's lawyer played a tape of Idema speaking to the office of Lieutenant General William G. Boykin, a former Delta Force commander serving as the undersecretary of defense for intelligence. Boykin had made headlines after suggesting, in uniform, that the war on terror was a struggle between the "Christian nation" of the United States and the satanic forces of Islam. In one of the tapes, a Boykin aide says, "We passed all your information to the J2 [intelligence] staff here and to DIA [the Defense Intelligence Agency]. And we were trying to protect our boss [Boykin] from getting associated with it, because he doesn't need any other scrutiny right now by the press." In another, an aide says, "I told General Boykin you called. I gave him the information." Although Idema could prove no written authorization for his activities, it was clear that some of the highest-ranking officials in the Pentagon knew what he was up to.

Idema's relationship with officials in the Afghan government, a patchwork of warlords, tribal interests, Northern Alliance commanders, and outright crooks without any discernible shared interests, did not fit the traditional role of mercenary. With the government so divided by factions, sometimes he seemed to be working against it, sometimes for it. At the trial, Idema's lawyer showed a tape in which Yunus Qanooni thanks Idema for thwarting the assassination attempt against him and offering the help of the Afghan government in Idema's private counterterrorism efforts. The trial's presiding judge, Abdel Basit Bakhtiari, echoed Qanooni's words when he declared in public, "You have saved the life of Minister Qanooni, and the people you have arrested were terrorists and Al Qaeda." Still, Idema was an outlaw so far as the governments of the United States and Afghanistan were officially concerned. In another age he might have been called a pirate.

When Idema entered Afghanistan, he cast his lot in with the Northern Alliance. After the fall of Kabul and the ousting of the Taliban, the old warlords from around the country—including the Northern Alliance commanders—jockeyed for influence. In their various designs for power, the warlords were inconsistently supported by the Americans. This exacerbated the instability. Afghanistan's central government became little more than a vehicle for the warlords, who'd assumed key positions, to usurp public money and channel foreign aid to their own private power bases. The old commanders raised thousands of private armies throughout post-Taliban Afghanistan, splintering the state into a thousand pieces.

Jack Idema's Task Force Saber 7 fit into the emerging post-Taliban feudal system. Idema was fighting state-identified terrorists. On several occasions, Idema called on ISAF (the NATO-led force, entirely separate from the U.S. military) bomb disposal squads to assist at houses he'd raided. The ISAF units, unable to tell the difference between Idema's squad and the American Special Forces presence more generally, found traces of explosives and suspicious electrical equipment at the locations Idema raided. Idema's outfit was really not that different from the other informal militias occupying the country: Task Force Saber 7 shared much with the warlords' private armies, the legions of private military contractors like DynCorp, Blackwater, and Triple Canopy, and the CIA and Special Forces paramilitaries themselves, who, like the others, weren't about to tell anyone who they were or what they were doing.

Idema's Task Force Saber 7 was just another private army (admittedly smaller) like those of the warlords; all thrived on the infusion of American dollars. The court eventually acquitted four Afghans caught with Idema after it turned out they were members of the Afghan army. And even as Idema sat in prison, the judge who'd sentenced him empathized with the rogue bounty hunter: "I'd like to be like Jack, because he is a very brave man," Bakhtiari told *The Times Online*. "I understand he had fought terrorism and I'm sorry he has been arrested. I feel the government of Afghanistan could have done more with him."

Jack Idema was reporting to Boykin's office at Rumsfeld's Pentagon. Just as the CIA was going through dramatic changes in its structure, managing everything from its new "expanded powers" to the legions of green-badgers it had brought on as private contractors, the Pentagon was also going through a huge change in the structure of its forces.

Humiliated by the Pentagon's inability to quickly deploy to Afghanistan immediately after 9/11 (leaving the CIA to take the lead role in the initial phases of the war), the defense secretary wanted a "leaner," more "agile" military. A key part of Rumsfeld's transformation was vastly expanding the size, scope, and powers of the Special Forces community. He'd requested a 35 percent budget increase for the Special Operations Command (SOCOM) between fiscal year 2003 and 2004, and changed SOCOM from being a "supporting command" to a "supported command": SOCOM went from being charged with supporting other combat commands' missions to being able to develop and implement missions on its own initiative. The change also removed a layer of bureaucracy between SOCOM and the secretary of defense: SOCOM would report directly to Rumsfeld rather than regional commanders.

In March 2004, Donald Rumsfeld won a bureaucratic turf battle over who would lead the war on terror, which had at that point been spearheaded by the CIA. The result was the 2004 Unified Command Plan, which designated the Special Operations Command as the "lead combatant commander for planning, synchronizing, and as directed, executing global operations" in the war on terror. In October 2004, SOCOM got even more power: An amendment to the defense authorization bill granted Special Forces the ability to recruit foreign paramilitaries, pay money to intelligence sources, and procure equipment and weapons from foreigners, powers only the CIA had previously held. In January 2006, the Joint Special Operations Command (which controls the black units) went from being a position for a two-star general to being a position for a three-star general.

Like the Justice Department's creation of "unlawful combatants" and the CIA's black site program, the newfound leadership role for the Special Forces community further removed the war on terror from democratic oversight and expanded the "we can do whatever we want" ethos of the black site program.

Unlike the CIA, the military doesn't do covert operations. The military does "clandestine" operations. On paper, the distinction is supposed to be the following: defined by law, "covert" actions are designed "to influence political, economic, or military conditions abroad, where it is intended that the role of the United States Government will not be apparent or acknowledged publicly." In other words, covert operations are operations whose sponsors are secret; the operation itself may be secret (such as bugging a foreign embassy) or out in the open (a propaganda campaign). In contrast, "clandestine" operations' details might be secret, but the existence of the operations wouldn't be denied after the fact (a hostage rescue, for example).

But there's another, more poignant, difference between the two: Covert actions require presidential findings before the action, and they have to be reported to Congress (a legacy of the Church and Pike hearings in the 1970s). Clandestine actions don't. The legislation dates back to Iran-Contra.

After the Iran-Contra scandal, Congress realized that they hadn't anticipated the possibility of covert actions being conducted outside the intelligence community, which the 1974 Hughes-Ryan Amendment applied to. In the Intelligence Authorization Act of 1991, Congress tried to plug this loophole by making the covert action reporting requirements apply to "any department, agency, or entity of the United States Government," including the military. There was, however, a significant exception built into the law: "Traditional . . . military activities or routine support to such activities" were exempted from the requirement. The conference committee report attached to the law describes "traditional" activities as including operations in "anticipation" of a military campaign. If a team of Navy SEALs, for example, infiltrated a country in order to disable its antiaircraft weapons in anticipation of a U.S.-led invasion, the mission wouldn't meet the requirements of a covert action. There's the rub: What does "anticipated" mean? Defense Department officials have left open the possibility that "anticipated" could mean "years in advance."

As the war on terror dragged on, the informal geography of the Afghan battlefield spread. Black sites, whose origins went back to a collection of shipping containers at Bagram, proliferated. The Salt Pit came first, then a black site in Thailand. Then the Dark Prison in Afghanistan, then sites in Poland and Romania. When the Eastern European sites closed in late 2005 after Human Rights Watch published their locations, the CIA created other black sites in locations that remain secret.

The black site prison program—off-the-books detention centers housing "ghost" prisoners outside the Geneva Conventions and outside the purview of the Red Cross—went far beyond its battlefield origins. It spread to other parts of the intelligence community and military. At Camp Nama in Iraq's Baghdad International Airport, a JSOC/CIA unit called Task Force 6-26 created a black site where Special Forces operatives abused ghost prisoners in a former Saddam Hussein torture chamber they called the

Black Room. A sign at the camp read NO BLOOD, NO FOUL, a reference to an adage military units stationed there had developed: "If you don't make them bleed, they can't prosecute for it." The Black Room was often the first place that a prisoner eventually bound for Abu Ghraib would be taken.

But the black sites were far more than a geography of secret places, unmarked airplanes, ever-changing code names, and undisclosed locations. They set a chain of events in motion: to keep the "aggressive interrogations" continuing, the Bush administration abandoned the Geneva Conventions; to keep the rendition flights and the black sites out of court, the Justice Department made frequent use of the state secrets privilege. To "legalize" the torture techniques the CIA used against the prisoners in its secret program, the Bush administration produced the infamous August 2002 "torture memos."

When the torture techniques pioneered in the CIA black sites migrated to Guantánamo Bay and Iraq, and culminated with the photos from Abu Ghraib, Congress passed the McCain Amendment. After signing the bill into law, Bush looked into a camera and said that the new law would make it "clear to the world that this government does not torture." In reality, it was quite the opposite. White was black.

First, the bill provided CIA officers with a defense against being prosecuted for engaging in torture. Second, it allowed for the use of evidence obtained under torture against terror suspects at Guantánamo Bay. Third, it stripped Guantánamo prisoners of their right to make habeas corpus appeals in federal courts. And finally, when Bush signed the bill, he added a signing statement declaring that the law's provisions would be interpreted "in a manner consistent with the constitutional authority of the President to supervise the unitary executive branch and as Commander in Chief and consistent with the constitutional limitations on the judicial power." In other words, the executive branch of government was claiming the right to ignore the law if it wanted to. The signing statement was the polite, legalistic version of the doctrine Khaled El-Masri had heard in the Salt Pit: "We are in Afghanistan, we can do whatever we want." The difference was that this was out in the open; it had become the law.

Almost a year later, something dramatic happened. On September 6, 2006, the Bush administration made a startling announcement: Fourteen "high-value" terror suspects held incommunicado in the CIA's network of secret prisons were being transferred to Guantánamo Bay, including the likes of Khalid Sheikh Mohammed, Ramzi bin al-Shibh, and Abu Zubaida. It was the first public admission that black sites existed, although the president declined to go into details.

Was this the end of the extraordinary rendition program? The black sites? The torture? Was this announcement an acknowledgment that the United States had been in violation of international laws and conventions and was now back on the right side of the law? No. Instead, it was the most aggressive declaration of the Salt Pit doctrine to date. The U.S. republic's system of checking the power of the executive with the power of the Congress and judiciary was being directly attacked.

A few months before Bush's announcement, the Supreme Court ruled in the *Hamdan* decision that the military tribunals the Bush administration had sought to convene were illegal because they were at odds with both the Geneva Conventions and the Uniform Code of Military Justice. In Justice Breyer's concurring opinion with the majority decision, he wrote, "Congress has denied the President the legislative authority to create military commissions of the kind at issue here. Nothing prevents the President from returning to Congress to seek the authority he believes necessary." The executive needed congressional approval for its military commissions. Against the backdrop of a looming election, the executive decided to raise the stakes.

In early 2006, law professor Mark Denbeaux undertook a comprehensive study, relying entirely on declassified Department of Defense documents, to describe the population of prisoners held at the controversial prison. His conclusions were stunning: Denbeaux found that 92 percent of the 517 prisoners then at Guantánamo Bay had not been al-Qaeda fighters; of those men, 42 percent had no clear connection to al-Qaeda and 18 percent had no connection to either al-Qaeda or the Taliban. Moreover, 86 percent of the prisoners hadn't even been captured by Americans: They had been brought to the U.S. military by bounty hunters in Afghanistan and Pakistan who'd been wooed by military advertisements exhorting potential freelancers, "Get wealth and power beyond your dreams. . . . You can receive millions of dollars helping the anti-Taliban forces catch al-Qaeda and Taliban murderers. . . . This is enough money to take care of your family, your village, your tribe for the rest of your life."

Denbeaux showed that not all the people at Gitmo were the "worst of the worst." The vast majority seemed to be nobodies. Years earlier, a CIA analyst had reached the same conclusion. Unlike Denbeaux's work, the CIA report's inconvenient conclusions stayed secret.

When the Bush administration announced its transfer of the fourteen "high-value" suspects from the CIA's black sites to Guantánamo Bay, it added new urgency to the proposed Military Commissions Act. Khalid Sheikh Mohammed, Ramzi bin al-Shibh, and many of their cohorts were indeed the real thing: These men had no qualms about killing thousands of civilians to serve their twisted interests. Their transfer to Guantánamo Bay was a direct challenge to the legislature: "If you want to put Khalid Sheikh Mohammed on trial, you'll have to authorize the military commissions." Moreover, to put these men on trial, the legislature would have to retroactively "legalize" their disappearances, their incommunicado detention, the black sites, the waterboarding, and the other forms of torture they'd been subjected to. The evidence against this cadre was hopelessly tainted by the circumstances that they'd been held under: Putting Khalid Sheikh Mohammed on trial was only possible by using evidence gleaned through torture.

The executive seemed to prevail. With a looming election, no one in Congress wanted to appear "soft on terrorism." The Military Commissions Act passed the Senate by a vote of 65 to 34 and the House with 253 to 168 votes. On October 17, 2006, President Bush signed the bill into law. The black site policies, in effect, turned white.

Almost invariably, covert operations are illegal. That's why they're *covert* operations. It's rare for a president to acknowledge the existence, much less the contents, of a black program. And that was what made the Bush administration's announcement terrifying for some. It would be naïve to think that the CIA hadn't been in the business of torture for a long time, either explicitly, as was the case in Vietnam, or by proxy, as had been the case in Central America during the 1980s. But the American government had never explicitly claimed the right to disappear and torture people. The Salt Pit doctrine, "We can do whatever we want," had migrated from being the war on terror's deepest, darkest, most secret dungeon, formalizing informality to become the United States' official and openly acknowledged modus operandi.

Once again, the secret world won. Bringing the war on terror's black geography into the light did not make it disappear. Instead, the secret world sculpted the surrounding state in its own image. Torture was now "legal." The black sites stayed open. And once again, the border between the black and the white dissolved. Everything became gray. It was hard to tell where one world ended and the other began.

Epilogue

Back in Las Vegas, the day is passing. The late afternoon's soft sunlight casts long red shadows on the airport tarmac, and the atmosphere's hazy cocktail of heat, dust, and pollution lends a warm yellow cast to the landscape. The Janet planes, with their white airframes and red stripes, are coming home. One after another, the 737s taxi to their special terminal on the west side of the airport and slide into their parking places. A man pushes a rolling staircase up to the plane's door, and a stewardess inside pops open the exit door. The day is over; the workers are going home. I'm watching the scene from my eighteenth-floor hotel room from about a mile away through the eyepiece of my telescope.

One by one, workers file down the staircase, onto the asphalt, through a door-sized opening in the chain-link fence surrounding the terminal, and into the parking lot. Their faces are blurry from this distance, but I can get a sense of what they look like. An overweight man with an orange T-shirt and suspenders wearing a black baseball hat walks slowly, putting his full weight into each step as if it's been a long day on the job. A young, thin man walks with a spring in his step to match his age. He's wearing a black and white sports jersey, perhaps the away uniform of the Oakland Raiders, and carrying a backpack. A heavyset woman with a white blouse and a blue fanny pack looks like someone you'd see at Disneyland or Yosemite corralling a herd of laughing children on a long weekend. A group of three trim thirtysomething white men wearing baseball hats and carrying duffel bags over their shoulders walk through the gate and pause for a moment to talk to each other before walking off to their respective pickup trucks on the far ends of the enclosed parking lot.

More than any other, this is the image I've returned to as I've thought about the secret world. This scene of hopeless banality. Sit outside a Wal-Mart during a shift change, and the scene would be more or less the same: Ordinary people slogging home after a day on the job.

The black world has sculpted the United States in numerous ways. Creating secret geographies has meant erasing parts of the Constitution, creating blank spots in the law, institutionalizing dishonesty in the halls of government, handing sovereign powers—what used to be the unlimited power of monarchs over their subjects and territories—to the executive branch, making the nation's economy dependent upon military spending, and turning our own history into a state secret.

Since Congress passed the Central Intelligence Act of 1949, exempting the CIA from accounting for its expenditures, the black budget has expanded to fund a roughly $50 billion intelligence industry and significant parts of the military. The black budget

created a "new normal," institutionalized the notion that the public has no right to know how their government spends their money.
Culturally, this "new normal" has become so ingrained that many
people would be shocked to learn that the Constitution says quite
explicitly that the government has to account for every dime of
taxpayer money it spends. The "power of the purse," which James
Madison regarded as "the most complete and effectual weapon
with which any constitution can arm the immediate representatives of the people, for obtaining a redress of every grievance, and
for carrying into effect every just and salutary measure," was
meant to reside in Congress, the branch of government most in-
clined to represent the popular will. The rise of the black budget
means that Congress, and the public, isn't "read into" the federal
budget. Each year, Congress, in a very real sense, signs off on an
official lie.

The black world's historical geography shows that where black
budgets manifest into a space, informal violence becomes the
norm. Whether it's the Air Force setting trenches of hazardous
waste on fire at a black site in Nevada, or the CIA helping to assassinate a long line of inconvenient democratically elected leaders,
from Mossadegh, through Lumumba to Allende, the black world
creates a legal "nowhere" that nourishes the worst excesses of
power. Oliver North would equate secrecy with legality when he
testified that "we operated from the premise that everything we
did do was legal." "Those bastards can do whatever they want,"
Stella Kasza had spit when asked about her dead husband. A few
years later, an interrogator at a black site outside Kabul would tell
rendition victim Khaled El-Masri, "We are in Afghanistan, we
can do whatever we want."

Covert actions, secret programs, and unlawful yet state-
sponsored violence, once revealed, have not just gone away. To expose the black world is not enough. Blank spots on maps have
generated blank spots in the law. When the Air Force lied about

the death of Judith Palya Loether's father and the Supreme Court went along with the cover-up, the state secrets privilege made it possible for future administrations to keep their alleged crimes out of court by simply crying "national security." The subsequent case history of the state secrets privilege reads like an encyclopedia of state malfeasance and cover-ups.

When covert actions and classified programs become public, their revelation is often used to legitimize their profoundly troubling purposes, to sculpt the state in their own image. Revelations of secret prisons and torture over the long course of the war on terror gave rise to the McCain Amendment and the Military Commissions Act, which retroactively promised to "legalize" disappearances and torture. When revelations of domestic spying by the NSA came out in *The New York Times*, the Bush administration got Congress to rewrite the Foreign Intelligence Surveillance Act in order to legalize the clearly illegal program. In another example of how secret, illegal programs sculpted policy in their own image, the misdeeds of Iran-Contra became a blueprint for executive power in the twenty-first century, as Dick Cheney himself acknowledged one day to reporters on Air Force Two.

But the black world and the hidden budgets that sustain it have changed American society in other, more subtle ways. At this moment, approximately *four million* people in the United States hold security clearances to work on classified projects. By way of contrast, the federal government employs approximately 1.8 million civilians in the white world. Each of those security-cleared workers spends their paychecks on clothes, housing, groceries, trips to Disneyland, restaurants, and all of the other things that people spend money on. This secondary spending, in turn, creates more jobs, an effect that economists call a "multiplier."

The black world, then, is much more than an archipelago of secret bases. It is a secret *basis* underlying much of the American economy. The black world, in other words, means jobs. Lots of jobs. Jobs for heavyset men in orange T-shirts and suspenders, for women wearing fanny packs, and for the supermarkets and movie theaters where workers stop to spend money on their way home from the job.

Contemporary trends to outsource the war on terror also mean jobs. Among the streets of Northern Virginia, the designer boutiques and inflated housing prices speak to the amount of money going to intelligence community contractors. A May 2007 report by the Senate Select Committee on Intelligence estimated that "the average annual cost of a United States Government civilian employee is $126,500, while the average annual cost of a 'fully loaded' (including overhead) core contractor is $250,000. . . . Given this cost disparity," said the committee, "the committee believes that the Intelligence Community should strive in the long-term to reduce its dependence upon contractors." But this hasn't happened.

It's no secret that since the Second World War, military spending has primed the American economy, a phenomenon some economists call "military Keynesianism." Ben Rich, the former chief of Lockheed's secret airplane factory, the Skunk Works, once said that it was an "open secret in our business . . . that the government practiced a very obvious form of paternalistic socialism to make certain that its principal weapons suppliers stayed solvent and maintained a skilled workforce."

Dwight Eisenhower spoke to the costs of it all when he came to office in the early 1950s:

> Every gun that is made, every warship launched, every rocket fired signifies, in the final sense, a theft from those who hunger and are not fed, those who are cold and are not clothed.
>
> . . . We pay for a single destroyer with new homes that could have housed more than 8,000 people. . . . This is not a way of life at all, in any true sense.

Upon his retirement eight years later, Eisenhower famously spoke of a rising "military-industrial complex." But he did not speak about the power of a black world complex. The secret world would grow more slowly, incrementally. Its scale would be hidden, its programs unaccounted for, its legitimacy rarely questioned.

Finally, the rise of state secrecy has transformed our national history into another blank spot. In my conversations with satellite observer Ted Molczan, I was struck by the way that he, in the tradition of astronomers going back to Brahe, Copernicus, Galileo, Kepler, and Newton, was able to look up into the night sky with a pair of binoculars and deduce hidden knowledge from observable phenomena. Although Molczan's observations are a powerful symbol of insisting on empirical truths in the face of power, much knowledge, especially when it comes to human affairs, doesn't work that way.

Human affairs don't follow Newton's laws of motion or Einstein's accounts of relativity. Unlike our colleagues in the "hard" sciences, those of us who traffic in the social sciences ("social studies" is probably a more accurate description), whether we're geographers, sociologists, policy makers, pundits, or interested members of the public, encounter a world where people can be fickle, inconsistent, unpredictable, and wont to ignore or chronically disprove whatever "rules" and predictions social scientists concoct. In order to understand the "big questions"—who we are, where we've been, and where we're going—those of us who study human affairs have to rely on historical interpretation, political and economic analysis, and cultural studies. In contrast to our colleagues in the physical sciences, social scientists have to rely on stories, libraries, archives, and vaults of records. To understand ourselves, in other words, we need access to our own histories.

Now recall that study by Harvard's Peter Galison mentioned in chapter 1. In terms of numbers of pages, more of our own recent history is classified than is not. Again, he concluded that the "classified universe . . . is certainly not smaller, and very probably much larger than the unclassified one." The dark world is already growing at a rate of 250 million classified pages in secret archives a year. Our own history, in large part, has become a state secret.

History and geography, it seems to me, cannot be easily separated from one another. The environments we live and work in, from our secret prisons to our universities, are in a very real sense the present past. We live in and among the institutions and spaces that have been bequeathed to us by what came before. But geography is more than the sedimented spaces produced in the recent and distant past. Geography also sculpts the future. The spaces we create place possibilities and constraints on that which is yet to come, because the world of the future must, quite literally, be built upon the spaces we create in the present. To change the future, then, means changing the material space of the present.

I must confess that when I began this project, I was seduced by blank spots on maps, by the promise of hidden knowledge that they seemed to contain. It was easy to imagine that if I could just find one more code name, if I only knew what the HAVE PANTHER project was (someone said it was a "dirty cat to clean up after"), if I knew the location of the next-generation CIA black sites, or if I could learn about the "really fast" thing they had out at Groom Lake during the 1980s, somehow the world itself would change for the better. *Something*, undoubtedly, would happen if these secrets came out into the open. History shows that revelation and change can often work in tandem, but revelation, in and of itself, accomplishes little.

Some of the black world's deepest secrets have indeed come to light over the last few years. The CIA has been operating, and continues to operate, a network of secret extralegal prisons at unknown places around the world. It has destroyed videotapes documenting the torture of terror suspects in American custody.

Off-the-books military teams secretly fund Sunni jihadist groups descended from those that perpetrated the attacks on the World Trade Center. The NSA has been flouting the law to surveil countless numbers of Americans. No doubt, these are all stunning revelations.

It's easy to imagine that the antidote to state secrecy is more openness, more transparency in state affairs. That is, no doubt, a crucial part of a democratic project. But transparency, it seems to me, is a democratic society's precondition; transparency alone is insufficient to guarantee democracy.

Just as the secret state has grown by creating facts on the ground, then sculpting the world around them in an attempt to contain the ensuing contradictions, the secret state only recedes when other facts on the ground block its path, when people actively sculpt the geographies around them. Over the course of researching and writing this book, I've met numerous people both within and outside of the secret state who are trying to do just that. In figures like Judith Palya Loether, who tried to reverse the *Reynolds* precedent when she learned that it was based on a lie, Lee Tien, whose measured arguments assert that judges should "get to see the secret sauce 99 percent of the time," and Ted Molczan, who meticulously documents the other night sky, and the military lawyers at Guantánamo Bay who're actively resisting what they see as unjust military courts, I see people actively working to prevent the secret state from spreading even further. In their efforts, I see people practicing democracy.

NOTES

Prologue

1: "We need to find an old man" See Trevor A. C. Paglen and Thompson, *Torture Taxi: On the Trail of the CIA's Rendition Flights* (Hoboken: Melville House, 2006).

4: "Every year, the United States" This number is a relatively conservative estimate based on a $30 billion "black budget" and an acknowledged low-end intelligence budget of approximately $40 billion.

4: "Approximately *four million*" Peter Galison, "Removing Knowledge," *Critical Inquiry* 31 (Autumn 2004); available at http://criticalinquiry.uchicago.edu/features/artsstatements/arts.galison.htm (accessed 12/20/2007).

4: "1.8 million civilians in the 'white' world" U.S. Department of Labor statistics. At http://www.bls.gov/oco/cg/cgs041.htm (accessed 12/19/2007).

4: "A 2004 study" Galison, "Removing Knowledge."

Chapter 1

9: "California had embarked" For the California prison system, see Ruth Wilson Gilmore, *Golden Gulag* (Berkeley: University of California Press, 2007).

9: "At Pelican Bay" "Former Inmate at Pelican Bay Wins Judgment Against State," *San Francisco Chronicle*, March 1, 1994, A18; *Madrid v. Gomez*, 889 F.Supp 1146, 1167, 1283 (N.D. Cal. 1995).

9: "At Corcoran State Prison" See Tim Cornwell, "Staged fights, betting guards, gunfire and death for the gladiators," *Independent*, August 22, 1996, international edition.

12: "As it turns out" Information in this paragraph from Laurence Bergreen, *Over the Edge of the World: Magellan's Terrifying Circumnavigation of the Globe* (New York: HarperCollins, 2003), 53–54; and Miles Harvey, *The Islands of Lost Maps* (New York: Random House, 2000).

12: "The Portuguese controlled" Harvey, *Islands*, xiv.

14: "In an October 12, 2001, memo" See Government Accounting Office, "Freedom of Information Act: Agency Views on Changes Resulting from New Administration Policy," September 2003, GAO-03-981; and Coalition of Journalists for Open Government, "the Ashcroft Memo," available at http://www.cjog.net/background_the_ashcroft_memo.html (accessed 02/05/2008).

14: "A few months later" See John Mintz, "Interrogating Abu Zubaida: Fact? Fantasy? Manipulation? Al Qaeda Figure's Tips Have Led to Two Alerts," *Washington Post,* April 27, 2002, sec. A.

14: "By 2003, classified" Dan Morgan, "Classified Spending on the Rise; Report: Defense to Get $23.2 Billion," *Washington Post,* August 27, 2003, sec. A.

14: "Vice President Dick Cheney's" Elisabeth Bumiller, "White House Letter; Shrinking from View but Still Looming Large," *New York Times,* November 26, 2001, sec. B.

15: "These oft-quoted" Max Weber, *Economy and Society* (1922), in H. H. Gerth and C. Wright Mills, eds. and trans., *From Max Weber: Essays in Sociology* (New York: Oxford University Press, 1958), 233–34.

15: "it is about how the United States" This formulation echoes the ideas of political theorist Carl Schmitt and numerous others. See Carl Schmitt, *Political Theology,* trans. George Schwab (Chicago: University of Chicago Press, 2006).

16: " 'Geography,' my friend" These were some of Allan Pred's signature lines, culled from his research statement on the geography department's Web site.

Chapter 2

21: "Known as 'Big Sky Ranch' " For Big Sky Ranch, see Dwayne Day, "Vandenberg Air Force Base," U.S. Centennial of Flight Commission. Available at http://www.centennialofflight.gov/essay/SPACEFLIGHT/VAFB/SP47.htm (accessed 05/01/2008).

23: "The NRO is one of those" For the National Reconnaissance Office, see Philip Taubman, *Secret Empire* (New York: Simon & Schuster, 2003). See also Jeffrey Richelson, *The Wizards of Langley* (Cambridge: Westview Press, 2001).

23: "On the afternoon" For USA 193 and FIA, see Noah Shachtman, "Rogue Satellite's Rotten $10 Billion Legacy," *Wired* Danger Room blog, February 20, 2008. http://blog.wired.com/defense/2008/02/that-satellite.html.

23: "A month after the launch" See Andrea Shalal-Esa, "Expensive New U.S. Spy Satellite Not Working: Souces," Reuters, January 11, 2007.

24: "After its initial launch" Data from amateur observers.

24: "The shoot-down was necessary" "DoD Succeeds in Intercepting Non-Functioning Satellite," DoD Press Release no. 1039-09, February 20, 2008.

24: "The official explanation" See John Barry, "A Flash in the Night Sky," *Newsweek* online, February 20, 2008.

24: " 'The claim there was a danger' " Pike quoted in James Oberg, "Sense, nonsense, and pretense about the destruction of USA 193," *Space Review,* March 3, 2008.

24: "On February 21" "Success of Satellite Hit Confirmed," *Washington Times,* Feb. 26, 2008.

26: "On January 21, 1959" Taubman, *Secret Empire,* 287

27: "Another story" "KH-1," *Encyclopedia Astronautica.* Available at http://www.astronautix.com/craft/kh1.htm (accessed 05/01/2008).

27: "Eleven subsequent Discoverer" William Burrows, *Deep Black* (New York: Random House, 1986), 109–10.

27: "Discoverer 13" Ibid.

27: "When the CORONA" "The Origin and Evolution of the Corona System," in Duane Day, ed., *Eye in the Sky* (Washington: Smithsonian, 1998), 192.

28: "The 3,600 feet of film" Taubman, *Secret Empire,* 322.

Chapter 3

35: "EG&G's history" Phil Patton, *Dreamland* (New York: Villard, 1998), 250–51.

36: "From time to time" Independent researcher Gary Sellani has several documents related to EG&G Special Projects, including copies of employment ads, at http://www.lazygranch.com/egg.htm (accessed 01/21/2008).

37: "When it created" David Loomis, *Combat Zoning* (Reno: University of Nevada Press, 1993), 9–10.

38: "Just north of Mercury" When Lockheed announced the existence of Polecat at the Farnborough Air Show on July 19, 2006, the company declined to mention where the aircraft had been tested. Aviation and defense journalists assumed that the craft had been tested at Groom Lake, but when Lockheed released a video of the UAV in flight, it was clear that it had been tested somewhere else. By paying close attention to the background details of the video, it was possible to deduce that Polecat had actually been tested at a new site at Yucca Dry Lake. Recent satellite photography of the dry lake confirmed the existence of a new facility at the site. See Jim Skeen, "Lockheed Offers Polecat peek," *Los Angeles Daily News,* July 26, 2006, available at http://aimpoints.hq.af.mil/display.cfm?id=12793 (accessed 03/02/2007). See also "Lockheed Martin's Skunk Works Reveals High Altitude Unmanned System," Lockheed Martin press release, June 19, 2006. For the Polecat video, see http://www.youtube.com/watch?v=bsowPKvcIxo (accessed 03/02/2007).

38: "A sprawling facility" See "Wing Infrastructure Development Outlook (WINDO) Environmental Assessment," Nellis Air Force Base, December 2005, available at http://budget.state.nv.us/clearinghouse/Notice/2006/E2006-241.pdf. For acceptance testing of electronic warfare assets, see "Final Acceptance Testing of the Texas Instruments (TI) ASR-8/ MTD (AN/GPN-25) at Tolicha Peak, Nevada," Radar Evaluation Squadron (Technical) (1954th) Hill Air Force Base, UT. October 15, 1980, available at http://stinet.dtic.mil/oai/oai?&verb=getRecord&metadataPrefix=html& identifier=ADA09 6292.

38: "But much about TPECR" See the Center for Land Use Interpretation's, CD-ROM *The Nellis Range Complex: Landscapes of Conjecture* (Culver City: CLUI, 2004).

39: "The Tonopah Test Range" For an early history of the TTR, see S. Hwang, et al., "1990 Environmental Monitoring Report, Tonopah Test Range, Tonopah, Nevada," Sandia Report SAND91-0593, UC-630, 1991, 2-1.

39: "For the last thirty years" See "Air Force Declassifies Elite Aggressor Program," USAF press release, 11/13/2006, available at http://www.af.mil/news/story.asp?storyID=123031752.

39: "In 1981, the newly created" Curtis Peebles, *Dark Eagles: A History of Top Secret U.S. Aircraft* (Novato: Presidio Press, 1999), 178.

40: "But the base at Tonopah" Peebles, *Dark Eagles,* 248.

40: "Sixty miles southeast" Powers quoted in Francis Gary Powers and Curt Gentry, *Operation Overflight* (New York: Holt, Rinehart and Winston, 1970), 28.

41: "Not that the 'DET. 3' name" Independent researcher Glen Campbell first uncovered the "DET. 3" designation. The story is told in Patton, *Dreamland,* 175.

41: "On the flights where" This has been documented in detail by independent researcher and military monitor Joerg Arnu at his Web site, http://www.dreamlandresort.com/info/janet_audio.html (accessed 1/20/08).

43: "The 'annihilation of space by time' " Karl Marx, *Grundrisse,* trans. Martin Nicolaus (New York: Penguin Classics, 1993), 539.

44: "The landings began" Paglen and Thompson, *Torture Taxi.*

45: "The name 'Tepper Aviation' " For Tepper Aviation, see Ted Gup, *The Book of Honor* (New York: Doubleday, 2000), 321–28; Allan George, "Airline Carrying CIA Guns to Unita," *Independent,* February 18, 1989; and Allan George, "US Weapons Boost Angolan Rebels," *Guardian,* June 25, 1990.

45: "The CIA created" Ted Gup, *The Book of Honor.*

45: "Another secret geography" Paglen and Thompson, *Torture Taxi.* See also Stephen Grey, *Ghost Plane* (New York: St. Martin's, 2006).

46: "It wasn't until 2006" Michael Isikoff and David Corn, *Hubris: The Inside Story of Spin, Scandal, and the Selling of the Iraq War* (New York: Crown, 2006), 6–9.

46: "According to Isikoff and Corn" Ibid.

47: "By the fall of 2002" Ibid., 153.

47: "In the fall of 2002" Ibid.

47: "Despite all the expense" Ibid., 211.

Chapter 4

50: " 'It is a soul-shattering silence' " Freeman Dyson, *Disturbing the Universe* (New York: HarperCollins, 2001), 128. Rebecca Solnit and John McPhee have both used this quote to describe the silence of the Basin and Range.

52: " 'Here, on the Humboldt' " Horace Greeley, *An Overland Journey from New York to San Francisco in the Summer of 1859*, Charles Duncan, ed. (London: Macdonald, 1963), 231; Reuben Cole Shaw, *Across the Plains in Forty-Nine*, Milo Milton Quaife, ed. (Chicago: The Lakeside Press, 1948), 135–36; Belknap quoted in John Walton Caughey, *California*, second ed. (New York: Prentice Hall, 1953), 251.

52: "On arriving at the sink of the Humboldt" Shaw, *Across the Plains*, 137–38; Vincent Geiger and Wakeman Bryarly, *Trail to California: The Overland Journal of Vincent Geiger and Wakeman Bryarly*, David Morris Potter, ed. (New Haven: Yale University Press, 1945), 189.

53: "One emigrant described the landscape" Geiger and Bryarly, *Trail to CA*, 85.

53: "The stretch was littered" Charles Glass Gray, *Off at Sunrise: The Overland Journal of Charles Glass Gray*, Thomas D. Clark, ed. (San Marino: Henry E. Huntington Library, 1976), 84.

53: "Later that day" Ibid.

54: "Milus Gay wrote" Quoted in Caughey, *California*, 251–52.

54: "Upon completing the" Quoted in Aldous Huxley, "The Desert," in Leonard Michaels, David Reid, and Raquel Scherr, eds., *West of the West: Imagining California* (San Francisco: North Point Press, 1989), 320.

54: "Forty-niner Alonzo Delano" Quoted in Kevin Starr, *Americans and the California Dream 1850–1915* (New York: Oxford University Press, 1973), 53.

54: "When William Lewis Manly" Quoted in Robert Glass Cleland, *From Wilderness to Empire* (New York: Alfred A. Knopf, 1959), 131.

54: "Lieutenant George Montague Wheeler" George Wheeler, "Preliminary Report Concerning Explorations and Surveys Principally in Nevada and Arizona," Corps of Engineers (Washington, D.C.: GPO, 1872), 11, 15, 16.

55: " 'All the tribes' " Ibid., 27.

55: "Wheeler possessed little sympathy" Ibid., 89.

55: "Per his own estimation" Ibid., 27.

55: "Despite his disdain" Ibid., 28.

55: "Development spelled ruin" Rebecca Solnit, *Savage Dreams* (Berkeley: University of California Press, 2000), 169.

55: "Cattle devoured" Ibid., 167.

55: "Slaughtered native peoples" Ibid.

56: "In the 1860s and '70s" Ibid. See also Brigham D. Madsen, *The Shoshoni Frontier and the Bear River Massacre* (Salt Lake City: University of Utah Press, 1995). The Bear River is in Southern Idaho, which is also traditional Shoshone territory.

56: " 'Nothing disappears completely' " Henri Lefebvre, *The Production of Space,* trans. Donald Nicholson-Smith (London: Blackwell, 1991), 229–30.

56: "The explosions were called" These thoughts echo Rebecca Solnit's. See Solnit, *Savage Dreams.*

58: "Shoshone legend holds" Paul Nellen, interview with Raymond Yowell, http://www.nativeweb.org/pages/legal/shoshone/.

59: "It's not clear whether" See Richard O. Clemmer, "Ideology and Identity: Western Shoshone 'Cannibal' Myth as Ethnonational Narrative," *Journal of Anthropological Research* 52, no. 2 (Summer 1996), 207–23.

59: "But the treaty of Ruby Valley" Solnit, *Savage Dreams;* Valerie Kuletz, *The Tainted Desert* (London: Routledge, 1998).

Chapter 5

64: "HAVE BLUE was built" Curtis Peebles, *Dark Eagles: A History of Top Secret U.S. Aircraft* (Novato: Presidio Press, 1999), 147–48.

65: "The HAVE BLUE program" Ibid., 151.

65: "Before its 1996 declassification" Ibid., 244–50.

66: "At the Gathering of Eagles" Flight Test Historical Foundation, "Out of the Black . . . Into the Blue," Gathering of Eagles 2004 Program, October 1, 2004; Peebles, *Dark Eagles,* 250.

67: "The section on Doug Benjamin" Ibid., 20.

68: "And then there was" Ibid., 22.

70: "A local paper" Anastasia Mercer, "Parents Don't Know What Pilot Son Did, but It Was Fantastic," *La Crosse Tribune,* September 27, 2004, http://www.lacrossetribune.com/articles/2004/09/27/news/z1pilot.txt (accessed 10/18/2005).

71: "In the 1960s" For biographical details on Birk, see "Frank T. Birk," *Aviation Week & Space Technology* 139, no. 6, August 9, 1993, 19. For Birk's early career, see Christopher Robbins, *The Ravens: The Men Who Flew in America's Secret War in Laos* (New York: Crown, 1987).

71: "According to Merlin" Peter Merlin, "Black Projects at Groom Lake: Into the 21st Century." Available at http://www.dreamlandresort.com/black_projects/black_projects_history.html (accessed 11/23/2007).

71: "The biography of" Ibid.; Pamela Parmalee, "Industry Outlook," *Aviation Week & Space Technology* 154, no. 20, May 14, 2001, 19.

71: "Then I found the biography" Lanni's biography has been subsequently taken offline. It remains on file with the author.

73: "major Air Force command" Air Force Materiel Command Web site, http://www.afmc.af.mil/units/.

74: "Born in 1889" David Kahn, *The Reader of Gentlemen's Mail: Herbert O. Yardley and the Birth of American Codebreaking* (New Haven: Yale University Press, 2004), 2; for Yardley's own book about the black chamber, see Herbert O. Yardley, *The American Black Chamber* (Annapolis: Naval Institute Press, 1931).

75: "As a telegrapher" Kahn, *The Reader*, 1.

75: "One slow night" Ibid., 11.

76: " 'I always assume that' " Quoted in James Bamford, *The Puzzle Palace* (New York: Penguin Books, 1983), 22.

76: "Yardley saw an opportunity" Kahn, *Reader*, 21.

76: "As the First World War" Bamford, *Puzzle*, 23.

76: "By the end of the war" Kahn, *Reader*, 50.

76: "With the end of World War I" Ibid.

77: "But there were stirrings" Bamford, *Puzzle*, 24.

77: "The budget for Yardley's" Ibid.

77: "The War Department's" Kahn, *Reader*, 54.

77: "submitted as a 'confidential memorandum,' " Bamford, *Puzzle*, 24.

77: "This early form" Ibid., 24–25.

77: "For the next ten years" Ibid., 25–26; Kahn, *Reader*, 87.

77: "The Radio Communication Act" Bamford, *Puzzle*, 28.

77: "Nonetheless, the Black Chamber" Ibid., 33.

78: "When Herbert Hoover" Ibid., 33–35.

78: "Or so it seemed" James Bamford, *Body of Secrets* (New York: Anchor, 2002), 1–3.

Chapter 6

80: "The conversation took" Richard Rhodes, *The Making of the Atomic Bomb* (New York: Simon & Schuster, 1986), 291–92.

81: "Szilard sketched out" Ruth Moore, *Niels Bohr: The Man, His Science, and the World They Changed* (Cambridge: MIT Press, 1985), 257.

81: " 'lest the Nazis learn' " Quoted in Rhodes, *Making of*, 294.

81: "The Danish scientist" Information on Bohr in this paragraph from Finn Aaserud, ed., *Niels Bohr Collected Works,* vol. 11, 6.

82: "As the physicists" Rhodes, *Making of,* 294.

82: "Since 1933, Bohr" Moore, *Niels Bohr,* 219–20.

82: " 'Using the word much' " Quoted in Ibid., 218–19.

85: "The whole conversation was moot" Ibid., 271.

85: "Such an undertaking" Rhodes, *Making of,* 294.

85: "The next month," Moore, *Niels Bohr,* 260.

85: "Back in Copenhagen" Ibid., 260–61.

85: "In April of 1940" Ibid., 275.

86: "In late August of 1943" Ibid., 299–301.

86: "On September 29" Ibid., 303–4.

86: "Upon his arrival" Ibid., 307.

86: "When Bohr set foot" Ibid., 320.

86: "This led to inevitable mishaps" Ibid., 320.

88: " 'What until a few years ago' " Aaserud, *Collected Works,* 105.

88: "Army security officers" See Richard Feynman, *Surely You're Joking, Mr. Feynman!* (New York: Norton, 1997), 114–17.

88: "Even Leo Szilard" William Lanouette with Bela Silard, *Genius in the Shadows: A Biography of Leo Szilard* (New York: Charles Scribner's Sons, 1992), 240.

88: "Moreover, the physicists" Quoted in Moore, *Niels Bohr,* 330.

88: "As Bohr learned" Rhodes, *Making of,* 379.

89: "At its height" See Jeff Hughes, *The Manhattan Project: Big Science and the Atom Bomb* (New York: Columbia University Press, 2003), 154.

89: " 'You see, I told you' " Rhodes, *Making of,* 501.

89: "Roosevelt secretly authorized" Rhodes, *Making of,* 379.

89: "Billions of dollars" See Leslie R. Groves, *Now It Can Be Told: The Story of the Manhattan Project* (New York: Harper and Brothers, 1962), 360–62.

89: "When Truman discovered" Tim Weiner, *Blank Check: The Pentagon's Black Budget* (New York: Warner Books, 1990), 20.

90: "With an eye toward preserving" Groves, *Now It Can,* 362–63.

90: "The future president" Rhodes, *Making of,* 623–26.

90: "The secrecy that went" Quoted in Edward Shils, *The Torment of Secrecy* (Chicago: Ivan R. Dee, 1996), 42.

91: "Bohr aggressively lobbied" Bohr quoted in Moore, *Niels Bohr,* 347.

91: "For Bohr, the only" Aaserud, *Collected Works,* 101–8.

92: "On August 26, 1944" Moore, *Niels Bohr,* 349–50.

92: "The meeting at Hyde Park" See Barton Bernstein, "The Uneasy Alliance: Roosevelt, Churchill, and the Atomic Bomb, 1940–1945," *Western Political Quarterly* 29, no. 2 (June 1976), 224–25; see also Moore, *Niels Bohr,* 352–53.

92: "Churchill was clearly" Quoted in Moore, *Niels Bohr,* 352.

92: "The meeting ended" Quoted in Bernstein, "Uneasy Alliance," 224.

93: "Secrecy had become" McGeorge Bundy, *Danger and Survival: Choices About the Bomb in the First Fifty Years* (New York: Random House, 1988), 76.

94: "As the war came to an end" See William Lanouette and Bela Silard, *Genius in the Shadows:* 293; see also Federation of American Scientists Web site at http://www.fas.org.

94: "In 1946, the federation" Dexter Masters and Katharine Way, eds., *One World or None,* (New York: Federation of American Scientists/McGraw-Hill, 1946).

95: "26.8 billion" This figure is based on the figure of $2.3 billion total for the Manhattan Project, as reported by Leslie Groves, and turned into 2007 dollars using the S. Morgan Friedman's Inflation Calculator at http://www.westegg.com/inflation.

Chapter 7

98: "Amateur satellite observing" For the history of Moonwatch, see W. Patrick McCray, *Keep Watching the Skies! The Story of Operation Moonwatch and the Dawn of the Space Age* (Princeton: Princeton University Press, 2008).

99: "The state-sponsored" Desmond King-Hele, *Observing Earth Satellites* (New York: Van Nostrand Reinhold Company, 1983), 107–8.

102: "The billion dollar satellite" Robert Wall, "Titan IV Flaws in Software," *Aviation Week & Space Technology* 151, no. 5, August 2, 1999, 31; William Harwood, "Military Satellite in Wrong Orbit," *Washington Post,* May 1, 1999, sec. A.

102: "In fact, they are so easy to mistake" See Anthony Eccles, "UFOs and the NOSS Problem," *Anomalist,* available at http://www.anomalist.com/features/Noss.html (accessed 08/20/2007); and "Recent Australian UFOs Were Just U.S. Navy Satellites," Listserv post at http://www.ufoinfo.com/roundup/v08/rnd0804.shtml (accessed 08/20/2007).

103: "Though the question itself" Jeffrey Richelson, *America's Secret Eyes in Space* (New York: Harper and Row, 1990), 231.

107: "From here, things get" Information taken from the Visual Satellite Observers Home Page at http://www.satobs.org/element.html (accessed 08/21/2007) and the Space-track.org page on TLE formats at http://www.space-track.org/tle_format.html (accessed 08/21/2007).

109: "The list ends with" See Gunther's Space Page, http://space.skyrocket.de (accessed 8/20/2007); and Elaine M. Grossman and Keith J. Costa, "Small, Experimental Satellite May Offer More Than Meets the Eye," *Inside the Pentagon,* December 4, 2003. Reprinted at http://www.globalsecurity.org/org/news/2003/031204-asat.htm (accessed 08/20/2007).

111: "The shuttle's pilot" For Casper's NASA biography, see http://www.jsc.nasa.gov/Bios/htmlbios/casper.html (accessed 08/28/2007).

111: "A blurb in" "Secret Mission," *Aviation Week and Space Technology* 132, no. 4, January 22, 1990, 23.

112: "An article in *Aviation Week*" "Soviets Claim Reconnaissance Satellite Launched by Atlantis Has Failed," *Aviation Week & Space Technology* 132, no. 13, March 26, 1990, 23.

113: "*The New York Times* eventually wrote" Warren Leary, "Space Shuttle Lifts Off with Secret Military Cargo," *New York Times*, November 16, 1990, sec. A.

115: "The story goes like this" See Allen Thompson, "A Stealth Satellite Sourcebook," 02/11/2007 version.

115: "Allen Thompson uncovered" See, for example, "Memorandum for Deputy of Technology/OSA; Subject: A Covert Reconnaissance Satellite," April 17, 1963, in Thompson, "Stealth Satellite Sourcebook."

116: "This is a relatively straightforward" There really was a design for a stealth aircraft carrier. See Ben Rich, *Skunk Works* (New York: Little, Brown and Co., 1994), 280.

119: "Legend holds that" Fred Watson, *Stargazer: The Life and Times of the Telescope* (Cambridge: Da Capo Press, 2004), 57.

119: "But early scientists" Ibid., 47.

120: "Fast forward 450 years" Quoted in Philip Taubman, *Secret Empire* (New York: Simon & Schuster, 2003), 213, 215.

120: "For his part, Eisenhower" Ibid., 214.

120: "On January 22, 1958" William Burrows, *Deep Black* (New York: Random House, 1986), 104.

121: "Since 1955, the Air Force" Ibid., 84, 90–91.

121: "After Sputnik, U.S. space" Ibid., 107.

122: "When the photographs" See "Memorandum for the Director of Central Intelligence; Plans for Handling Satellite Photography (CORONA)," August 24, 1960, available at http://www.gwu.edu/~nsarchiv/ NSAEBB/NSAEBB225/doc05a.pdf.

123: "On August 26, 1960" Memorandum for the Secretary of State, Secretary of Defense, Attorney General, Chairman, Atomic Energy Commission, Director of Central Intelligence, August 26, 1960, available at http://www.gwu.edu/~nsarchiv/NSAEBB/NSAEBB225/doc05b.pdf; http://www.gwu.edu/~nsarchiv/NSAEBB/NSAEBB225/doc05c.pdf.

123: "TALENT KEYHOLE was just" National Reconnaissance Office, "The Retirement of BYEMAN," *Security Newsletter* 4, August/September 2004, available at http://www.gwu.edu/~nsarchiv/NSAEBB/NSAEBB225/ doc06.pdf.

123: "The CIA's Photographic Interpretation" Steve Vogel, "Charting a Military Course; After Cartographic Consolidation, Mapping Agency Is Aiding Forces in the Balkans," *Washington Post*, May 9, 1999, sec. A; Na-

tional Geospatial-Intelligence Agency Web page: http://www.nga.mil/
portal/site/nga01/index.jsp?epi-content=GENERIC&itemID=91a8353e5
cbd0110VgnVCMServer3c02010aRCRD&beanID=1629630080&viewID=
Article; Jeffrey Richelson, *The US Intelligence Community,* 5th ed. (Boulder: Westview Press, 2008), 51.

124: "Throughout the U-2, CORONA" Richelson, *US Intelligence Community,* 38.

124: "By the time the NRO's existence" Commission on the Roles and
Capabilities of the United States Intelligence Community, "Preparing for
the 21st Century: An Appraisal of U.S. Intelligence," February 13, 1996, ch.
13, available at http://www.fas.org/irp/offdocs/report.html.

Chapter 8

128: "As the arch-spy" Robert Baer, *Sleeping with the Devil* (New York:
Three Rivers Press, 2003), 6.

128: "On May 22, 1999" *Florida Today* article quoted from SeeSat-L list
at http://satobs.org/seesat/May-1999/0321.html.

129: "It took almost three years" Allan Thompson, "A Stealth Satellite
Sourcebook."

131: "Using the SRP analysis" SeeSat-L post, August 2002.

132: "This mission reminds me" http://satobs.org/seesat/Aug-2002/0075.
html.

132: "And so, Molczan" This section is based on a close reading of more
than a decade of Listserv posts to the SeeSat-L list.

134: "A researcher named Anthony Kenden" Anthony Kenden, "Was
'Columbia' Photographed by a KH-11?" *Journal of British Interplanetary Society,* February 1983, 73–77.

134: "In June of 1983" See Curtis Peebles, *Guardians* (Novato: Presidio,
1987), 137.

135: "In late 2004, the MISTY" Dana Priest, "New Spy Satellite Debated on Hill," *Washington Post,* December 11, 2004, sec. A.

135: "In the summer of 2007" Noah Shachtman, "Head Spook Kills
Off Lame Spy Sat," *Wired* Danger Room blog, June 22, 2007, http://blog.
wired.com/defense/2007/06/head-spook-kill.html (accessed 05/01/2008).

136: "After McConnell's statement" Mark Mazzetti, "Spy Director
Ends Program on Satellites," *New York Times,* June 21, 2007, sec. A.

136: "It later came out" Walter Pincus, "Nominee Defends Ending
Programs; Kerr Testifies About Satellite Contracts," *Washington Post,* August 2, 2007, sec. A.

Chapter 9

138: "In January 2003" Statement: Mark Klein, April 6, 2006. Available at http://www.wired.com/science/discoveries/news/2006/70621; see also "Spying on the Home Front," *Frontline,* PBS, aired May 15, 2007.

140: "Tien's case, however" "Judge's Refusal to Dismiss EFF's Spying Case Sets Stage for Congressional Showdown," Electronic Frontier Foundation Press Release, July 21, 2006, available at http://www.eff.org/news/archives/2006_07.php#004843 (accessed 07/19/2007).

141: "authoring a classified legal opinion" James Risen and Eric Lichtblau, "Bush Lets U.S. Spy on Callers Without Courts," *New York Times,* December 16, 2005, sec. A.

141: "Yoo told Fox News" Fox News, January 30, 2006. Transcript available at http://www.foxnews.com/story/0,2933,183179,00.html (accessed 02/14/2008).

144: "Powell claimed that the" Charles Hanley, "Powell's Case for Iraq War Falls Apart 6 Months Later," Associated Press, August 11, 2003; "The Man Who Knew: Ex-Powell Aide Says Saddam-Weapons Threat was Overstated," *60 Minutes,* February 4, 2004. Transcript available at www.cbsnews.com/stories/2003/10/14/60II/main577975.shtml.

144: "'Satellites and intercepts can't'" Robert Baer, *See No Evil* (New York: Three Rivers Press, 2003), 18, 140.

147: "The 1980s were boom times" George C. Wilson, "Air Force Plans to Hide Secret Fighter; Billion-Plus Program Also Would Arm 'Stealth' Radar-Evader," *Washington Post,* March 21, 1987, sec. A.

147: "The pages of public accounting" Bill Keller, "Defense Department Seeks More Money for Secret Weapons, Analyst Says," *New York Times,* February 12, 1985, sec. B, 24; for code names, see Bill Arkin, *Code Names* (Hanover: Steerforth Press, 2005).

147: "Somewhere in an unmarked hangar" John Tirpak, "The Robotic Air Force," *Air Force Magazine* 80, no. 9, September 1997; for Quartz, see Richelson, "United States Intelligence Community," 39.

148: "Air Force officers at" Richard Leiby, "Secrets Under the Sun," *Washington Post,* July 20, 1997, sec. F.

148: "A chronic cough" Author's interviews with Stella and Nancy Kasza, Las Vegas, NV; Leiby, "Secrets Under the Sun."

149: "When Frost died" Leiby, "Secrets Under the Sun."

150: "The lawsuit had several" Ibid.

150: "Responding to the lawsuit": Keith Rogers, "National Security Defense Cut from Groom Lawsuits," *Las Vegas Review Journal,* November 11, 1994, available at http://www.reviewjournal.com/webextras/area51/1994/lawsuits/security.html (accessed 07/09/2007).

150: "Next, the Air Force" Robert Granader, "Privilege an Obstacle in Groom Lake Suit: Government Refuses Even to Name Secret Air Base in

Litigation Over Pollution," *American Bar Association Journal* 28, September 1995, 81.

150: "The court holds that federal" *Frost v. Perry,* no. CV-S-94-714-PMP (RLH), 919 F. Supp. 1459, D. Nev. March 6, 1996.

151: "In November 1998" Keith Rogers, "High Court Keeps Groom Lake Secret," *Las Vegas Review Journal,* November 3, 1998, http://www.reviewjournal.com/lvrj_home/1998/Nov-03-Tue-1998/news/8525455.html (accessed 8/16/2005).

Chapter 10

152: "It began outside Waycross, Georgia" Barry Siegel, *Claim of Privilege* (New York: Harper, 2008), 45–48.

153: "There was Secret Project MX-397" For the XP-59a, see Curtis Peebles, *Dark Eagles: A History of Top Secret U.S. Aircraft Programs* (Novato: Presidio, 1995); for Project X-Ray, see Jack Couffer, *Bat Bomb* (Austin: University of Texas Press, 1992).

153: "Robert Palya had written an engineer" This account, and much of the following account in general, is based on a series from the *Los Angeles Times*; see Barry Siegel, "The Secret of the B-29: How the Death of Judy's Father Made America More Secretive; A plane crashes at the dawn of the Cold War, and the government seeks a special legal privilege. Its claim sows the seeds of the Patriot Act," *Los Angeles Times,* April 18, 2004, sec. A.

155: "U.S. District Court judge" Quoted in Siegel, "Secret of the B-29."

157: "The Vinson court was composed" See Henry Abraham, *Justices, Presidents, and Senators.* (Lanham: Rowman and Littlefield, 1999), 160.

157: "the *Youngstown Sheet & Tube Co. v. Sawyer*" For an account of the Sawyer case, see Maeva Marcus, *Truman and the Steel Seizure Case: The Limits of Presidential Power* (New York: Columbia University Press, 1977).

157: " 'One is the ballot box' " Quoted in Louis Fisher, *In the Name of National Security.* (Lawrence: University of Kansas Press, 2006), 3.

157: "Pine flat-out rejected" Ibid., 93–94.

157: "The Supreme Court concurred" Ibid., 94.

158: " 'The court itself must determine' " Quoted in ibid., 111.

158: "He went on to state" Quoted in ibid., 112.

158: "The executive would henceforth" Ibid., 113.

159: "In his analysis" Ibid., 119.

159: "Judy Palya Loether grew up" Author interview with Judith Palya Loether, 07/19/2007.

160: "One day in February" Ibid.

160: "As Loether spent night" Accident report quoted in appendix to Biddle filing, 66a; Barry Siegel, "The Secret of the B-29: A Daughter Discovers What Really Happened," *Los Angeles Times,* April 19, 2004, sec. A; Michael Freedman, "Daughters of the Cold War," *Legal Affairs* (online edition), January/February 2004, available at http://www.legalaffairs.org/issues/January-February-2004/story_freedman_janfeb04.mspaccessed07/17/2007; Biddle appendix, 22a.

160: "Loether went from" Author interview with Loether.

161: "After more time on the Internet" Ibid.

161: " 'I am interested in' " Qutoed in Siegel, "Secret of the B-29."

162: "In the early 1980s, Alger Hiss" Megan Rosenfeld, "Alger Hiss: Pleading His Cause—Still," *Washington Post,* November 9, 1980, sec. L; David Remnick, "Alger Hiss Goes Ungently into That Good Night; Tired, Nearly Blind and 81, the Demon of Modern Conservatism Still Seeks Vindication," *Washington Post Magazine,* October 12, 1986, sec. W; for Korematsu, see Annie Nakao, "Overturning a Wartime Act Decades Later," *San Francisco Chronicle,* December 12, 2004, sec. D.

163: " '*United States v. Reynolds* stands exposed' " Petition for a Writ of Error Coram Nobis to Remedy Fraud Upon This Court. In Re Patricia J. Herring et al. in *United States v. Reynolds.*

163: "After receiving Brown's petition" For Olson, see Joe Conason, "Ted Olson? You've Got to Be Kidding," Salon.com, February 6, 2001, available at http://archive.salon.com/politics/feature/2001/02/06/olson/index.html (accessed 07/18/2007).

163: "In 2001, his wife was killed" Neil Lewis, "Barbara Olson, 45, Advocate and Conservative Commentator," *New York Times,* September 13, 2001, sec. A.

163: "Back in 1950, Olson wrote" Quoted in Siegel, "Secret of the B-29."

164: "Finally, argued Olson" Quoted in ibid.

164: "In other words, Olson's argument" Fisher, *National Security,* 94.

164: "A few months later, Olson went on" See Linda Greenhouse, "Justices to Hear Case of Detainees at Guantanamo," *New York Times,* November 11, 2003, sec. A.

00: " 'The motion for leave' " Quoted in Siegel, "Secret of the B-29."

165: "To avoid the consequences" U.S. District Court for the Eastern District of Virginia, *El-Masri v. Tenet,* Civil Action No. 1:05-cv-01417-TSE-TRJ, March 13, 2006.

165: "In every case where" See "Reply of United States of America to Plaintiff's Opposition to United States' Invocation of State Secrets Privilege," *Maher Arar v. Ashcroft et al.,* Case No. 04-CV-0249-DGT-VVP, April 4, 2005.

165: "Government whistleblower" See Barry Siegel, "State Secret Overreach," *Los Angeles Times,* September 16, 2007, available at http://

www.latimes.com/news/opinion/la-op-siegel16sep16,0,4846280.story (accessed 09/19/2007).

166: "The court itself must determine" Quoted in Fisher, *National Security,* 112.

Chapter 11

169: "Author David Ovason writes" David Ovason, *The Secret Architecture of our Nation's Capital: The Masons and the Building of Washington, D.C.* (New York: Harper, 2002), 334–49.

171: "The NRO built the complex" Pierre Thomas, "Spy Unit's Spending Stuns Hill; $310 Million Facility Secretly Sprouts Up Near Dulles Airport," *Washington Post,* August 9, 1994, sec. A.

172: "I located the P.O. box" Names and flight records come from "Direccion General de la Guardia Civil 1701a Comandancia Illes Balears Compania Puerto—Aeropuerto Palma," Diligencias Numero: 065/06, March 23, 2005, 72. The document is the file from the police investigation.

172: "Both of these men now have" John Goetz, Marcel Rosenbach, and Holger Stark, "CIA Arrest Warrants Strain US-German Ties," *Der Spiegel,* June 25, 2007, available at http://www.spiegel.de/international/germany/0,1518,490514,00.html (accessed 01/30/2008).

174: "Inside the NCTC" Lawrence Wright, "The Spymaster," *New Yorker,* January 21, 2008.

175: "At a February 2008" Federal News Service, "Hearing of the House Permanent Select Committee on Intelligence; Subject: Worldwide Threats," February 7, 2008.

176: "Three quarters of the people working" For the privatization of the intelligence community, see Tim Shorrock, *Spies for Hire* (New York: Simon & Schuster, 2008).

176: "The scale of privatization" Ibid., 16.

176: "At the Pentagon" Ibid., 15.

176: "Private intelligence recruiters" Greg Miller, "Spy Agencies Outsourcing to Fill Key Jobs; Contractors, many of them former employees, are doing sensitive work, such as handling agents. A review of the practice has been ordered," *Los Angeles Times,* September 17, 2006, sec. A.

176: "This didn't start on September 12, 2001" Remarks by Vice President Al Gore, opening session for International REGO Conference, January 14, 1999, available at http://clinton2.nara.gov/WH/EOP/OVP/speeches/interego.html; for privatization of the intelligence community during the 1990s, see Shorrock, *Spies for Hire.*

177: "It happens at every level" Tim Shorrock, "The spy who came in from the boardroom: Why John Michael McConnell, a top executive at a private defense contractor, should not be allowed to run our nation's intelligence agencies," Salon.com, available at http://www.salon.com/newsfeature/2007/01/08/mcconnell/.

177: "Booz Allen's offices" Donald L. Barlett and James B. Steele, "Washington's $8 Billion Shadow," *Vanity Fair,* March 2007, available at http://www.vanityfair.com/politics/features/2007/03/spyagency200703; http://investors.saic.com/phoenix.zhtml?c=193857&p=irol-newsArticle& ID=894561&highlight= (Saic press release); Scott Shane, "US: Uncle Sam Keeps SAIC on Call for Top Tasks," *Baltimore Sun,* October 26, 2003.

178: "If CIA front companies" http://www.abraxascorp.com/; accessed 12/18/2007; http://www.spectal.com/; accessed 12/18/2007; Defense Group Incorporated Web site: http://www.defensegroupinc.com/cira/organization.htm, (accessed 12/18/2007).

178: "Even *unclassified* intelligence-related" See "Secrecy News," FAS Project on Government Secrecy, vol. 2007, no. 124, December 18, 2007.

179: "Here are some random line items" Defense Department Budget Request, Fiscal Year 2007, OMA-V1, 187; AFD -070209-062, 117; AFD-070209-061,138; OPA-34, 150.

182: "Steven Kosiak, an analyst" See Steven Kosiak, "Classified Funding in the FY 2009 Defense Budget Request," June 17, 2008, available from http://www.csbaonline.org.

182: " 'The black budget is like' " Author interview with Steven Kosiak, November 11, 2005.

183: "The language is deliberately unambiguous" For the constitution and the black budget, see William Banks and Peter Raven-Hansen, "The Statement and Account Clause as a Constitutional Limit on Black Budgets," in *National Security Law and the Power of the Purse* (New York and Oxford: Oxford University Press, 1994), 100–5.

183: " 'The people,' argued George Mason" Quoted in Tim Weiner, *Blank Check* (New York: Grand Central Publishing, 1990), 215.

184: "Nonetheless, there are precedents" Act of 1 July 1790, 1 Stat. 129 (1790).

184: "Niels Bohr's 'huge factory' " Alice L. Buck, "A History of the Atomic Energy Commission," U.S. Department of Energy, DOE/ES-0003, July 1983.

Chapter 12

186: "It was 1947 and the House Chambers" For a historical overview of the Capitol's architecture, see William Allen, *History of the United States Capitol* (Washington, D.C. GPO, 2001). The description here of the 1949 architecture comes from 412–15.

187: "Truman's secretary of state" Dean Acheson, *Present at the Creation: My Years in the State Department* (New York: Norton, 1969), 214;

Rhodri Jeffreys-Jones, *The CIA and American Democracy,* 2nd ed. (New Haven: Yale University Press, 1989), 40; Tim Weiner, *Blank Check* (New York: Grand Central Publishing, 1990), 115, 116.

188: "Section 102 of the National Security Act" Thomas Powers, *The Man Who Kept the Secrets* (New York: Alfred A. Knopf, 1979), 29.

188: "The OPC was, in short" Quotes from Weiner, *Blank Check,* 117.

188: "But NSC-10/2 contained" Ibid.

189: "Curiously, the agency" Jeffreys-Jones, *CIA,* 42.

189: "In the meantime," Weiner, *Blank Check,* 116.

189: "Finally, and most importantly " Jeffreys-Jones, *CIA,* 59–60.

189: "Congressman Vito Marcantonio" Quotes from these proceedings are taken from *Congressional Record* 95, part 2, 81st Congress, 1st session, February 21, 1949–March 18, 1949, 1943–1947.

190: "The Central Intelligence Agency Act" Ibid., 60.

191: "The Hollywood blacklist" Joseph Losey interview at http://www.moviecrazed.com/outpast/losey.html.

191: "Revelations that the CIA" For the heroin trade, see Alfred McCoy, *The Politics of Heroin,* 2nd ed. (New York: HarperCollins, 2003), 288.

192: "On the Senate floor" Quoted in Weiner, *Blank Check,* 128.

192: "On June 17, 1972, police arrested" Ibid., 131.

194: "Helms suspected that Schlesinger's" Powers, *The Man Who Kept the Secrets,* 314.

194: "Before leaving office, Helms" Ibid.

194: "Schlesinger's tenure at the CIA" Ibid., 322–23.

194: "On April 15, 1973, John Dean" Ibid., 329–30; Weiner, *Blank Check,* 131–32.

195: "When Schlesinger found out about" Weiner, *Blank Check,* 132.

196: "HUGE CIA OPERATION REPORTED" Seymour Hersh, "Huge CIA Operation Reported Against Antiwar Forces, Other Dissidents in Nixon Years," *New York Times,* December 22, 1974, sec. A.

196: "On January 27, the Senate voted" John Prados, *President's Secret Wars* (Chicago: Ivan R. Dee, 1996), 333–34; also Jeffreys-Jones, *CIA,* 199.

196: "William Colby is one of the more" See John Prados, *Lost Crusader* (Oxford: Oxford University Press, 2003), 38–39.

197: "On one hand, there was William Colby" For the Phoenix program, see Douglas Valentine, *The Phoenix Program* (New York: William Morrow, 1990).

197: "During Colby's confirmation hearings" Prados, *President's,* 325.

197: "On the other hand, water-cooler gossip" Prados, *Lost Crusader,* 2.

197: "According to his memoirs" William Colby, *Honorable Men* (New York: Simon & Schuster, 1978), 399.

198: "Before the Rockefeller Commission" Colby, *Honorable Men,* 400.

198: "Drawing from his experience" Ibid., 407.

199: "Richard Helms, Colby's old boss" Richard Helms, *A Look Over My Shoulder* (Novato: Presidio Press, 2004) 429.

200: "In June of 1975, the Rockefeller Commission" Quoted in Weiner, *Blank Check,* 137.

200: "During the hearings, DCI Colby" Church Report Book I, 369, 370, 371.

200: " 'It is clear,' concluded the Committee" Ibid., 373.

201: "Colby and Helms advanced" Ibid., 51, 52, 55, 82.

201: "George Bush concurred" Bush's comments weren't made in person but were entered into the record in a written form.

201: "No one from the intelligence community" Ibid., 383.

202: ""The real fear on both sides" Quoted in ibid.

202: "In conclusion, the Church Committee" Ibid.

202: "In 1998, the Federation of American Scientists" CIA press release no. 03-98, March 20, 1998; Scott Shane, "Official Reveals Budget for U.S. Intelligence," *New York Times,* November 8, 2005.

203: "When the 9/11 Commission took up" National Commission on Terrorist Attacks Upon the United States, *9-/1 Commission Report* (Washington, D.C.: GPO, 2005), 410.

203: " 'Secrecy, while necessary' " Ibid., 103.

203: "To combat the secrecy and complexity" Ibid., 416.

203: "The executive branch stuck" "Secrecy News," 10/30/2007; 10/22/2007.

204: "Nonetheless, the bill passed" Walter Pincus, "Intelligence Budget Disclosure is Hailed," *Washington Post,* October 31, 2007, sec. A.

204: "Although Congress compelled" For the other parts of the intelligence community whose budgets are not disclosed, see U.S. Intelligence Community, "The Intelligence Budget Process," http://www.intelligence.gov/2-business_nfip.shtml.

204: "Reluctant disclosures from the" See Laura Heaton, "Intel. Budget may be buried in PowerPoint," United Press International, June 6, 2007. See also Raelynn Hillhouse, "Office of Nation's Top Spy Inadvertently Reveals Key to Classified National Intel Budget," The Spy Who Billed Me blog, June 4, 2007, available at http://www.thespywhobilledme.com/the_spy_who_billed_me/2007/06/exclusive_offic.html (accessed 05/01/2008).

205: "In a different PowerPoint presentation" Hillhouse, http://www.thespywhobilledme.com/the_spy_who_billed_me/WindowsLiveWriter/DIA-contractor-v-emp.gif (accessed 05/01/2008).

206: "In other words, the DIA was warning" Walter Pincus, "Defense Agency Proposes Outsourcing More Spying," *Washington Post,* August 19, 2007, sec. A.

206: "Even executives at private intelligence" Quoted in Sebastian

Abbot, "The Outsourcing of U.S. Intelligence Analysis," http://newsini-tiative.org/story/2006/07/28/the_outsourcing_of_u_s_intelligence (accessed 12/18/2007).

Chapter 13
209: "One day in 2004, Joe was sitting" Conversations with Bryan; see also Joseph Bryan, "We've Got a Bigger Problem Now," unpublished manuscript, 2007.
212: "If Your Solutions's intent" Michael Dobbs, "Negroponte's Time in Honduras at Issue; Focus Renewed on Intelligence Pick's Knowledge of Death Squads in 1980s," *Washington Post,* March 21, 2005, sec. A; "Nomination of John Negroponte," *Congressional Record,* September 14, 2001 (Senate), S9431-S9433.
213: "Battalion 316 was the brainchild" Gary Cohn and Ginger Thompson, "When a wave of torture and murder staggered a small US ally . . . ," *Baltimore Sun,* June 11, 1995.
213: "As Alvarez rose to power in Honduras" See William Leogrande, *Our Own Backyard* (Chapel Hill: University of North Carolina Press, 2000), 30–31.
214: "On Honduras's northern border" Cohn and Thompson, "When a wave of torture."
214: "Beginning in the early 1970s" "Nunca Mas (Never Again)," CON-ADEP (National Commission on the Disappearance of Persons) report, 1984, available at http://web.archive.org/web/20031004074316/nuncamas.org/english/library/nevagain/nevagain_001.htm (accessed 05/02/2008); Alejandro Teitelbaum, "Represión en argentina y memoria larga," Argenpress, April 10, 2006, available at http://www.argenpress.info/notaold.asp?num=029406 (accessed 05/02/2008).
214: "Alvarez stressed theme" Quoted in Cohn and Thompson, "When a wave of torture."
215: "Binns feared the Argentines" Jack Binns, *The United States in Honduras* (Jefferson: McFarland and Company, 2000), 13; On Operation Charly, see María Seoane, "Los secretos de la guerra sucia continental de la dictadura," *El Clarin,* March 24, 2006, available at http://www.clarin.com/suplementos/especiales/2006/03/24/l-01164353.htm (accessed 07/09/2007); also Martha Honey, *Hostile Acts: US Policy in Costa Rica in the 1980s* (Gainesville: University of Florida Press, 1994), and Cohn and Thompson, "When a wave of Torture."
217: "Learning of the disappearances" Binns, *United States,* 200.
217: "Washington had already warned" Ibid., 163.
218: "In the white world" William Smith, "Things are Moving," *Time,* August 15, 1983, available at http://www.time.com/time/print-

out/0,8816,949720,00.html (accessed 07/06/2007); see also Leogrande, *Our Own Backyard*, 316–17.

218: "The BIG PINE exercises" Leogrande, *Our Own Backyard*, 318; "GIs Dig in for Honduras Maneuvers," *New York Times*, August 21, 1983, sec. 1; Michael Getler, "Hondurans Uneasy Over U.S. Military; Some Interests Diverge in 2-Front Effort," *Washington Post*, April 7, 1985, sec. A.

219: "Responding to the hostage situation" Steven Emerson, *Secret Warriors* (New York: Putnam, 1988), 12.

219: "Within hours of the failed rescue attempt" Holloway Report, available at http://www.gwu.edu/~nsarchiv/NSAEBB/NSAEBB63/doc8.pdf (accessed 12/02/2007); Emerson, *Secret Warriors*, 14; Holloway Report, vi.

220: "To fill the need for highly trained" "The 160th Special Operations Aviation Regiment (Airborne) Fact Sheet," at http://www.soc.mil/160soar/soar_home.htm (accessed 05/02/2008); for the 160th SOAR, see Michael Durant and Steven Hartov, *The Night Stalkers* (New York: Putnam, 2006).

220: "The Night Stalkers had a black counterpart" Emerson, *Secret Warriors*, 45–47.

220: "The Army created other black units" Jeffrey Richelson, "Truth Conquers All Chains: The U.S. Army Intelligence Support Activity, 1981–1989," *International Journal of Intelligence and Counterintelligence* 12, no. 2, April 1, 1999, 168–200(33); for the ISA, see Michael Smith, *Killer Elite: The Inside Story of America's Most Secret Special Operations Team* (New York: St. Martin's, 2008).

221: "In February 1982, SEASPRAY" Emerson, *Secret Warriors*, 90.

222: "Bill Casey, who assumed the CIA helm" For portraits of Bill Casey, see Bob Woodward, *Veil* (New York: Simon & Schuster, 1987); and Joseph E. Persico, *Casey* (New York: Viking, 1990).

222: "Casey chose former Rome station chief" Duane Clarridge with Digby Diehl, *A Spy for All Seasons* (New York: Scribner, 1997), 197–98; Cohn and Thompson, "When a wave of torture."

223: "The long-held fiction" Holly Sklar, *Washington's War on Nicaragua* (Boston: South End Press, 1988), 114.

223: "Casey first heard of the black army units" Emerson, *Secret Warriors*, 135–36, 149.

224: "The new black military units" Ibid., 150.

224: "September 8, 1983, saw two lightweight planes" Jeff Gerth, "On the Trail of a Latin Mystery, C.I.A. Footprints," *New York Times*, October 6, 1983, sec. A; Sklar, *Washington's War on Nicaragua*, 149–50.

225: "The same day as the Managua" Chamorro Affidavit, quoted in Sklar, *Washington's War on Nicaragua*, 151.

225: "One of the problems of having" Emerson, *Secret Warriors*, 94–96.

225: "With YELLOW FRUIT" Ibid., 96–97; for address, see ibid., 165.

226: "At YELLOW FRUIT's Annandale office" Tim Weiner, *Blank Check*, 184–88.

226: "The document called for a three-point plan" Emerson, *Secret Warriors*, 152.

227: "Congress tried to definitively" Leogrande, *Our Own Backyard*, 330–33.

227: "Barry Goldwater, chair of the Senate Intelligence Committee" Woodward, *Veil*, 320, 333.

227: "In 1982, Congress had passed" Boland quoted in Sklar, *Washington's War on Nicaragua*, 175.

228: "Fortunately for the group of people who'd" Emerson, *Secret Warriors*, chapter 17.

Chapter 14

229: "It didn't used to be as easy" Wendy Griffin, "Aguacate Air Base Brings Back Contra Memories," *Honduras This Week*, February 28, 2000, online edition available at http://www.marrder.com/htw/feb2000/nation al.htm (accessed 07/06/2007); Lydia Chavez, "U.S. and Honduras Are Still Playing Game on Nicaragua Rebels," *New York Times*, July 8, 1984, sec. 1; also Robert McCartney, "Honduras Bars Role in Aid; Contras to Receive Money Elsewhere," *Washington Post*, August 28, 1985, sec. A.

230: Names have been changed to preserve privacy.

233: "There was, however, another possibility" Walsh Iran-Contra Report, 166.

233: "The Enterprise started unraveling October 5, 1986" Dominic Streatfeild, *Cocaine: An Unauthorized Biography* (New York: Picador, 2003), 326.

233: "Eugene Hasenfus was the only survivor" Peter Ford and Lionel Barber, "Man Held by Nicaragua Says He Worked for the CIA," *Financial Times*, October 10, 1986, sec. 1; Lawrence E. Walsh, *Firewall: The Iran-Contra Conspiracy and Cover-Up* (New York: Norton, 1998), 21.

234: "At the crash site, the Nicaraguans" Julia Preston, "Clandestine Missions Described; Honduran Airfields Used by Planes Supplying Contras," *Washington Post*, October 17, 1986, sec. A.

234: "Felix Rodriguez was a longtime CIA operative" CIA Debriefing of Felix Rodriguez, June 3, 1975, available through the National Security Archive at http://www.gwu.edu/~nsarchiv/NSAEBB/NSAEBB5/che15_1. htm (accessed 02/15/08).

234: "Rodriguez's partner at Ilopango" Anne Louise Bardach and Larry Rother, "A Bomber's Tale: Part I: Taking Aim at Castro," *New York Times*, July 12, 1998; Holly Sklar, *Washington's War on Nicaragua* (Boston: South End Press, 1988), 274; for Posada's CIA history, see "Luis Posada Carriles, the Declassified Record," National Security Archive Briefing Book no. 153, May 10,

2005, available at www.gwu.edu/~nsarchiv/NSAEBB/NSAEBB153, (accessed 02/15/2008); Sklar, *Washington's War on Nicaragua,* 274; Alexander Cockburn and Jeffrey St. Clair, *Whiteout: The CIA, Drugs, and the Press* (New York: Verso, 1999), 294.

235: "In 1998, Posada claimed" Bardach and Rother, "A Bomber's Tale"; "No Deportation for Cuban Militant," BBC News, September 28, 2005. Available at http://news.bbc.co.uk/2/hi/americas/4289136.stm (accessed 02/18/2007).

235: "Headquartered at a restricted section" Walsh, Iran-Contra Report, 166.

235: "When Nicaraguan authorities" Julia Preston and Joe Pichirallo, "Phone Calls Suggest Exile Tied to Resupplying Contras; Fugitive Contacted Spouse in Miami," *Washington Post,* October 31, 1986, sec. A.

235: "Continuing the CIA's off-the-books" Michael Gillard, "Former MOD Minister Helps Out Arms Company Chief," *Observer,* November 13, 1994.

236: "According to Senate Iran-Contra" Inouye quoted in Weiner, *Blank Check,* 203.

236: "The statistics confirm Marcos's analysis" Douglas Farah, "Look at Us Now—We Are Worse Off than Ever," *Washington Post,* June 1, 1993, sec. A.

237: "In a 2007 report, the United Nations concurred" "Report of the Working Group on the use of mercenaries as a means of violating human rights and impeding the exercise of the right of peoples to self determination: Addendum: Mission to Honduras," Ms. Amanda Bevavides de Perez, chairperson, February 20, 2007, 5, 17.

238: "Aboard an Air Force Two" Office of the Vice President, "Vice President's Remarks to the Traveling Press, Air Force Two, En route, Muscat, Oman," December 20, 2005, available at http://www.whitehouse.gov/news/releases/2005/12/20051220-9.html (accessed 06/08/2007).

239: "In the majority opinion" "Report on the Congressional Committees Investigating the Iran-Contra Affair with Supplemental, Minority, and Additional Views," H. Rept. no. 100-433; S. Rept. no. 100-216 (Washington, D.C.: GPO, 1987), 13–22.

239: "Dick Cheney's office authored the minority opinion." Ibid., 545; 583–85.

240: "In early 2005, according to Seymour Hersh" Seymour Hersh, "The Redirection," *New Yorker,* March 7, 2007.

Chapter 15

243: "Identification cards dangling from their necks" For background on KBR, see Dan Brody, *The Halliburton Agenda* (New York: Wiley, 2005). For military contract figures, see USAspending.gov.

244: "KBR's charter plane from Dubai departed" Account of Bagram from Dan Ephron, "Life at Bagram," *Newsweek* online, July 5, 2007, available at http://www.msnbc.msn.com/id/19619662/site/newsweek/ (accessed 07/30/2007).

244: "Kabul International Airport is an entirely different affair" Tamim Ansary, "An Afghan-American Speaks," Salon.com, September 14, 2001, available at http://archive.salon.com/news/feature/2001/09/14/afghanistan/ (accessed 07/30/2007); Michael R. Gordon, Eric Schmitt, and Thom Shanker, "Scarcity of Afghanistan Targets Prompts U.S. to Change Strategy," *New York Times,* September 18, 2001, sec. A.

245: "Violence, like the traffic rules" Peter Beaumont, "US Pulls Out Karzai's Military Bodyguards," *Guardian* (UK), November 24, 2002, available at http://www.guardian.co.uk/world/2002/nov/24/afghanistan.peterbeaumont (accessed 07/30/2007).

249: "In the hours after 9/11" Richard A. Clark, *Against All Enemies: Inside America's War on Terror* (New York: Free Press, 2004), 24.

249: "CIA Director George Tenet envisioned" Bob Woodward, *Bush at War* (New York: Simon & Schuster, 2002), 50.

249: "The weekend following the attacks" Ibid., 76.

249: "Tenet's proposal was a vision of the future" Ibid., 76–78.

250: "The CIA director's vision" Ibid., 76–77.

250: "On Monday, September 17" Ibid., 101.

250: "The CIA spearheaded the American invasion" Gary Schroen, *First In* (New York: Presidio, 2005); for Schroen's earlier career, see Steve Coll, *Ghost Wars* (New York: Penguin, 2005).

251: "Within a few weeks, Schroen's team" Michael Smith, *Killer Elite* (New York: St. Martin's, 2006), 215–16; Schroen, *First In*; for Schroen's earlier career, see Coll, *Ghost Wars*; for the early stages of the Afghanistan invasion see Schroen, *First In,* and Gary Bernstein with Ralph Puzzullo, *Jawbreaker* (New York: Crown, 2005).

251: "Other major Northern Alliance commanders" For the Northern Alliance, see Coll, *Ghost Wars*; Smith, *Killer Elite,* 215; "National Commission on Terrorist Attacks Upon the United States," 146. For Sayyaf, see John Anderson, "The Assassins," *New Yorker* June 10, 2002, 72; and Schroen, *First In,* 117.

252: "As American teams of Special Forces" Dana Priest, "CIA Holds Terror Suspects in Secret Prisons," *Washington Post,* November 5, 2005, sec. A.

252: "Alberto Gonzales, John Yoo, and Jay Bybee" John Barry, Michael Hirsh, and Michael Isikoff, "The Roots of Torture," *Newsweek,* May 24, 2004, 26; Jane Mayer, *The Dark Side* (New York: Doubleday, 2008).

253: "The first was Guantánamo Bay" Karen Greenberg and Joshua Dratel, eds., *The Torture Papers* (Cambridge: Cambridge University Press,

2005), 25–28, 29–37; for Guantánamo Bay, see Derek Gregory, "Vanishing Points: Law, Violence and Exception in the Global War Prison," in Derek Gregory and Allan Pred, eds., *Violent Geographies: Fear, Terror and Political Violence* (New York: Routledge, 2006); and Amy Kaplan, "Where Is Guantánamo," *American Quarterly* 57:3 (2005), 831–58.

254: "A second solution to the White House's geography problem" Paglen and Thompson, "Torture Taxi."

254: "From the beginning, Guantánamo Bay" James Risen, *State of War* (New York: Free Press, 2006), 29.

254: "For the CIA, Guantánamo Bay" Ibid., xx.

Chapter 16

256: "By the time we arrived" Carol Leonnig and Eric Rich, "US Seeks Silence on CIA Prisons," *Washington Post,* November 4, 2006, sec. A.

256: "Laid Saidi, an Algerian man" Craig Smith and Souad Mekhennet, "Algerian Tells of Dark Term in U.S. Hands," *New York Times,* July 7, 2006; Paglen and Thompson, "Torture Taxi."

256: "The former prisoners give similar" "Declaration of Khaled El-Masri in Support of Plaintiff's Opposition to the United States' Motion to Dismiss or, in the Alternative, for Summary Judgement," *El-Masri v. George Tenet,* Civil Action No. 1:05cv1417-TSE-TRJ. El-Masri's statement was originally written in German—direct quotes are from the English translation provided in the court documents. In some cases, I've relied on El-Masri's original statement in German when it contained untranslated details.

257: "As he recounted in his diary" Portions of Binyam Mohammed's account were reprinted in the *Daily Mail,* December 11, 2005, available at http://www.dailymail.co.uk/pages/live/articles/news/news.html?in_article_id=371330&in _page_id=1770 (accessed 06/06/2006).

258: "Accounts from other prisoners" Prisoner accounts provided by Clive Stafford Smith's office, Binyam Mohammed.

259: "A Red Cross report on the prison" David Cloud, "Red Cross Cited Detainee Abuse Over a Year Ago; Agency Filed Complaints About Abu Ghraib Prison Months Before U.S. Probe," *Wall Street Journal,* May 10, 2004, sec. A.

261: "Jack Idema's military career" Peter Bergen, "Shadow Warrior," *Rolling Stone* 974, May 19, 2005, 56–88.

262: "During this same time" Ibid.

263: "From time to time" Christina Lamb, "The Strange Story of Tora Bora Jack," *Times* online, August 8, 2004, available at http://www.timesonline.co.uk/tol/news/article466759.ece (accessed 05/02/2008).

264: "A spokesperson for the Defense Department" Quoted in ibid.

265: "Boykin had made headlines" For Boykin, see Richard Leiby,

"Christian Soldier," *Washington Post,* November 6, 2003, sec. C. Quotes from Bergen, "Shadow Warrior."

265: "Idema's relationship with officials" Bergen, "Shadow Warrior."

00: "When Idema entered Afghanistan" For a remarkable account of warlordism in post-Taliban Afghanistan, see Sarah Chayes, *The Punishment of Virtue* (New York: Penguin, 2006).

266: "Jack Idema's Task Force Saber 7" Nick Meo, "Vigilante Fooled NATO into Helping Raids," *Independent* (London), July 5, 2004, 18.

266: "Idema's Task Force Saber 7 was just another" Lamb, "Strange Story."

267: "A key part of Rumsfeld's transformation" Jennifer D. Kibbe, "The Rise of the Shadow Warriors," *Foreign Affairs,* March/April 2004.

267: "In March 2004, Donald Rumsfeld" Jennifer D. Kibbe, "Covert Action and the Pentagon," *Intelligence and National Security* 22:1, 57–74.

268: "Unlike the CIA, the military doesn't" Kibbe, "Rise of the Shadow Warriors"; Alfred Cumming, "Covert Action: Legislative Background and Possible Policy Questions," Congressional Research Service Report #RL33715, updated October 11, 2007.

268: "After the Iran-Contra scandal" Kibbe, "Rise of the Shadow Warri.ros."

269: "As the war on terror dragged on" Human Rights Watch Statement on U.S. Secret Detention Facilities in Europe, November 7, 2005, available at http://www.hrw.org/english/docs/2005/11/07/usint11995.htm (accessed 02/18/08).

269: "The black site prison program" Eric Schmitt and Carolyn Marshall, "In Secret Unit's 'Black Room,' a Grim Portrait of US Abuse," *New York Times,* March 19, 2006.

270: "But the black sites were" See The Torture Papers; *El-Masri v. Tenet; Arar v. Ashcroft;* For the torture memos, see Dana Priest and R. Jeffrey Smith, "Memo Offered Justification for Use of Torture," *Washington Post,* Tuesday, June 8, 2004, sec. A.

270: "First, the bill provided CIA" http://www.whitehouse.gov/news/releases/2005/12/20051230-8.html.

271: "Almost a year later" The full text of Bush's speech is available at http://www.whitehouse.gov/news/releases/2006/09/20060906-3.html.

271: "In Justice Breyer's concurring opinion" The text of Breyer's opinion is available at http://www.law.cornell.edu/supct/html/05-184.ZC.html.

272: "In early 2006, law professor" Mark Denbeaux et al., "Report on Guantanamo Detainees: A Profile of 517 Detainees," Seton Hall University, February 8, 2006; see also John Simpson, "No surprises in the war on terror," BBC News, February 13, 2006, available at http://news.bbc.co.uk/2/hi/middle_east/4708946.stm (accessed 1/05/2007).

272: "Denbeaux showed that not all" Jane Mayer, *The Dark Side* 183–85.

Epilogue

276: "The " 'power of the purse' " Federalist No. 58.

276: "Oliver North would equate secrecy with legality" North quoted in Weiner, *Blank Check*, 210.

277: "At this moment, approximately *four million*" Peter Galison, "Removing Knowledge," *Critical Inquiry* 31 (Autumn 2004); U.S. Department of labor statistics at http://www.bls.gov/oco/cg/cgs041.htm (accessed 12/19/2007).

Pg. 332: "Contemporary trends to outsource" "Intelligence Authorization Act for Fiscal Year 2008," Senate Report 110-75, 110th Congress, 1st Session, May 31, 2007.

278: "Ben Rich, the former chief of Lockheed's" Rich, Ben with Leo James, *Skunk Works* (New York: Back Bay Books, 1994), 306.

278: "Dwight Eisenhower spoke" Dwight David Eisenhower, "The Chance for Peace," speech given to the American Society of Newspaper Editors, April 16, 1953.

279: "Upon his retirement eight years later" Farewell speech of President Dwight Eisenhower, January 17, 1961.

279: "Now recall that study by" Galison, "Removing Knowledge."

281: "Off-the-books military teams" For U.S.-funded Sunnis, see Seymour Hersh, "The Redirection," *New Yorker,* March 5, 2007.

281: "It's easy to imagine that the antidote" Here I'm echoing Keenan's argument about mobilizing shame. See Thomas Keenan, "Mobilizing Shame," *South Atlantic Quarterly* 103, no. 2/3, Spring/Summer 2004, 435–49; for visibility as a precondition of knowledge, see Michel Foucault, *The Order of Things* (New York: Vintage, 1973), 53–55.

ACKNOWLEDGMENTS

This book would not have been possible without the support of far too many people and institutions to mention here. Numerous people have served as guides, mentors, interlocutors, and supporters over the course of this project. Ruth Wilson Gilmore, Gillian Hart, Jean Lave, Ananya Roy, and Michael Watts read and provided invaluable feedback on this manuscript. My immensely talented brother, Jack Paglen, spent weeks reviewing, fine-tuning, and providing helpful commentary on this project. Michael Light provided the quiet and beautiful space in the desert where much of this book was written. More than anyone, the late geographer Alan Pred took me under his wing and provided a unique combination of freedom, guidance, and encouragement.

None of this work would have been possible without the support of the geography department at U.C. Berkeley, the Berkeley Center for New Media, the art department at Berkeley, Claudia Altman–Siegel, Bellwether Gallery, Greg Hopkins, Allison Kave, Elisabeth Schneider, and Becky Smith.

Other people who were instrumental in realizing this project include: Joe Bryan, Kelly Burdick, Lauren Cornell, Kurt Cuffey, Apsara DiQuinzio, Aaron Gach and CTM, Ken Goldberg, Suzanne Guthrie, Renee Green, Adriene Jenik, Thomas Keenan, Shiloh Krupar, Yates McKee, Julia Meltzer, Peter Merlin, Greg Niemeyer, Marisa Olson, Patrick Paglen, the Pred Family, G. W. Schulz, Rebecca Solnit, Elizabeth Thomas, A. C. Thompson, Nato Thompson, David Thorne,

Richard Walker, Anne Walsh, and Benjamin Young. Praba Pilar was a constant source of support and inspiration.

I want to thank my agent, Ted Weinstein, for helping to conceive, guide, shape, and realize this project from the very beginning, and Stephen Morrow, my editor at Dutton, who was simply outstanding.

INDEX

PLU'S